LEARNING FROM COMPARING
new directions in comparative educational research

Volume 2   Policy, Professionals and Development

LEARNING FROM COMPARING
new directions in comparative educational research

Volume 2
Policy, Professionals and Development

EDITED BY
Robin Alexander
Marilyn Osborn
& David Phillips

SYMPOSIUM BOOKS

Symposium Books
PO Box 65 Wallingford, Oxford OX10 0YG, United Kingdom

Published in the United Kingdom, 2000

ISBN 1 873927 63 0

Typeset in Melior by Symposium Books
Printed and bound in the United Kingdom by Cambridge University Press

Contents

PART THREE

Education Professionals Compared

COMPANION VOLUME

LEARNING FROM COMPARING:
new directions in comparative educational research

Volume 1: Contexts, Classrooms and Outcomes

Edited by Robin Alexander, Patricia Broadfoot & David Phillips

ISBN 1 873927 58 4   Symposium Books 1999

Preface

This is the second of two volumes bearing the general title *Learning from Comparing: new directions in comparative educational research.* The books are the outcome of a programme of seminars which took place over the period 1997–99 and were funded by the United Kingdom Economic and Social Research Council (ESRC). The seminars were organised by the Centre for Research in Elementary and Primary Education, the Centre for Curriculum and Assessment Studies and the Centre for Comparative Studies in Education, located, respectively, at the universities of Warwick, Bristol and Oxford.

The full background and rationale to this project are outlined in the introduction to Volume I. Suffice it to say here that the seminars provided a forum for international representatives from the constituencies of research and policy – 'research providers' and 'research users' in today's research accounting jargon – to come together in order to reassess and perhaps help to redirect comparative educational research as a theoretical and empirical activity.

The initiative was prompted not just by a sense that this kind of appraisal would be helpful to the field's intellectual vitality, but also in response to several rather more particular developments. Educational discourse, as an aspect of the more general globalisation of ideas, has become increasingly internationalised, though it is clear that this trend makes considerable assumptions about how well ideas generated in one national context will travel to others. International comparisons of educational systems, policies, practices and outcomes, sometimes well conceived but as often not, now feature regularly as an adjunct to national policy and programmes of bilateral or multilateral aid. Such comparisons encompass fields like pedagogy, assessment and teacher professionalism about which, traditionally, comparative educationists have had surprisingly little to say and for which the methodology of comparison may not be as rigorous as it ought to be. And there are particular dangers attaching to the application of these sorts of analysis in the context of the relationship between the world's richer and poorer nations.

The two books contain revised versions of all the papers given at the seminars together with contributions which were commissioned subsequently in order to extend the analysis. Like Volume 1, Volume 2 is in three sections, each of which corresponds to a seminar theme. As the sequence of seminars was determined by operational contingencies as well as logic, readers will need to take both volumes together in order to appreciate that the six themes are less random than might be apparent from a brief glance at the contents of Volume 2 alone.

In this volume, then, we consider three broad questions. How, in an international context, can educational policies validly be researched and compared and what can be learned from the exercise (Part 1)? What can comparative research contribute to education in developing countries and how is the relationship between research, development and education best understood (Part 2)? What can we learn by studying comparatively the work of those professionals who are at the cutting edge of education, especially teachers, inspectors and teacher trainers (Part 3)?

The trio who initiated this project (Robin Alexander, Patricia Broadfoot and David Phillips) and the colleagues who joined with them in organising the seminars (Colin Brock, Marilyn Osborn and Michele Schweisfurth) would like to thank the many others who were involved: the two hundred or so seminar participants, some of whom were prepared to travel halfway round the globe to take part; those who produced papers for the seminars and then rewrote them for the two volumes of *Learning from Comparing;* those who provided additional papers; the ever-patient Roger Osborn-King of Symposium Books; and the Economic and Social Research Council, who funded the enterprise.

The Editors

PART ONE

The Comparative Study
of Educational Policy

Introduction: the comparative study of educational policy

DAVID PHILLIPS

The comparative context for educational policy can be illuminating in a number of ways. It can, *inter alia*:

- demonstrate possible alternatives to policy 'at home';
- provide insights into the processes of policy formation;
- clarify means of successful implementation used elsewhere; and
- serve to warn against adopting certain measures.

Comparativists have long contemplated the possibilities for policy 'borrowing'; indeed, one of their principal contributions has been the ability – through detailed accumulated knowledge and understanding of education in other countries – to provide policy-makers with objective analysis which should serve to prevent the simplistic adoption of practices merely because they are perceived to be successful elsewhere. The recent history of education abounds with examples of references by politicians and administrators to features of other education systems which might be copied 'at home'. Often such enthusiasms are supported by *ad hoc* reports, quickly put together by teams visiting the foreign countries in question. Joanna Le Métais explains among other things in her valuable analysis what the pitfalls are for fact-finding missions, among them the telling point that 'a visit usually does not reveal coherence between intention and implementation, the degree of success and any unintended consequences'.

In 1989, I edited a special issue of the journal *Comparative Education* (Vol. 25, No. 3) on the topic of 'Cross-national Attraction in Education'. I invited specialists to write on why it was that their countries were interested in features of education in specific other countries, and I then asked experts from those 'target' countries to respond to the enthusiasms shown. It was clear that a high degree of scepticism becomes evident when such an exercise is undertaken. Often commentators in the countries whose experience is being held up as an example to be emulated are quite astonished that others should be interested in what they are doing. There has clearly been a lack of critical edge, a failure to investigate the downside, in outsider perception of what is happening in other – supposedly instructive – contexts.

The naïve assumptions on the part of policy-makers seeking what Joanna Le Métais calls in her article the 'quick fix' approach to the solution of problems in their home countries ignore, of course, the central importance of context, pointed out so eloquently by Michael Sadler at the turn of the century. That context is changing rapidly, and Val Rust in his opening contribution describes the complex shifts in globalisation and localisation which are challenging our assumptions about the centrality of the nation state in education. 'Comparative Education must contribute a more enlightened dialogue about policy formation and implementation within this turbulent, global context', he writes, and his article is a finely argued analysis of the complexities with which comparativists need to wrestle if they are to provide policy-makers with evidence that can challenge their idealised solutions based on selected aspects of the foreign experience.

What comparativists can do is to produce analysis which attempts to be both explanatory and predictive in nature, which tries to account for phenomena in education being as they are (with due regard to the complexities of context – historical, political, cultural, religious, economic, linguistic, geographical, etc.) and which endeavours to assess the potential those phenomena suggest for other settings.

Mary-Louise Kearney, from the wealth of experience she has as a higher education specialist in a multilateral organisation, provides us with many examples of the kind of reports and studies – often undertaken over long periods – that properly inform policy discussion about the future of a domain as intricate as higher education.

Between them, the three contributors to this section of our present volume provide a wide range of illuminative coverage of the theoretical and practical dimensions to the role that comparative education can and should have in the formulation of a country's educational policy.

Education Policy Studies and Comparative Education

VAL D. RUST

Introduction

Education policy studies is a subfield of a more comprehensive group of specialisations known variously as public policy, public administration, or policy studies. Education policy specialists concentrate on policies related to education and endeavour 'to ensure that education occurs in the public interest' (Taylor et al, 1997, p. 2). Education policy studies is somewhat marginal as an academic field, though in recent years it has made strides towards legitimacy. Our task here will be to assess how comparative education might interface with education policy studies to the benefit of both fields.

Unfortunately, comparative educators are seldom identified with education policy studies, even though they have a strong history of work in the field. In the USA, the educators who initiated the journal *Educational Policy* were comparative educators at SUNY (State University of New York) Buffalo, and many of the articles appearing in the journal have cross-national content.[1] The SUNY Buffalo situation reflects a general tendency among comparative education specialists, at least in the USA. In 1998 the Comparative and International Education Society (CIES) fundamentally revised its constitution, and the purposes section now makes explicit reference to policy.[2] A recent UCLA (University of California in Los Angeles) study surveying authors contributing to *Comparative Education*, the *Comparative Education Review* and the *International Journal of Educational Development* between 1985 and 1995 found that more than two-thirds deemed their research to be policy oriented (Rust, undated).

There is certainly potential for comparative education specialists to play a more visible role in the field of policy studies; and it is useful to elaborate on the kinds of contributions they might make. First, one norm of the field of comparative education is that cross-nations studies always attend to the dynamic relationships tying education and society together. In contrast, David Halpin (1994, pp. 202–205) explains that education policy studies specialists who examine a policy issue in more than one nation usually fail to place that issue in its proper 'historical, social, political and economic' context. Consequently, this type of comparative analysis usually misses the mark. Halpin's criticism of policy studies research that takes a cross-national perspective is warranted. Policy studies specialists engaging in comparative analysis too often fail to apply basic principles that a beginning student of comparative education will have learned about the relationship between schooling and society. Comparative educators are aware that education must be interpreted in terms of national forces and factors outside the school. They are trained to be conscious of the dangers of selectively looking for examples somewhere in the world that reconfirm initial bias, of glossing over subtleties and contradictions marking any education system, and of formulating prescriptive policy to be applied anywhere and everywhere.

Second, comparative education specialists try to develop a clear balance between theory and practice in their work. According to Charles D. Raab (1994), a major weakness of the education policy studies literature is that it is 'descriptive and evaluative', and as these studies pile up, questions of broader theoretical interest remain unexplored. In contrast, comparative educators, from the beginning of their field, have stressed that description is destitute unless it contributes to the development of analytic models and theory (see, for example, Kandel, 1933; Hans, 1949; Bereday, 1964). Of course, theory is also poor if it is developed without appropriate touch points with social reality. Although comparative education is not exonerated from a tendency to be descriptive and evaluative, it is a field reflecting a healthy theory orientation that can serve to counterbalance inevitable descriptions and evaluations. In the UCLA survey we asked authors to indicate where their study fell along a five-point Likert scale between theory and practice. The responses, shown in Figure 1, indicate attempts at a clear balance between a theory and a practice orientation:

Theory	1	2	3	4	5	Practice
	7%	31%	29%	20%	11%	

Figure 1. UCLA survey of theory/practice in comparative education.

Third, whereas comparative education has long identified itself with the basic social sciences, the field of education policy studies has remained isolated from policy studies in other professional fields such as public administration and from the social sciences in general (Troyna, 1994). There is, indeed, a general gap between the study of politics and the study of education. However, the field of comparative education has always been relatively healthy in this regard. The first editor of *Comparative Education Review*, George Z. F. Bereday, was a political scientist. The UCLA survey indicates that more than 60% of the authors appearing in the major comparative education journals claim the discipline base of their study to be sociology, political science, economics, or history. It is clear that there is a close identity between works in comparative education and the social sciences, and comparative educators are well situated to cross the gap between education and those social science fields most closely related to policy studies.

Fourth, whereas comparative education has been able to overcome its most critical ideological divisions, as Troyna (1994) reminds us, the field of education policy studies is becoming more and more divided along deep fault lines: conflict vs equilibrium theories, theory vs practice, objective science vs subjective knowledge, rationalism vs humanism. In contrast, comparative education has learned successfully to cope with the natural divisions in its field. In the 1950s and 1960s, comparative education was rather homogeneous in its theoretical and methodological orientation but in the next two decades tremendous fault lines appeared. The field was first challenged by various conflict orientations that undercut the hegemonic control that so-called equilibrium orientations held over the field (Paulston, 1976). The struggle opened the way for the emergence of other protest movements, for instance, feminists (Kelly & Nihlen, 1982; Stromquist, 1990), who attacked the field and education in general for supporting the dominance of males and the male point of view. In the 1970s, some comparative education scholars challenged the field for being too theoretical and failing to give sufficient attention to educational practice, to reforming the curriculum, and to improving instructional practice through comparative evaluation studies. Anthropologists such as Lawrence Stenhouse (1979) and Richard Heyman (1979) claimed that comparative education ought to be less concerned with scientific generalisations and predictions than with understanding the everyday life of the school. Other anthropologists, including Vandra Masemann (1990), recognised the legitimacy of science but attempted to give credence to personal, intersubjective knowledge and to introduce ethnomethodological approaches into comparative education.

Still other scholars argued that the field give more attention to humanistic concerns such as global understanding, world harmony and peace (Fraser & Brickman, 1968). Recently, various ideological and disciplinary orientations, including various post-structural theories (Cherryholmes, 1988) and postmodern theories (Rust, 1990), have challenged critical theorists and others who argue that while the 'project of the Enlightenment' has not been particularly successful, academics should revitalise its ideals, 'feeble as they may be' and 'not declare the entire project of modernity a lost cause' (Habermas, 1983).

I have briefly charted multiplying developments within comparative education, which fragmented the field just as education policy studies continues to be fragmented. However, in the past decade comparative educators have been successful in overcoming these divisions and the field has been moving towards integration (Paulston, 1992, 1993; Rust, undated). The so-called paradigm wars of the 1970s and 1980s have been replaced by a more eclectic and sharing orientation, where scholars recognise that each perspective is but a partial perspective. Communities within our field are no longer as disputatious and divisive as they were, but scholars representing differing perspectives now rely on each other to provide a fuller picture or map of social reality, and of education taking place in that reality. This situates comparative education well to contribute to a resolution of some of the problems facing education policy studies.

Fifth, the most important insight comparative education can contribute to education policy studies is to help that field bring a comparative perspective to the models it has come to rely on. Most important among comparative insights is the realisation that any given policy model is often more than a simple competitor among theoretical options; rather, that certain policy models are more suitable for explaining change in a given situation while other policy models are more suitable in another. Comparative analysis confirms that individual theoretical orientations rarely have universal application to social reality; they more often replicate certain norms and practices in specific countries or cultures. In other words, policy models, and even the theories on which they are based, are not as much about universal truth and reality as they are about culturally conditioned judgements and culturally shaped constructs (Rorty, 1979). For example, this is clearly apparent with regard to interest intermediation models. Pluralism has taken root in countries such as Great Britain and the USA, where political practices take for granted the active role of interest groups. Conversely, models of democratic corporatism characterise the policy formation processes of the Scandinavian countries, Germany and France, for instance, and it would be inappropriate to claim that one theoretical orientation has greater universal validity than the other. Rather, a comparative perspective helps us see that we are dealing more with models of actual practice than with universal theoretical orientations.

Education Policy Models in Comparative Perspective

The major categories of policy processes are policy formation and policy implementation.[3] We shall deal here only with policy formation, though it must be understood that policy implementation could be subjected to a similar treatment.

Scholars explain policy formation processes through bureaucratic or institutional factors, environmental factors, or a combination of the two. Bureaucracy-oriented models are based on the assumption that forces in the formal organisations of the state define policy and these models explain how that takes place. Environmental-oriented studies operate on the assumption that the major policy processes take place outside the formal organisations of the state. Interest groups are usually identified as those power blocks that influence formal policy-makers. Of course, certain models account for both bureaucratic and environmental factors. One such approach would be the so-called cognitive-structuralist or mind-set approach developed by Samuel Culbert (1996).

Although a number of models that explain policy formation through institutional or bureaucratic factors have been developed, I shall mention only four. Many scholars give weight to various versions of individualism and claim that the bureaucracy is little more than a collection of individuals who make collective, competitive, or divided decisions based on the power they hold in the bureaucratic hierarchy (Nordlinger, 1981). Other scholars advocate a so-called institutional politics model based on the assumption that various public bureaucracies operate as self-conscious political actors whose major aim is to advance their own department, bureau, or programme within the larger governmental structure (Simon et al, 1972). Still other scholars advocate a scientific management model that relies on the work of efficiency experts and is based on the assumption that actors in any organisation can behave rationally and according to the dictates of a highly centralised power structure in achieving specified goals, increasing production, and operating at a high level of efficiency.[4] Finally, other scholars advocate the so-called human relations model that stresses the needs of individuals for group identification and focuses as much on psycho-social norms and behaviours as it does on goals, production, and efficiency.

Scholars who focus on environmental factors usually rely on what is known as interest intermediation, but which takes various forms, including the pluralist, the corporatist and the Marxist models. The pluralist model is centred on the idea of political relationships among a multiplicity of voluntary interest groups competing for power and influence, though within a social framework of laws and values. Although interest groups are seen as non-hierarchically ordered, some accounts refer to an element of structural inequality and covert exercise of power (Bachrach & Baratz, 1962).

Democratic corporatism, a second interest intermediation model, emphasises the significance of interest groups, but rather than emphasising competition between interest groups, as in the pluralist model, a structured pluralism is portrayed in which the state is seen to act with corporate groups in policy formation (Cawson, 1982). There is a 'mutual interdependence and interpenetration of the public and private sectors' (Olsen, 1981) because government and private interests are seen as partners. Governments in corporatist states rely on special interest groups to supply information, hold their members in check, and contribute directly to decision-making. In return, the major interest groups are granted a representational monopoly of their spheres (Lembruch & Schmitter, 1982). In terms of education, professional groups in a corporate system work not only to gain sectional advantages, but they help maintain the authority and legitimacy of the system as a whole (Rust, 1990).

The third emphasis falls within the Marxist camp, and a common feature of Marxist groups is a view of the state as a political, social and cultural agency that reinforces and reproduces capitalist social relations. However, in advanced capitalist society, the state is seen to be drawn increasingly into relatively unmanageable conflicts of interest. Rising public expenditure on education, for example, is sanctioned because the state must respond to popular demand for better provision and to the training requirements of employers. But as both public expenditure and the taxation to fund it increase, the probabilities of social crisis, which may even affect the legitimacy of elected government itself, are thought to increase (Weiler, 1989b).

The comparative education insights regarding the policy models just outlined not only have cross-national value, but a comparative perspective provides some advantage in assessing policy change within a single country. Irvent Torres (1998), for example, examined the reform process at a single community college in the USA. He began by reviewing the current educational reform movement, which began after *A Nation at Risk* (Gardner, 1983) appeared in 1983; he identified three major phases of this reform process. The first phase (1983–91) was characterised by a top–down, rational, scientific management approach to educational reform where experts were called on to tell us what was to be done to our schools. The second phase (1992–96) abandoned this approach and moved in the direction of a decentralisation of authority and a dispersion of power to parents (parental choice) and the private sector. The third phase (1997–present) has begun to emphasise the notion that education is an industry and that learning, teaching and governance ought to be perceived as a profit-driven enterprise. Torres found that the reform strategies of the college replicated the more general reform phases: scientific management to human relations management to corporate management. This suggests that policy formation models are always contingent but are useful even in times of rapid change.

Under certain circumstances, where policies remain lodged within a national context, the conventional policy study models may remain appropriate even during times of change. Policy-makers may even change their mode of policy formation and implementation to the detriment of the nation state in question. From my vantage point, this is what has happened in Norway. The conventional education policy formation strategy in Norway, known generally as democratic corporatism (Rust, 1990), is a long and difficult process but it ensures that a policy enjoys a high level of consensus, and those expected to implement the reforms usually maintain a strong sense of ownership. Because the process takes a number of years to complete, recent Norwegian ministers of education have complained that is too slow and have argued that some other mechanism is necessary to address quickly changing needs. The Norwegian Department of Education has chosen to become more aggressive in its change orientation and to short-circuit the conventional policy formation model. That is, a drawn-out review of policy and policy revision no longer takes place and no trial programmes are instituted. The advantage of this new model is that it requires less time to formulate new policy (Briseid, 1995). However, the disadvantages are that little consensus is gained in the reform proposals and those expected to implement policy play almost no role in defining the policy. In other words, they have no sense of ownership. This new policy formation strategy was behind the recently adopted Reform 94, a secondary school endeavour. Consequently, it is not surprising that Reform 94 has been controversial and many professionals have subverted its intentions (Rust, undated).

A number of nation states are finding that globalising and localising forces necessitate changing the policy formation process, but the new models of policy formation they have adopted have been within the framework of well-known models. In Korea, for example, where education policy has been until recently almost entirely driven by a statist, bureaucratic model, the country has come under increasing pressure to open up its markets in general and its educational system in particular. This has occurred as foreign commercial firms have become established in the country and have demanded that the firms themselves be allowed to provide appropriate, non-Korean education and training for their Korean employees. Pressure has also come from those crafting free trade agreements, particularly the Uruguay Round General Agreement on Tariffs and Trade (GATT). And so, in 1993, the Korean Government decided to open up its educational market by allowing foreign institutions to establish management training, English language and other programmes in the country. This policy change came about because the education policy formation process shifted from a statist to a corporatist model that emphasises a tripartite accommodation between business, state and intellectual elites (Kim, 1997). Another example, that replicates the shift taking place in Korea, was a recent USA–Japan partnership, where a statist model also gave way to a corporatist model.

The Japanese Government entered into a corporatist relationship with industry, and education was intended to promote the local economy, stop the flow of young people to Tokyo, and respond to American universities that were raising money and recruiting students (Institute of International Education [IIE], 1997).

I would like to turn now to special issues confronting both specialists in comparative education and education policy studies and explore how the two fields might work together to resolve some of these issues. I would like to do this within the context of a major challenge faced by both comparative education and education policy studies: globalisation and localisation.

Globalisation and Localisation

On the surface, globalisation and localisation appear to be divergent processes, but they are seen by most scholars as being complementary. Giddens (1995, pp. 80–81) reminds us that globalisation is really about the transformation of time and space and increasingly engages not only large-scale systems but also local bodies and individuals. According to David Held (1991, p. 9), globalisation marks 'the intensification of worldwide social relations which link distant localities in such a way that local happenings are shaped by events occurring many miles away and *vice versa*'. Both Giddens and Held claim that today the local is integrally tied to the global, and the global to local.[5] It is a mistake to argue that one can be disentangled from the other, as is assumed by authors such as Jerry Mander and Edward Goldsmith (1992). Our technological world provides instant access to almost every corner of the globe through the use of electricity, electronic signals, paper, wheels, roads and wings. These enable social relations – economic, cultural and political – to form transnational connections. These are transnational because the relations involved do not rely on state territories and state frontiers. Whereas international relations embody the notion of relationships and transactions between nations, global relations imply that economic, political and cultural activities have disengaged themselves from territorial authority and jurisdictions (Hobsbawm, 1994; Giddens, 1995; Waters, 1995) and have begun to transcend the nation state and to function according to more immediate imperatives and interests.

To this point, the greatest interest has been shown towards economic globalisation, which interpreters claim emerged after the end of the 1960s. The global economy is seen to have transcended national economies and is dominated by market forces run by 'transnational corporations that owe allegiance to no nation state and locate wherever in the globe market advantage dictates' (Hirst & Thompson, 1996, p. 1). Interpreters claim that the economy of the world is now driven by some

600 mega-firms that account for more than 20% of the world's economic production. Few of these firms are nationally based. Let us take a single example: Japanese auto firms. Ford owns 25% of Mazda; Honda cars are increasingly built in the USA and shipped even to Japan; General Motors is the largest single stockholder of Isuzu (Toffler, 1990, pp. 460–461). Economic globalisation is intrinsically bound up with capitalist development and has been variously described as 'McDonaldisation', 'Coca-Colaisation', 'Toyotism' and 'Post-Fordism', but these characterisations refer mainly to the value system behind economic globalisation, including an emphasis on economic efficiency and a tendency towards homogenising practices (see, for example, Barber, 1995; Wilms, 1996).

Parallel with the development of multinational industries is the development of a global electronic finance market that exchanges more than a trillion dollars a day. This market has little to do with trade but is oriented almost entirely towards speculation in currency and paper money (Bergsten, 1988). The financial markets are pushing giant mergers of financial institutions as well as a surge in new charters of local institutions that address speciality needs and small businesses.

Malcolm Waters (1995) reminds us that globalisation goes far beyond economic processes and includes political and cultural processes as well. A common political culture has emerged in the eyes of people such as Francis Fukayama (1992), who claims that the collapse of communism and the authoritarian right has resulted in global political liberalism. A global economy signals the surrender of sovereignty on the part of nation states and the emergence of larger political units (European Union), multilateral treaties (North American Free Trade Association [NAFTA]), and international organisations (United Nations, International Monetary Fund). The rational consequence of these trends would be a system of global governance, with the decline of state powers and authority (Held, 1991, pp. 207–209). Such a scenario seems reasonable, but actual political developments are not so clear. While state autonomy is in decline, as yet no global political unit is in place that regulates and coordinates economic globalism. Further, if one judges the current orientation of the European Union (Baneth, 1993), it is unclear if regional political units are compatible with economic globalism.

The so-called myth of globalism also includes the notion of cultural globalisation. We speak now of a global village, with its intimate variety of 'neighbourhoods' that can be visited in person, on the television screen, or via the Web. At the end of 1998, 72 million Americans (33% of the adult population) had direct home or office access to the Internet, while 6.5 million people in Britain (16%), and 11.5 million Japanese (13.4%) had direct access. Up to 350,000 American teachers have on-line access. Now via the Internet I can visit the Haiti International Boutique at the Haiti Global Village International Mall or buy hand-woven clothes from Guatemala. Or I can attend Robert Schuller's Crystal Cathedral Church service while I am working in Azerbaijan. Or from my living room I can find people of like mind and heart, and in neighbourly fashion, show them how to bake a pie or fix a leaking roof. Besides having instant access to the virtual world, through global travel I can visit these neighbourhoods in person. By 1989 one billion passengers had travelled each year by air; by the end of this decade that figure will reach two billion (Naisbitt & Aburdene, 1990, p. 119).

The globalisation process includes the increasing development of binational and transnational orientations, including a multiplicity of involvements – familial, friendship, social, organisational, religious, and political – that span across borders (Schiller et al, 1994). Illustrative are the contacts millions of Mexicans living in the USA maintain with their families, neighbourhoods and culture in Mexico (Monkman, 1997); or the contacts growing numbers of vagabond professionals maintain as they float from place to place teaching English, working as international consultants, or serving as relief and development specialists throughout the world.

While travel is often seen as a privilege of the wealthy, today we are witnessing movements of vast numbers of refugees, internally displaced persons (IDPs) and immigrants. The number of refugees in the world has doubled in the past decade and has increased by a factor of six in the past two decades (United Nations Development Programme [UNDP], 1994), and the number of individuals displaced within the borders of their own nations is growing even more rapidly, an increase that portends a significant growth in refugees themselves, because internal migration is a common first phase prior to international migration. While refugees and IDPs are usually a political form of migration, immigrants are typically those who migrate for economic reasons (Hein, 1993).[6] They constitute a much larger group than do refugees and IDPs, and in many instances their plight may be just as great. In the mid-1990s it was estimated that about 200 million people (2% of the earth's inhabitants) were living outside their country of birth or citizenship.

More characteristic of our incipient global culture are revolutionary improvements in telecommunications and computerisation. Almost a quarter of a century ago, Daniel Bell (1973) claimed that the world's value system is now driven by mass media, from the West and North to the rest of the world, including television programmes, movies, books and newspapers. Charles Jencks (1987, p. 75) claims we now live in a 24-hour 'information world' where people not only consume information every minute of the day, but up to 75% of the workforce of the developed countries is now employed for the purposes of information production and distribution (Toffler, 1990). However, it would be a mistake to identify cultural globalisation with cultural integration (Archer, 1985), although at some abstract level we might speak of integration at least in terms of the means of communication and interaction and what Roland Robertson (1992) describes as the compression of the *world* and an intensified consciousness of the whole. There is growing evidence, however, that beyond these superficial uniformities, cultures are increasingly growing and changing in different directions. According to Hannertz (1990, p. 2376), the world 'is marked by an organisation of diversity rather than by a replication of uniformity. No total homogenisation of systems of meaning and expression has occurred, nor does it appear likely that there will be one at any time soon'. This claim is also accompanied by recent theoretical orientations, including complexification theory, self-organisation theory, the theory of fractal sets, and chaos theory, that suggest substantial local variation within the framework of broader, universal developments (Jantsch, 1980; Shieve & Allen, 1982; Eisler & Loye, 1987; Prigogine & Stengers, 1984).

The globalising and localising trends have important implications for education. There is persuasive evidence that education is becoming more and more uniform. The goal of every country is to have all children attend school for a certain period of time. The schools are vertically age-graded and divided into primary, lower secondary and upper secondary levels. Teachers increasingly possess post-secondary teaching credentials. Essentially the same curriculum is taught in every environment. Children are trained to contribute to the global economy (see, for example, Meyer & Hannan, 1979).

Simultaneous with globalising tendencies in education, strong localising forces are promoting revitalisation of local cultures and economies (Schriewer, 1998). Individual and cultural needs are incorporated into the abstractly uniform curriculum in such a way that diversity and uniqueness are encouraged. Local narratives and stories are highlighted but increasingly appreciated. Difference is encouraged and rewarded (Mander & Goldsmith, 1992).

In spite of these ongoing globalisation and localisation processes, the nation state remains important, with educational policy responses by and large the responsibility of the state. And the importance of the state does not appear to be waning, though we are finally beginning to recognise that the concept of the nation state is far more complex than the model provided by modern Europe with its relatively fixed boundaries and populations. For example, the small nations of the Caribbean are populated largely by people whose family networks and loyalties transcend boundaries (Wiltshire, 1992).

Nationalism continues to be reinforced by a number of forces. On the one hand, international and global political bodies have relatively little formal authority, which remains in the hands of the nation state. On the other hand, local forces reinforce the status of the nation state in that they attempt to divide states into smaller 'national' units, as has occurred in Czechoslovakia, the Soviet Union and Yugoslavia, or they attempt to gain a greater share of power and influence over policy in the existing nation state. The World Wide Web page of the Zapatista Front of National Liberation in Mexico illustrates how a small group of guerrillas in the jungles of Chiapas, Mexico can mobilise the world against an entire nation state in favour of their 'national' agenda. However, that effort does not signal the death of Mexico, but a power struggle over who will control Mexico.

We return now to comparative education and policy studies. While comparative education can be a great contributor to education policy studies, both fields face great theoretical and practical challenges arising from radical changes taking place in the world. I would like to cast these challenges within the context of a globalising and localising world.

Need for a New Paradigm of Change

Globalising and localising processes require a reassessment of the change paradigms social scientists have come to rely on. The social sciences have proved to be inadequately prepared to predict and to interpret changes occurring in the world, as observers of recent developments in eastern Europe can attest. The collapse of the Soviet empire was so abrupt that social scientists were as surprised as political analysts and the media. Their tools of analysis had not given them the slightest insight into the processes of changes at work. The realisation of this fact provides a major challenge to comparative education, which has taken pride in its reliance on the social sciences.

Although the emergent paradigm is as yet unclear, I think certain overlapping features have already begun to manifest themselves. First, social science theory has generally taken for granted that the larger social context is stable or in a state of revolution, while the actual world finds itself in a state of ongoing, continuous turbulence. According to Eric Hobsbawm (1994, pp. 534–551), the sciences in general have seen change as one of 'bourgeois improvement and progress, continuity and gradualism dominated the paradigms of science'. In those periods of calm and gradualism, we tended to view turbulence and chaos as frightening and disorienting, but we are beginning to recognise that social systems are actively dissipative in nature (Schieve & Allen, 1982). That is, they must continually renew themselves or they die. My point is that disequilibrium is beginning to be seen as a condition under which development and growth take place. Turbulence is precarious, but it has great positive potential (Prigogine & Stengers, 1984). Second, since the 1970s, conflict and change entered into the laboratories and now we speak comfortably about catastrophe, complexification and chaos, and have even developed theoretical perspectives such as fractal concepts (Oliver, 1992), chaos theory (Gleick, 1987; Lorenz, 1993), and catastrophe theory (Saunders, 1980). These perspectives caution scholars from complete reliance on linear science and suggest that points of bifurcation, indeterminance and feedback loops appear that demand a view of an indivisible, dynamic and organic world. It has led us to break the conventional links science has made between causality and predictability, and the new paradigm includes the notion that historical and social development is neither coherent and amenable to complete explanation, nor can it be predicted (Hobsbawm, 1994, pp. 541–542).

Third, it is becoming increasingly clear that the research tradition of separating social, political and economic institutions from local groups, institutions and individuals in the form of macro-studies as opposed to micro-studies is not only arbitrary but it distorts our ability to understand the nature of social processes. The new paradigm requires that researchers simultaneously account for the global, the national and the local. Fourth, the spontaneous transformation of systems, including education, is forcing us to take seriously the notion that systems have a self-organisation capacity that includes their ability to adjust to extensive external shifts (Jantsch, 1980; Shieve & Allen, 1982). From this vantage point, organisation is not necessarily something imposed by some larger authority or by a defined power but includes a self-organisation process of a myriad of individual acts that constitute almost an unconscious organising capacity (Foucault, 1980).

In the remainder of this article I would like to explore specific issues related to globalisation and localisation that neither comparative education nor education policy studies have adequately addressed. I maintain that these issues can only be adequately explained and policies related to the issues appropriately adopted if they are approached from the vantage point of the incipient paradigm of change. I shall discuss the telecommunications revolution, the increasing migration of people in the world, the local school as an actor in policy formation, and policy models for the developing world.

The Telecommunications Revolution and Education

Illustrative of the changes that are taking place in the world is the so-called telecommunications revolution, which is confronting both comparative educators and policy studies specialists with difficult educational dilemmas and opportunities. The Internet illustrates what most people would consider to be a positive turbulence in that it provides the possibility that any person can interact with another person, anywhere in the world, as easily as if that person were sitting directly in front of the other. This has created tremendous educational possibilities. Finland, for example, has incorporated email into its foreign language education programmes, so that students might interact directly with young people whose mother tongue is the language being studied. The implications for education policies are great. Educators are finally able to talk about genuine equality of educational opportunity, at least in terms of accessibility. Those who have long been disadvantaged because they were living far removed from centres of learning now have direct access to those centres. In New Mexico, for example, remote high schools are engaged in interactive instruction through two-way video hook-ups with community colleges, which provide instruction in the most current courses available anywhere. One of the major breakthroughs in education is that institutions of higher learning are no longer some distant place of advanced learning. They are becoming increasingly integrated into the everyday life of schoolchildren. In North Carolina, for example, Appalachian State University has joined with private enterprises such as AT & T and Southern Bell to provide rural high schools with the most current concepts and information (Dalin & Rust, 1996, p. 116).

Technology has moved so quickly that it promises soon to give learners access to information, wherever and whenever the learner wishes to access that knowledge. Already, major projects are being developed that aim to make that promise a reality. The European Union, for example, had taken the initiative to develop the so-called DELTA project, which attempts to provide direct and remote access to learning resources throughout Europe. With a budget of 100 million dollars in 1994 alone, it draws 174 organisations together to focus on more than 300 subprojects intending to facilitate networks of information (Collis & de Vries, 1994).

While the DELTA project is marvellous, the new technology promises to engulf the entire world. With telecommunications developments, the necessity of schools remaining in large complexes is quickly becoming obsolete. It is possible to bring people together in face-to-face meetings from almost anywhere on the globe. The local school appears to be much too confining in face of a world open to all. It is not yet clear what kinds of educational policies are possible given the runaway nature of communications technology, but it is clear that nation states cannot behave in the future as if they were self-contained and isolated from the rest of the world. Meaningful policies must be global in nature, because the information age knows no national boundaries.

Education policies can no longer be seen as creatures of the public sphere. They must also take into account the role of the commercial and corporate world. For example, one company that has targeted its efforts toward schools has been the Apple Classroom of Tomorrow projects (ACOT, 1993). One of ACOT's beacon projects has been at a rural Blue Earth School District, in Minnesota. All grades participate to some extent, but the main focus has been on the upper grades of primary school. For example, each sixth grader shares a computer at school with one other student, and each of these students has a computer at home for the entire school year. The impact has been impressive. Entirely new mathematics and language arts programmes have been instituted that allow students to move ahead as quickly as their ability and motivation permits. A problem-solving course has been developed that compels students to become globally aware as they attack local problems. The base of this course is a rich, global database that allows students access to information about those problems on a global level. Creativity is stressed through the use of graphics and sound capabilities by the computer. Such innovations required a whole set of new skills, including keyboarding skills, knowledge of word processing programmes, use of databases and graphics packages.

But the policy issues go beyond curriculum and instruction. In fact, the school itself is now in question. It is clear that the modern school is modelled after modern industrial institutions. The modern school is now as obsolete as the modern factory. Comparative educators and policy studies specialists must work together in designing an educational system that satisfies the new technology and educational imperatives of young and old alike.

State Policy Models in a World of Migration

Another phenomenal change taking place in the world, one that exemplifies disorientation and dislocation, is the growing tendency for people to relocate themselves. An axiom of modern education has been that the nation state is responsible for education within the borders of its domain. During the past 200 years people have thought in terms of educational systems structured by nation states that behaved as if they were stable, autonomous, self-sufficient entities. But, does this assumption hold for a turbulent, globalised world? I think not, unless some sort of super state emerges, which certainly has not yet occurred, although some kinds of international formations have taken place, including the United Nations. The most striking relations over the past decades have been those indicative of a growing regionalisation, giving us acronyms such as ASEAN (Association of South East Asian Nations), NAFTA (North American Free Trade Agreement), and APEC (Asia-Pacific Economic Cooperation). The primary model for regional coalitions comes from western Europe, where the European Union has taken the lead in redefining national sovereignty by forging what some people call 'Fortress Europe' (Aho, 1994). The European Union has established an impressive model for education within a free trade agenda. Article 126 of the Maastricht Treaty, signed in 1992, gives priority to education within the European Union and Article 128 stresses that the Treaty intends to 'contribute to the flowering of the cultures of the Member States, while respecting their national and regional diversity and at the same time bringing the common cultural heritage to the fore'. In other words, the European Union is structured in such a way that national autonomy is respected, though member states harmonise details of education in a manner similar to the German Standing Conference of Ministers of Education (McLean, 1989).

This is no small matter. The German Standing Conference has entered into a multitude of agreements that signal an increasing centralisation of authority, as the East Germans discovered when these education agreements were imposed on the five new German states in 1991 (Rust & Rust, 1995, pp. 163–167). The European Union came into being in part from a recognition that European countries are increasingly multinational. Up to 15% of the Europeans are living in a country where they do not enjoy citizenship, and these people are beginning to gain a voice in public affairs. This condition is not exclusive to Europe, since the world itself is becoming characterised by increasing numbers of IDPs, refugees, and immigrants; these developments raise crucial education policy issues.

Policy issues surrounding IDPs are most likely to evoke consensus about who is responsible for their education. Even though IDPs are dispossessed, they are so within their own conventional national borders and they remain subject to legal and moral conditions that prevailed prior to the events leading to their displacement. In most instances, a crisis represents a temporary displacement. The 1998 hurricane in Central America has led to the displacement of more than 3.2 million people, but efforts are under way to restore them to their original homes. In Somalia, no generally accepted political authority is found, and so it is difficult to define the legal and moral mandates necessary to ensure adequate educational service for displaced persons, even though they have remained in Somalia. In Rwanda, one ethnic group is intent on exterminating another and it would be foolish to assume that the state will act responsibly regarding everyone's educational welfare. In Azerbaijan, international relief agencies care for the 1.2 million IDPs, providing schooling, textbooks and other resources. The Ministry of Education acts as a hindrance to educational provision, because it at times blocks attempts of relief agencies to provide basic schooling needs for the IDPs (Rust, 1994).

Educational provision for refugees is usually complicated. The 1951 United Nations Convention on the status of refugees claims that educational services are the responsibility of the country of asylum (United Nations High Commissioner for Refugees [UNHCR], 1993, Article 92). However, it has become increasingly clear that refugees create difficult authority issues. Many governments in the developing countries are unable or unwilling to provide universal primary education for their own children, and so they establish discriminatory policies regarding children who hold refugee status. In Burundi, for example, Rwanda children must score 20% higher than Burundi children to qualify for secondary schooling privileges. Even with the assistance of international agencies, many countries often do not have the infrastructure, resources, trained personnel, and even willingness to provide educational services to refugee children, and when educational services are provided to refugees, it is difficult to define what level of education ought to be provided. Should refugees be given the same education as is found the host country? Should they be offered the same curriculum and language of instruction as those in the host country? Can refugees demand a higher level of general education than they enjoyed in their homeland? These are not easily resolved issues and the answers usually depend on the situation. Further complicating the issue, refugee groups often do not wish to have their children subjected to a foreign educational enterprise. Do they have the right to demand their own separate schools, teachers, textbooks and programmes? Cambodian and Vietnamese refugees were placed in settlements within Indonesia and cared for by international agencies. The Indonesian Government allowed these agencies complete control over the educational programmes they set up. Should such a policy be adopted everywhere?

If immigrants were strictly people migrating from one country to another with the intention of remaining permanently in the new country, few ethical problems would be found regarding the proper educational jurisdiction over them. However, large numbers of immigrants migrate with the intention of remaining only for a short period of time. The European guestworker situation is a good case in point. Guestworkers were invited to migrate on a temporary basis, with the understanding that they would not remain. However, history has demonstrated that the workers brought their spouses with them, they had children, and large numbers of them became permanent residents or immigrants in the strict sense of the term. In countries such as Germany, Sweden and Great Britain, the state itself exercised complete control over immigrant children, although some sense of cooperation with foreign governments was maintained. For example, West German authorities worked diligently with foreign consulates that provided not only resources and teachers but input into the definition of language and culture programmes for the children of guestworkers (Willke, 1975). Monkman (1997) has shown that US policies regarding the education provided for Mexican children is based on the assumption that they ought to be Americanised, while the Mexicans themselves, even while they wish to learn English, are much more transnational in their orientation and resist being exclusively Americanised.

Policies are written and enacted that do not always do justice to the reality of the situation of our changing, global world, and comparative education must contribute a more enlightened dialogue about policy formation and implementation within this turbulent, global context. Transnational education policies are inevitable; however, multinational and national policy orientations are, by definition, high risk because no one really knows how they will affect local conditions. Grand schemes must begin to include more local, organic policy processes.

Schools as Part of the Equation of Change

While comparative educators are actively involved with policy issues regarding globalisation, many have failed to recognise the importance of localisation. Those who have focused on localisation are usually committed to radical change and give almost all their attention to issues such as the resurgence of local cultural identities, ethnicities, grass roots movements and alternative life-style groups (Arnove & Torres, 1999). They have deliberately neglected the role of the school, because they see it as an instrument of the larger social, economic and political context, serving the functions assigned to it (Carnoy & Levin, 1976). However, the role of the school should not be forgotten; all the national and global forces, including new policies and administrative measures decided by educational authorities, meet in one place: the school.

Education policy specialists have long given attention to the school. But the models they have developed have focused almost exclusively on policy implementation rather than policy formation (see, for example, Dalin, 1978, 1994). Schools are usually seen as the targets of education policy, and little thought has been given to them as participants in policy formation. One movement that in some respects contradicts this general observation has been the 'populism' of Thatcherism in Britain that has given some life to the idea of participatory policy formation (McLean, 1989).

The American Research and Development (R & D) experience illustrates the consequence of treating schools as instruments of larger societal forces. Based on their experience with agricultural extension programmes, where extension agents go to farms and help farmers adopt new farming processes, the American Federal Government established a general education R & D policy requiring a hierarchy of institutions. At the top of this hierarchy is the university, which engages in basic educational research. Education R & D centres would transform the basic research products into practical educational programmes. Regional laboratories would make the educational programmes culturally and locally relevant. Finally, informed, rational teachers would recognise the advantages of the new programmes and incorporate them into their school activities. Of course, the design has been a failure. The blame has usually been directed towards the teachers for 'resisting' change and failing to adapt. However, changing schools is far more complex than introducing a new corn seed or variety of sugar beet. Tensions continue between state education offices and local schools because the schools are still seen as recipients of state mandates rather than as partners in change (Dalin & Rust, 1983).

The rhetoric of educational reform in England suggests that the English may be more enlightened than the Americans, in that the Education Reform Act of 1988 intended to create alliances between the Department of Education and Science and the local schools (McLean, 1989). Unfortunately, a decade of experience with this Act has confirmed that the Department has exercised its 'latent powers' by centralising most authority and imposing its decisions on the schools. In other words, the English schools enjoy no more autonomy than the American schools.

Certain school policy models are finally beginning to give credence to localised, personal endeavours. In Western Germany, scholars such as Hans-Günter Rolff (1991, 1992) are relying on self-organisation theory (Jantsch, 1980; Shieve & Allen, 1982) that views the schools themselves as the primary agents of school change and grass-roots initiators of more general school policy. Rolff claims, however, that the authority structure above the schools plays a vital role if self-organisation efforts are to succeed. Central authorities must provide support, consultation, training, communication, etc. to cultivate and encourage school change.

Unfortunately, relationships between state ministries and local schools usually remain top–down in nature. Let me cite an example from the former Soviet Union and another from Eastern Europe. Azerbaijan is undergoing a so-called educational transformation similar to that of the other republics of the former Soviet Union, though when we look at the Azerbaijan school, very little has changed. Teachers remain subject to a highly authoritarian, uniform, centralised and corrupt system of education. Even the higher education institutions must gain permission of the Ministry of Education to change a department chair or alter a programme in any way. Organisationally, Azerbaijan continues to maintain its unified, comprehensive school. This means its curricular programme is as uniform and as tightly controlled as it ever was under socialist ideology.

Having visited scores of schools in Azerbaijan, I must interject a note of hope. The most interesting indicator of change in Azerbaijan is the rise of diversity outside the official governmental structure. A number of small, individual efforts are taking place both in the private sector and in the public sector, where educators are taking steps on their own and have initiated broader discussions of how to improve the situation in the schools. Throughout Azerbaijan, individual school initiatives have sprung up, serving as sources of pride and renewal. Of course, many efforts fail, but others succeed and flourish. Out of this has come a spark of hope, but that hope will only be realised if schools begin to participate with authorities above them in formulating policies. If reform occurs, it will probably come in large measure from the bottom and work its way up in the system, but to this point the formal bureaucracy impedes more than it facilitates school improvement.

Another case in point is Eastern Germany following the collapse of the Soviet Union. In 1989 the command system collapsed overnight, creating a total vacuum of authority from the Minister of Education down to the local school leaders. Remarkably, the schools not only continued to function but each school began to mobilise itself, and its faculty engaged in efforts to rethink their entire programme and develop a new, more appropriate form and content of education. Of course, after it became clear that East Germany would be 'Westernised', these individual plans were disregarded and a top–down imposition of West German schooling took place (Rust & Rust, 1995).

The Azerbaijan and East German developments suggest that models of policy studies must begin to take account of small, individual innovations by people who are not intent on bringing about changes in the big picture. They are simply professionals who are trying to improve themselves and their classroom or school, although their inspiration often springs from broader messages in the media and developments in the local community about the way things can be (Abbott, 1991). In other words, the school's community is rapidly becoming the global village of which the school is now an integral part.

Policy Models and the Developing Countries

In some respects, conventional policy models have gained a place in certain parts of the developing world. Latin America has a strong tradition of corporatism, although this type of interest intermediation has little in common with what I have labelled democratic corporatism and more in common with authoritarian versions of state corporatism (Schmitter, 1974). However, it is particularly difficult to apply conventional policy-making models to certain situations in the developing world. In sub-Saharan Africa, countries inherited or adopted educational policies reflecting colonial attitudes; policy formation processes almost always reflect continuing involvement of former colonisers and foreign aid agencies. Nearly 40 years after political independence, most sub-Saharan countries find themselves more 'grown than developed'. Even when developed jointly with government officials, policy documents are perceived by those in the local bureaucracy to belong to the donor agency and as exogenous to local policy-making. The national capacity for policy formation remains uninstitutionalised and episodic mainly because the policy foundation set by national procedures is quickly submerged under a flood of donor-generated country plans, sector studies, feasibility studies and staff appraisal reports that drive new investment and shape educational policy (Soumaré, 1998).

Let me discuss the implications of this issue regarding the country of Mali, where the Ministry of Basic Education recently adopted

Education Project IV. Aminata Soumaré (1998) studied the policy formation process in Mali and was dismayed to find almost no involvement on the part of local decision-makers in the process and almost no initiatives coming from national ministry officials, who were neither engaged in a process of developing their own reform agenda nor did they really read and try to understand the documents being developed by international agencies. Let us consider Soumaré's observations in the context of two interest intermediation models.

Within the pluralist model, the legitimate role of the Ministry of Basic Education is perceived to be that of a respondent to the needs and wishes of interest groups in the society. The Ministry is expected to coordinate, but not be the primary source of education policy. From a pluralist perspective, the task of the Ministry is to play a passive role and to respond to external forces that provide the impetus for change.

Within the democratic corporatist model, the state itself, as expressed in the Ministry, takes an active and initiating role in establishing education policy, but it does this in explicit partnership with major economic and representative social organisations such as business, labour, the professions, the churches, or, indeed, professional organisations of educators.

At first glance it might appear that the pluralist model best describes the passive role of the Ministry in Mali, while the main forces for change come from outside the bureaucracy. However, the infrastructure such a model depends on is so underdeveloped in Mali that the organisations to which the Ministry might be responsive are not internal to the country but are international, such as the World Bank. This situation is apparently frustrating and not effective; literacy has fallen, not risen, education has foundered, not flourished. Further, the confidence of educators in their own effectiveness and roles has been undermined by alien agencies.

If the pluralist model is inappropriate, so is the corporatist model. First, a 'corporatist' government takes an active role in policy formation and implementation, but in Mali the Ministry is not functionally active. The second requirement of the model, that the government form alliances with organised groups within the nation, is also not found in Mali. And, again, the agencies with which the Ministry is aligned are international, not national. Soumaré advocates a type of corporatist model in that she recognises that the Ministry officials are not strong enough to deal with international agencies on their own, and she feels that they ought to build ties with other agencies, both within and outside the government of Mali itself, such as the Ministry of Health, which has some history of adequate planning and use of statistics. Other agencies might be farmers' associations, educational groups, religious groups and village chiefs. Fundamentally, the decision-makers within the Ministry could come to realise that such alliances do not undermine, but rather strengthen, its own position, especially *vis-à-vis* international aid agencies, by facilitating more relevant and effective educational change rooted deep within the culture of Mali. However, from my vantage point, the overriding presence of international agencies negates the adoption of either the pluralist or corporatist model and necessitates the development of a model that incorporates both the international agency factor and global forces in general into the policy formation process (Guthrie, 1994).

Concluding Remarks

Comparative education is well situated to contribute to the further development of education policy studies. On the one hand, comparative education can contribute to many of the current difficulties policy studies is experiencing, particularly to help contextualise cross-national policy activities, to help policy studies move from a practice-oriented field to one relying heavily on social science theory, to assist policy studies specialists overcome their ideological and theoretical divisions and to gain a firmer grounding of the policy studies models being used in the field. On the other hand, comparative education can work closely with education policy studies because both address the challenges presented by globalising and localising developments. However, to accomplish these challenges, comparative educators must further develop their own transnational competence (IIE, 1997).

Notes

[1] The initial editors were Philip G. Altbach, Gail P. Kelly, Hugh G. Petrie and Lois Weis, when the journal was first published in 1986.

[2] ARTICLE I, Section 3 stipulates the Purposes of CIES and subsections b and e have strong policy implications: (a) promote teaching and research in comparative and international education in institutions of higher learning in both domestic and international contexts; (b) foster application of comparative theories and research in applied settings; (c) facilitate publication and dissemination of comparative, cross-cultural, interdisciplinary and international studies contributing to interpretation of developments in the field of education in their broad and interrelated political, economic and social context; (d) encourage educational and cultural exchanges; and (e) promote and foster understanding of how educational policies and programmes can improve social and economic development.

[3] J. R. Hough (1984) defines four main phases in the policy process: (1) issue emergence and problem identification; (2) policy formulation and authorisation; (3) policy implementation; and (4) termination or change of policy. Thomas R. Dye (1981) outlines five phases: (1) identifying

problems; (2) formulating policy proposals; (3) legitimating policies; (4) implementing policies; and (5) evaluating policies. Each of these phases is also usually conceptualised as having additional steps or phases.

[4] Most of these orientations stress policy based on a scientific and technological foundation. Formation Phase might have the following steps. First, a problem area must be identified. Next, goals and priorities must be specified. Third, all alternative courses of action are listed, and the potential impacts of each are identified. Fourth, some decision criteria or some decision rules are adopted. Finally, a decision is made which maximises the attainment of the goals.

[5] Globalisation and localisation must also not be confused with centralisation and decentralisation, which are connected with the administrative structure of systems such as education. See, for example, Weiler (1989a) for a comparative discussion of decentralisation.

[6] Many immigrants do not initially come to a country for the purpose of permanent residence. In Europe, for example, since World War II, the largest immigration has been that of so-called 'guestworkers', most of whom eventually remained permanently.

References

Abbot, John (1991) *The Creation of Effective Modern Learning Communities: constructivism in practice*, Management Analysis Paper (MAP). Oslo: International Movements Towards Educational Change (IMTEC).

Apple Classroom of Tomorrow Project (1993) *Apple Classroom of Tomorrow Project*, IMTEC School Year 2020 MAP no. 501. Oslo: IMTEC.

Aho, C. Michael (1994) 'Fortress Europe': will the EU isolate itself from North America and Asia? *The Columbia Journal of World Business*, 29(3), pp. 32–39.

Archer, Margaret (1985) The Myth of Cultural Integration, *British Journal of Sociology*, 36, pp. 333–353.

Arnove, Robert F. & Torres, Carlos Alberto (Eds) (1999) *Comparative Education: the dialectic of the global and the local*. Lanham: Rowan & Littlefield.

Baneth, Jan (1993) *'Fortress Europe' and Other Myths about Trade*. Geneva: World Bank.

Bachrach, Peter & Baratz, Morton S. (1962) Two Faces of Power, *American Political Science Review*, 56, pp. 947–952.

Barber, Benjamin (1995) *Jihad vs. McWorld*. New York: Times Books.

Baolnc-Szanton, Crisina (1994) *Nations Unbound: transnational projects, postcolonial predicaments and deterritorialized nation-states*. Luxembourg: Gordon & Breach.

Bell, Daniel (1973) *The Coming Post-industrial Society*. New York: Basic Books.

Bereday, George Z.F. (1964) *Comparative Method in Education*. New York: Holt, Rinehart & Winston.

Bergsten, C.F. (1988) *America in the World Economy: a strategy for the 1990s.* Washington, DC: Institute for International Economics.

Briseid, Ole (1995) Comprehensive reform in Upper Secondary Education in Norway: a retrospective view, *European Journal of Education*, 30, pp. 323–332.

Carnoy, Martin & Levin, Henry (Eds) (1976) *The Limits of Educational Reform.* New York: McKay.

Cawson, Alan (1982) *Corporatism and Welfare.* London: Heinemann.

Cherryholmes, Cleo H. (1988) *Power and Criticism: poststructuralism investigations in education.* New York: Columbia University, Teachers College.

Collis, B. & de Vries, P. (1994) New Technologies and Learning in the European Community, *T.H.E. Journal*, 21, pp. 83–87.

Culbert, Samuel (1996) *Mind-set Management: the heart of leadership.* New York: Oxford University Press.

Dalin, Per (1978) *Limits to Educational Change.* London: Macmillan.

Dalin, Per (1994) *Skoleutvikling: teorier for forandring.* Oslo: Universitetsforlaget.

Dalin, Per & Rust, Val D. (1983) *Can Schools Learn?* London: NFER–Nelson.

Dalin, Per & Rust, Val D. (1996) *Towards Schooling for the Twenty-first Century.* London: Cassell.

Dye, Thomas R. (1981) *Understanding Public Policy.* Englewood Cliffs: Prentice-Hall.

Eisler, R. & Loye, D. (1987) Chaos and Transformation: implications of nonequilibrium theory for social science and society, *Behavioral Science*, 32, pp. 53–65.

Foucault, Michel (1980) *Power/Knowledge.* New York: Pantheon.

Fraser, Stewart E. & Brickman, William W. (Eds) (1968) *A History of International and Comparative Education.* Glenview: Scott, Foresman & Co.

Fukuyama, Francis (1992) *The End of History and the Last Man.* New York: Free Press.

Gardner, David P. (1983) *A Nation at Risk: the imperative for educational reform.* Washington, DC: The National Commission of Excellence in Education.

Giddens, Anthony (1995) *Beyond Left and Right: the future of radical politics.* Cambridge: Polity Press.

Gleick, James (1987) *Chaos: making a new science.* New York: Viking.

Guthrie, Gerard (1994) Globalization of Educational Policy and Reform, *International Encyclopaedia of Education.* Oxford: Pergamon.

Habermas, Jürgen (1993) Modernity – an incomplete project, in Hal Foster (Ed.) *The Anti-aesthetic: essays on postmodern culture*, pp. 3–15. Seattle: Bay Press.

Halpin, David & Troyna, Barry (Eds) (1994) *Researching Education Policy: ethical and methodological issues.* London: Falmer Press.

Hannertz, Ulf (1990) Cosmopolitans and Locals in World Culture, *Theory, Culture and Society*, 7, pp. 237–251.

Hans, Nicholas (1949) *Comparative Education: a study of educational factors and traditions.* London: Routledge & Kegan Paul.

Hein, Jeremy (1993) Refugees, Immigrants, and the State, *Annual Review of Sociology*, 19, pp. 43–59.

Held, David (Ed.) (1991) *Political Theory Today.* Stanford: Stanford University Press.

Heyman, Richard (1979) Comparative Education from an Ethnomethdological Perspective, *Comparative Education*, 15, pp. 241–249.

Hirst, Paul & Thompson, Grahame (1996) *Globalization in Question.* Cambridge: Polity Press.

Hobsbawm, Eric (1994) *The Age of Extremes: a history of the world, 1914–1991.* New York: Pantheon.

Hough, J.R. (Ed.) (1984) *Educational Policy: an international survey.* London: Croom Helm.

Institute of International Education (1997) *Towards Transnational Competence: rethinking international education.* New York: Institute of International Education.

Jantsch, Eric (1980) *The Self-organizing Universe.* Oxford: Pergamon.

Jencks, Charles (1987) *What Is Post-modernism?* New York: St Martin's Press.

Kelly, Gail & Nihlen, A. (1982) Schooling and the Reproduction of Patriarchy, in Michael Apple (Ed.) *Cultural and Economic Reproduction in Education*, pp. 162–180. London: Routledge & Kegan Paul.

Kim, Anna (1997) Free Trade and Education in Korea, PhD dissertation, University of California, Los Angeles.

Lembruch, Gerhard & Schmitter, Philippe C. (Eds) (1982) *Patterns of Corporatist Policy-making.* Beverly Hills: Sage.

Lorenz, Edward N. (1993) *The Essence of Chaos.* Seattle: University of Washington Press.

Mander, Jerry & Goldsmith, Edward (Eds). (1992) *The Case against the Global Economy: and for a turn toward the local.* San Francisco: Sierra Club Books.

Masemann, Vandra. (1990) Ways of Knowing, *Comparative Education Review*, 34, pp. 465–473.

Mclean, Martin. (1989) Populist Centralism: the 1988 Education Reform Act in England and Wales, *Educational Policy*, 3, pp. 233–244.

Meyer, John & Hannan, Michael T. (1979) *National Development and the World System.* Chicago: University of Chicago.

Monkman, Karen (1997) Transnational Migration, Gender Relations, and Learning Processes: Mexican adults constructing lives in California, PhD dissertation, University of California, Los Angeles.

Naisbitt, John & Aburdene, Patricia (1990) *Megatrends 2000: ten new directions for the 1990s.* New York: Avon Books.

Nordlinger, Erik (1981) *On the Autonomy of the Democratic State.* Cambridge MA: Harvard University.

Oliver, Dick (1992) *Fractal Vision: put fractals to work for you*. Carmel IN: SAMS Publishing.

Olsen, Johan P. (1981) Integrated Organizational Participation in Government, in Paul C. Nystrom & William H. Starbuch (Eds) *Handbook of Organizational Design*, pp. 493–510. Oxford: Oxford University Press.

Paulston, Rolland G. (1976) *Conflict Theories and Social and Educational Change: a typological review*. Pittsburgh: University of Pittsburgh.

Paulston, Rolland G. (1993) Comparative Education as an Intellectual Field: mapping the theoretical landscape, *Comparative Education*, 23, pp. 101–114.

Prigogine, I. & Stengers, I. (1984) *Order out of Chaos: man's new dialogue with nature*. New York: Bantam Books.

Raab, Charles D. (1994) Where We Are Now: reflections on the sociology of education policy, in David Halpin & Barry Troyna (Eds) *Researching Education Policy: ethical and methodological issues*, pp. 17–30. London: Falmer Press.

Robertson, Roland (1992) *Globalization: social theory and global culture*. London: Sage.

Rolff, Hans-Günter (1991) Schulentwicklung als Entwicklung von Einzelsculen? Theorien und Indikatoren von Entwicklungsprozessen, *Zeitschrift für Pädagogik*, 37, pp. 865–886.

Rolff, Hans-Günter (1992) Die Schule als besondere soziale Organisation – Eine komparative Analyse, *Zeitschrift für Sozialisationsforschung und Erziehungssoziologie*, 12 Jahrgang, Heft 4, pp. 306–324.

Rorty, Richard (1979) *Philosophy and the Mirror of Nature*. Princeton: Princeton University.

Rust, Val D. (1990) The Policy Formation Process and Educational Reform in Norway, *Comparative Education*, 26, pp. 13–25.

Rust, Val D. (1994) Relief Education: a new imperative in Azerbaijan, *Azerbaijan International*, Summer, pp. 24–25.

Rust, Val D. & Rust, Diane (1995) *The Unification of German Education*. New York: Garland.

Rust, Val D. (in press) *Reform 94 in Norway*.

Rust, Val D. (undated) Theory in Comparative Education.

Saunders, P. (1980) *An Introduction to Catastrophe Theory*. Cambridge: Cambridge University Press.

Schieve, William C. & Allen, Peter M. (Eds) (1982) *Self-organization and Dissipative Structures: applications in the physical and social sciences*. Austin: University of Texas Press.

Schmitter, Phillipe C. (1974) Still the Century of Corporatism? *Review of Politics*, 36.

Schriewer, Jürgen (1998) World-system and Interrelationship-networks, in T.S. Popkewitz (Ed.) *Educational Change and Educational Knowledge*. Albany: State University of New York Press.

Simon, Herbert A., Smithburg, Donald W. & Thompson, Victor A. (1972) *Public Administration*. New York: Knopf.

Soumaré, Aminata (1998, unpublished manuscript in press) Educational Reform for Social Change Calls for Reform in the Decision Making Culture in Africa.

Stenhouse, Lawrence (1979) Case Study in Comparative Education: particularity and generalization, *Comparative Education*, 15, pp. 5–10.

Stromquist, Nelly (1990) Gender Inequality in Education: accounting for women's subordination, *British Journal of Sociology of Education*, 11, pp. 137–154.

Taylor, Sandra, Rizvi, Fazal, Lingard, Bob & Henry, Miriam (1997) *Educational Policy and the Politics of Change.* London: Routledge.

Tofler, Alvin (1990) *Powershift.* New York: Bantam.

Torres, Irvent Rolando (1998) American Educational Reform from 1978 to 1998: a case study of institutional reform in a college district, PhD dissertation, University of California, Los Angeles.

Troyna Barry (1994) Reforms, Research and Being Reflexive about Being Reflective, in David Halpin & Barry Troyna (Eds) *Researching Education Policy: ethical and methodological issues*, pp. 1–14. London: Falmer Press.

United Nations Development Programme (UNDP) (1994) *Human Development Report, 1994.* New York: Oxford University Press.

United Nations High Commissioner for Refugees (UNHCR) (1993) UNHCR Guidelines on Refugee Children, in Geraldine van Bueren (Ed.) *International Documents on Children*, pp. 350–386. Dordrecht: Martinus Nijhoff.

Waters, Malcolm (1995) *Globalization.* London: Routledge.

Weiler, Hans (1989a) Education and Power: the politics of educational decentralization in comparative perspective, *Educational Policy*, 3, pp. 31–44.

Weiler, Hans (1989b) Why Reforms Fail: the politics of education in France and the Federal Republic of Germany, *Journal of Curriculum Studies*, 21, pp. 291–305.

Willke, Ingeborg (1975) Schooling of Immigrant Children in West Germany, Sweden, England: the educationally disadvantaged, *International Review of Education*, 21, pp. 357–400.

Wilms, Wilford W. (1996) *Restoring Prosperity: how workers and managers are forging a new culture of cooperation.* New York: Random House.

Wiltshire, Rosina (1992) Implications of Transnational Migration for Nationalism: the Caribbean example, in Linda Busch, Nina Glick Schiller & Cristina Szantaon-Bolanc (Eds) *Toward a Transnational Perspective on Migration: race, class, ethnicity, and nationalism reconsidered*, pp. 175–187. New York: New York Academy of Sciences.

Snakes and Ladders: learning from international comparisons

JOANNA LE MÉTAIS

A parliamentary committee, concerned about the level of school failure, decided to explore strategies adopted overseas. Supported by civil servants, they undertook a fact-finding mission which covered the status of teachers, the role and methods of inspection, developments in information and communications technology, and class size. The programme comprised meetings with the 'great and the good' and practitioners and two school visits – and lasted four days. The experience was a rich one; all those they met spoke of the effectiveness of their activities, despite the difficult circumstances.

When they returned home, committee members enthused about what they had seen and introduced some elements into their education policies.

Unlike the fairy tale, they did not all live happily ever after: practitioners were less than enthusiastic about yet another innovation, the 'bright idea' failed to deliver the desired results, and the politicians were left wondering why.

Concerned about the levels of school failure, a parliamentary committee decided to explore strategies adopted overseas ...

This experience is not uncommon. In the introduction to the specification for its Future Governance Programme, Lessons from Comparative Public Policy, the Economic and Social Research Council states:

Cross-national experience is having an increasingly powerful impact upon policy makers, as governments look to other countries for new ways of organising and delivering public services, and as international obligations upon nations to follow practices developed elsewhere become more pervasive. (ESRC, 1998)

Researchers in cross-national education, particularly those involved in policy research, should be pleased to see the raised profile of their work. Why, then, do we surround our work with so many health warnings? Is it professional preciousness or concern about the ways in which lessons from overseas are learned and applied? We are not alone in expressing such concerns:

> *cross-national lessons are often based upon a superficial understanding of programmes and institutions and of the conditions that contribute to their success or failure. Valid lessons from cross-national experience can only be drawn on the basis of the systematic applications of knowledge about how policies and institutions work. (ESRC, 1998)*

This article contends that the relationship between policy-makers and comparative research is like the familiar game where the apparent progress promised by the roll of the dice can be undermined by landing on a snake. It presents different approaches to gathering and using information about overseas policy and practice and discusses ways in which policy-makers and researchers can overcome the constraints under which they work to derive maximum benefit from their efforts.

Three Snakes

I describe the first three approaches to cross-national lessons as 'snakes' because they distance us from our objectives.

The 'Quick Fix'

This is a common reaction to the publication of a report or cross-national study, especially when the national performance is less than good. For example, when the Third International Mathematics and Science Study (TIMSS, Keys et al, 1996) was published, governments in the United Kingdom and in Australia declared their intention to increase the time students spend on mathematics. This satisfied the demand for instant action, but failed to discriminate between the different elements of mathematics to be taught or the differential performance of students.

It also ignored the limitations of international surveys of educational achievement, arising from methodological and practical problems, research design, sampling and missing information (see, for example, Reynolds & Farrell, 1996).

The Imported Solution or 'Transplant'

This searches for *the* key initiative, which may be transplanted from another country and, when implemented, will transform the nation's students into high performers.

Reynolds (1996, 1997a, 1997b) attributes the success of Oriental students in international studies to whole-class interactive teaching, and the Numeracy Task Force report (Department for Education and Employment [DfEE], 1998) accordingly recommends the adoption of such methods. However, the recommendations do not secure the 'important' factors identified in the research that underpins the proposals, namely:

- the high status of teachers, and the use of specialist teachers who have up to one-third of their time out of the classroom in Pacific Rim countries; and
- homogeneous teaching groups and qualifications which require students to pass in a range of subjects in Germany and the Netherlands (Reynolds & Farrell, 1996, pp. 554–556).

Moreover, Korean and Japanese educators who have participated in our research (O'Donnell et al, 1998) have stressed the role of the evening 'crammers' in the students' success, suggesting that in some cases the 'day school' is perceived as relatively unimportant. Without proper consideration of this supplementary/alternative schooling, and other contextual factors, we cannot be confident of a causal relationship between teaching method and outcome.

The Pick and Mix Package

Compacts were introduced in 1998 to motivate disadvantaged young people living in inner cities to make best use of the education and training opportunities in order to reach their full potential (Saunders et al, 1995, p. iv). The scheme involves employers and secondary school students in a 'compact' or contract, whereby employers guarantee a job to students who have met agreed attendance and performance targets. It was based on a similar project, which a group of businessmen and educators from the Inner London Education Authority had seen in Boston (Martineau, 1988). It was piloted in London and, within the year (before the pilot was evaluated), the scheme was introduced in 54 settings across the country.

Implementation factors. These variations were intentional and included:

- the operation of the scheme in 54 urban areas instead of one;
- the introduction of compacts alongside a range of education–business partnerships which had been established for different purposes,

instead of the creation of partnerships specifically for the Compact programme; and

- the adaptation of criteria for trainees over time and according to local circumstances (which did not apply in the single-city Boston model).

Circumstantial factors. These factors were outside the control of the Programme Directors and industrial partners and included:

- the institutional and curricular changes arising from the implementation of the Education Reform Act 1988;
- the economic prosperity – which made job guarantees seem feasible – gave way to economic recession, which made job guarantees virtually impossible and so an alternative guarantee (a place in further education) was offered; and
- extrinsic motivation: a guaranteed job with training, or a guaranteed place in further education (which was a less powerful motivating force).

Although there were beneficial outcomes, the factors already outlined meant that the evaluation of the Compact scheme between 1990 and 1994 showed that it differed considerably between settings and in some cases bore little resemblance to its conception and the Boston model (see Richardson, 1993). It is therefore not possible to make generalised claims for a 'programme' whose characteristics varied locally and over time (Saunders et al, 1995).

The weaknesses of the three 'snake' approaches are:

- the application of a 'solution' without due consideration of the problem. For example, the benefits of 'an extra hour of mathematics a day' depend on the nature of the activities to be undertaken and the needs of the students involved;
- insufficient consideration of the contexts and influences within which educational systems operate;
- failure to create the organisational and supportive structure on which an initiative depends, for example, teacher non-contact time and mechanisms for ensuring homogeneous teaching groups to support new teaching styles, and the creation of the specific education industry partnerships which gave rise to the development of the Compact programme; and
- the use of a programme name (e.g. Compacts) to designate an adapted form may create inaccurate impressions of the effectiveness of the schemes on which it was based.

Climbing the Ladders – five steps to effective learning from abroad

This rather negative description may lead one to dismiss overseas experience and, consequently, lose the potential benefits. Whilst international studies may simply confirm cultural differences without bringing about improvements in our own system, evaluating our performance relative to others can help to avoid two weaknesses of self-review: uncritical acceptance of traditional problems and traditional solutions, and undue influence of local and current priorities. Such external evidence takes us beyond the task of understanding other systems and moves us towards identifying causes and suggesting ideas and priorities for action *within our own context.* It must be borne in mind, however, that changes may be difficult to implement, have significant ramifications for other aspects of the service and may involve choices between different resource priorities.

1. Setting the Objectives

The first priority is to set the objectives, which may involve choices, for example, between developing individual potential and securing the achievement of minimum targets by all students, or increasing the number of students who achieve the higher grades at General Certificate of Secondary Education (GCSE). Whilst these objectives are not necessarily mutually exclusive, the focus of attention and resources on one area may involve a corresponding reduction in another.

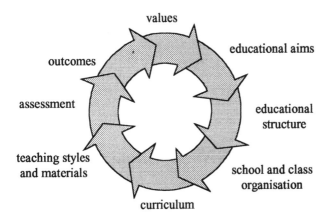

Figure 1. Areas of policy focus.

2. Finding the Focus

Policies and strategies aimed at raising standards have focused on different aspects of the education service, which may be broadly characterised as input, process or output measures. In choosing the focus of their initiatives, policy-makers always have to take into consideration the current (inherited) situation in each of the areas (see Figure 1) and the impact which a reform may have on students part-way through the educational cycle.

3. Exploring the Options

A study of the characteristics which are perceived to contribute to the relative success of high-performing countries can make a constructive contribution. This approach is facilitated by the exposure of policy-makers and practitioners to overseas experiences through visits and meetings, as well as through printed and electronic media. However, each of these sources has strengths and limitations as a basis for policy-making, as I shall discuss.

Visits and meetings. As all educators know, personal experience makes the most powerful and lasting impact. Policy-makers are no exception to this rule, which doubtless accounts for the popularity of fact-finding missions. Their effectiveness as data collection exercises is affected by:

- the desire of receiving countries to show off their successes rather than to dwell on their failures;
- the tendency to schedule a series of presentations, which does not allow scope for detailed exploration of the context, implementation and *unintended* outcomes of policies;
- the rapid rate of change in education policy, which means that the initiatives presented may themselves be too new for a reasoned evaluation to have taken place;
- the fact that politicians are not specialists in education, and, equally, the 'specialist' in the relevant areas may not be available at the scheduled time; and
- the need for interpretation between languages, which affects the quality of understanding and of discussion.

There is often a tendency to 'maximise' the benefits of a visit covering a number of themes (as in the aforementioned example), which exponentially increases the problems. The better targeted the visit, the richer the information.

As a result, a visit *can* tell us the purpose and the nature of the initiative, the factors affecting its success and whether any evaluation has taken place. A visit usually *does not reveal* coherence between intention and implementation, the degree of success and any unintended consequences.

Cross-national meetings are also increasing. For example, ministers and senior officials in the European Union have a cycle of regular meetings which helps them build up an understanding of one another's systems as part of the cooperative striving for more effective education throughout the Union. But the constraints are similar to those applying to visits and, especially in the case of ministerial meetings, education decisions must be considered in the broad political and economic context.

Printed and electronic media. Much, not to say most, information has traditionally been obtained through published documents: official publications, research reports etc. These raise problems of access (language, timescale and cost), quality (accuracy, completeness and currency), impartiality and comparability. Whilst increasing access to the Internet speeds up the process and reduces the cost, the other questions remain.

Subject to these reservations, the Internet can make a considerable contribution to our information pool. For example, a single UNESCO site [1] offers links to international education organisations, ministries of education, comparative education societies and institutions, educational research and academic institutions, education journals, conferences and meetings. Secondly, subject only to language constraints (and many sites now have English language pages), access to ministry and other documents is virtually instant and free. Thirdly, research findings become available, even in refereed journals, within weeks rather than months.

4. Evaluating the Options

Before adoption, initiatives should be evaluated in terms of their effectiveness – in the originating country and elsewhere – and in terms of the characteristics, factors and context which contribute to their success or failure. Attention should also be given to exploring any unintended outcomes.

The speed and extent of educational change may mean that the initiative under consideration may not yet have been evaluated. In any case, it is important to assess proposed strategies in the light of other research findings. For example, Reynolds's (1997a) support for 'whole class interactive teaching, where the teacher is the centre of the class and instructs the class for about 90 per cent of the lesson time' is not supported by Jensen (1998), who argues that:

> *when teachers insist on holding students' attention, they miss the fact that much learning comes through indirect acquisition, such as peer discussion or environmental stimuli. By making excessive attentional demands on students, teachers can create resentful learners. Ultimately, brain-compatible teachers may engage learners' attention only 20 to 40 per cent of the time and still do a great job. Teachers need to keep attentional demands to short bursts of no longer than the age of their learners in minutes ... teachers ought to spend*

> *55–80 per cent of their time allowing students to process*
> *information. (Jensen, 1998)*

It is notoriously difficult to isolate *the* factor which is responsible for success, particularly when a series of reforms have been introduced concurrently or within a short timescale (as has been the case in England and Wales).

Outcomes attributed to specific educational policies may, equally, result from unrelated contextual influences. For example, does an increase in staying-on rates result from relevance of curricula or from a lack of jobs? Contextual influences apply at different levels. Political, economic, cultural, social, linguistic and religious influences may operate at national or regional level. Whilst, individually and collectively, they may contribute to educational performance, these aspects cannot be readily 'imported' alongside an initiative. However, by examining the articulation between the elements, we may find ways of creating similarly supportive links within our own society.

The staff, students and their parents constitute the immediate school community and their values, attitudes and resources affect the way in which the school and its students set and achieve their objectives. Here again, it is worth examining strategies which have been found to promote effective partnerships between the three groups in different contexts.

Finally, we are not alone in having a proportion of young people who have not achieved the standards which society considers essential for a happy and productive adult life. If, as Tomlinson & Kalbfleisch (1998) contend, 'the one size fits all approach to classroom teaching is ineffective for most students and harmful to some', then it may be more helpful to take our focus beyond mainstream provision and examine the ways in which countries make provision for the 'context' of students 'at risk'.

In some cases, the contributory factors may not be immediately apparent. For example, Cataldi (1994) and Diaz (1985) argue that a strong knowledge of two languages may make a positive contribution to students' educational achievement by developing mental flexibility, concept formation and a metalinguistic awareness. This benefit may not be apparent to those who take their bilingual environment for granted. It is here that general studies of students' learning provide valuable insights.

A study of unintended outcomes is essential. The emotional or social 'cost' of a policy may outweigh its academic benefits. For example, whilst the achievements of students in Japan and Korea are often cited as examples to emulate, the consequences in terms of pressure on young people or convergent thinking patterns may not be desirable.

5. *Making and Supporting the Choices*

Linking progress to purpose is essential. The race to be 'top of the league' may not be in students', or in a country's, best interest. There is enormous scope for demotivation, given that only one country can 'win'. Moreover, educational *purpose* is an important determinant of progress. It is therefore necessary to use the comparative information on possible outcomes, in order to address questions such as the following.

- What does the nation want its achievements to be?
- Does the nation want to do (equally) well in all subjects?
- Can performance be improved in all subjects, or only in one at the expense of others?
- What effect would pursuing higher performance in (for example) science, English and mathematics have on the overall breadth of the curriculum?

To what extent does the success of an initiative depend on circumstances which we can re-create? Whilst it may be possible to raise the perceived status of teachers (through the creation of a General Teachers' Council and increasing salaries), the respect for their profession engendered by the traditional Oriental regard for learning is more difficult to secure.

In terms of cost, whilst staff training is an accepted cost of innovation, are we able and willing to resource up to 33% non-contract time? It is argued that in England and Wales teachers' energy is channelled into the production of worksheets rather than classroom instruction and marking (Reynolds & Farrell, 1996). Are we prepared to remedy this situation, and underline the importance of textbooks to students, by issuing them with a set of new textbooks in each school year, as is the case in Japan?

Back in the Real World

Understanding the Pressures

Politicians operate under considerable pressure. Research findings and survey reports seldom appear at the most propitious political and budgetary moment. Media reports tend to sensationalise, often taking a negative view, and clamour (on behalf of the people) for 'solutions' or, at the very least, 'action'.

Whilst education is a long-term activity offering limited scope for instant reforms and no instant outcomes, the electoral cycle is limited and no government can bank on being returned to office. Thus, to be politically attractive, education policies must not only contribute to a long-term benefit, but must show results in the medium or even short term.

At the same time, all reforms have resource implications. A compromise must be sought between competing demands. Which of the government's duties and services should take priority? A carefully balanced decision may be derailed by yet another exposure of the vulnerabilities of the aged, the homeless or the sick.

Meeting the Needs

In this context, it clearly is not helpful to offer detailed findings 'next year', however impeccable the research. Equally, in the light of what has already been said, whilst anticipation of results from research in progress, or extrapolations from foreign contexts may hold out a promise, there is no guarantee that it will be fulfilled.

The optimum solution therefore lies in a combination of research and information activities which can be drawn on in different ways, and at short notice, to inform policy decisions.[2] The combination would include:

- ongoing collection of information on systems and policies and contexts in different countries (to inform cross-national meetings or visits and contextualise survey results) and, by giving alternative examples, stimulate analysis of our own educational provision;
- in-depth studies of curriculum and teaching, to identify the theoretical basis, and help evaluate the likely effectiveness, of new initiatives; and
- short-term case studies to evaluate initiatives and identify the characteristics and circumstances which contribute to their success.

The outcomes would be characterised by:

- targeted recommendations and implications, based on findings;
- brief supporting evidence; and
- any contextual notes which are essential for understanding national distinctions.

Building Partnerships

For this approach to work:

- both sides would need to invest time in identifying needs and clarifying processes;
- communication would need to be ongoing to take account of changes in policy and priorities; and
- there must be mutual trust and a collaborative approach as a foundation for achieving best fit within imperfect circumstances.

Conclusion

If we wait for perfection, we would never embark on anything. We therefore need to look for a best-fit compromise between political imperatives and quality research. The most important contributor is ongoing dialogue whereby we can clarify objectives, explain constraints and identify opportunities.

Notes

[1] http://www.ibe.unesco.org/News/Link/links.htm#mined

[2] See Le Métais (1998).

References

Cataldi, J.R. (1994) Bilingualism and Early Language Acquisition – great assets, *National Association of Secondary School Principals Bulletin*, 78, pp. 62–64.

Department for Education and Employment (DfEE) (1998) *The Implementation of the National Numeracy Strategy. The Final Report of the Numeracy Task Force.* London: DfEE. Available on-line: http://www.open.gov.uk/dfee/numeracy/chapter1.htm Chapter 1.

Diaz, R.M. (1985) *The Intellectual Power of Bilingualism* (ERIC Document Reproduction Service No. ED 283 368).

Economic and Social Research Council (ESRC) (1998) Specification for *Future Governance Programme: lessons from comparative public policy*. Swindon: ESRC.

Jensen, E. (1998) How Julie's Brain Learns, *Educational Leadership*, 56, pp. 41–45.

Keys, W., Harris, S. & Fernandes, C. (1996) *Third International Mathematics and Science Study, First National Report. Part 1: Achievement in Mathematics and Science at Age 13 in England.* Slough: National Foundation for Educational Research.

Le Métais, J. (1998) Contrasting Approaches to Comparative Education Research, paper presented at the British Association for International and Comparative Education (BAICE) Inaugural Conference: Doing Comparative Education Research: issues and problems. University of Reading, 12 September.

Martineau, R. (1988) How We Got Going with Compact, *CBI News*, 27 May – 9 June. London: Confederation of British Industry.

O'Donnell, S., Le Métais, J., Boyd, S. & Tabberer, R. (1998) *INCA: the International Review of Curriculum and Assessment Frameworks Archive*, 2nd edn (CD-ROM). London: Qualifications and Curriculum Authority. Also available on-line at: http://www.inca.org.uk

Reynolds, D. (1996) The Truth, the Whole-class Truth, *The Times Educational Supplement*, 7 June, p. 21.

Richardson, W. (1993) Employers as an Instrument of School Reform? Education-business 'compacts' in Britain and America.

Reynolds, D. (1997a) East–West Trade-off, *The Times Educational Supplement*, 27 June, p. 21.

Reynolds, D. (1997b) Good Ideas Can Wither in Another Culture, *The Times Educational Supplement*, 12 September, p. 17.

Reynolds, D. & Farrell, S. (1996) *Worlds Apart? A Review of International Surveys of Educational Achievement Involving England.* London: Office for Standards in Education.

Saunders, L., Morris, M., Stoney, S. with Schagen, I. & Sims, D. (1995) *National Evaluation of Urban Compacts.* Sheffield: Employment Department.

Tomlinson, C. & Kalbfleisch, M.L. (1998) Teach Me, Teach My Brain: a call for differentiated classrooms, *Educational Leadership*, 56, pp. 52–55.

Higher Education: polemic and policy imperatives

MARY-LOUISE KEARNEY

Introduction

The current trends and new challenges facing higher education imply the need to rethink its role and mission, identify new approaches and set new priorities for future development. (UNESCO, 1995, Foreword)

The purposes of this article are:

- to review the various challenges affecting higher education policy;
- to assess aspects of the diversification option; and
- to emphasise the role of partnerships in future action.

Today, it might be said that the ongoing crisis in higher education has reached a watershed. Certainly the moment for profound review seems to have arrived, as is witnessed by the recent studies and major reports on the present and future health of this sector undertaken by several major institutions, notably, UNESCO (1995) *Policy Paper for Change and Development in Higher Education*, The World Bank (1994) *The Lessons of Experience* and the Organisation for Economic Cooperation and Development (OECD) (1998a) *Rethinking Tertiary Education,* (UNESCO, 1999) the Final Report of the World Conference on Higher Education, and (World Bank/UNESCO, 2000) *Higher Education in Developing Countries: peril and promise* (Report of the Independent Task Force). The outcomes of their respective analyses have sparked debate in countries across all regions which are seeking effective and innovative policies to deal with the current socio-economic issues affecting their development.

Indeed, for many in the higher education community, the rate of recent change has been not only unprecedented but also largely unforeseen. Consequently, systems and institutions are obliged to face issues of growing gravity for which solutions are urgent. In this regard, and although the polemic will doubtless continue, sound policy imperatives to ensure quality and relevance must be constructed. This heralds an era of real change where benefits must be available to all parties concerned. What are the risks? Who are the stakeholders? While not proposing any definitive answers, this article will offer comments on the current mood of the debate.

For this purpose, a basic definition of higher education, already nearly a decade old, will be that adopted by the General Conference of UNESCO at its twenty-seventh session in 1993:

> *All types of studies, training or training for research at the post-secondary level, provided by universities or other post-secondary establishments that are approved as institutions of higher education by the competent state authorities.*

In addition, the new opportunities for non-formal learning resulting from the impact of information technology must also be fully recognised when discussing policy imperatives for higher education.

Present Policy Challenges

> *To manage, even generate, quickening change while ensuring stability has itself become one of the policy challenges of today. Education, broadly conceived, is both a defining characteristic of modern societies and a key strategic means for realizing desired change. (OECD, 1998, p. 17)*

Major Issues

These can be listed as follows:

- the impact of massified higher education;
- the resulting need to diversify its provision;
- reduced resources;
- the task of maintaining quality and relevance;
- the potential of new technologies for teaching and learning; and
- the phenomenon of internationalisation.

By now, these questions have been extensively debated by national and institutional policy- and decision-makers across all regions. The problems are largely the same but the means of resolving them differ significantly, due to varied national capacities and socio-economic conditions. Moreover, governments and higher education institutions (especially universities) do not see these questions in the same light.

This, of course, is the source of the polemic. These issues warrant some specific attention because closer agreement on purpose and process amongst the main parties involved has become necessary.

National and institutional priorities. For governments, the principal task must be to ensure a national context which facilitates democracy, social stability, economic development, cultural tolerance and equity of opportunity for all citizens. Even if the present trend is towards reduced and leaner government, sustainable national and international development depend to a large extent on five crucial elements:

- *a foundation of law*
- *a benign policy environment (including macro-economic stability)*
- *investment in people and infrastructure*
- *protection of the vulnerable*
- *safeguard of the natural environment. (World Bank, 1997, p. 4)*

To attain these objectives, education has become essential – i.e. knowledge, skills, information, values, communication and exchange. Above all, there must be equality of educational opportunities to avert social exclusion and resulting deprivation for all groups of the population. While differing socio-economic levels may continue to exist, equity must permeate policy orientations so as to permit all citizens to enjoy an adequate lifestyle and to formulate aspirations for their own future advancement. More pragmatically, social failure is costly for countries and so must be avoided if possible. In the past, a more buoyant labour market could accommodate those who did not succeed in the more rigid examination at the end of secondary studies. In contrast, jobs are more technical and skilled in today's context. Thus, it is necessary to rethink secondary schooling so as to diversify the competences acquired by students who complete this level.

These social realities have obliged governments to review their investment in education at all levels in order to achieve a better balance amongst these in terms of their contribution to social development. In effect, this and other areas of social policy investment constitute a real juggling act for governments and have become the chief target of criticism and even opprobrium on the part of the electorate.

For higher education institutions, the perspective has been somewhat different. It is widely accepted that this sector is of paramount importance for social and economic development. According to the World Bank:

> *Institutions of higher education have the main responsibility for equipping individuals with the advanced knowledge and skills required for positions of responsibility in government, business and the professions. (1994, p. iv)*

This particular definition would certainly apply to universities once described by Benjamin Disraeli as places 'of light, liberty and learning' where minds and characters were moulded on the basis of proven intellectual ability. But, today, the definition might also hold valid for more vocationally-oriented institutions which provide training in a range of work-related fields of competence.

For a long time, this dichotomy between education (in the sense of research-based teaching) and training (in the sense of skill acquisition) dominated the debate on higher education. However, this has undergone rapid change in the last 5 years due to the much greater demand for post-secondary education and to the changing nature of society in general and of work in particular. As a result, the whole concept of higher education and of its missions and methods of delivery is now under serious discussion by industrialised and developing countries alike so as to adapt to the reality of the 'learning society' – i.e. one which invests adequately in education and training for its citizens throughout life.

Dealing with Massified Higher Education

Of course, it is clear that increased demand for post-secondary education and training is simply the inevitable result of enhanced participation at the lower levels of the system. To some extent, this is true since governments have striven to universalise basic and secondary instruction within their formal educational systems. A glance at gross enrolment ratios in countries with widely differing development levels can corroborate this argument (see Tables I and II).

Primary education	1985 (%)	1995 (%)
Afghanistan	20	49
Guatemala	76	84
Israel	97	99
Samoa	104	116

Table I. (Source: *World Education Report*, UNESCO, 1998a.)

Secondary education	1985 (%)	1995 (%)
Saudi Arabia	42	56
Botswana	29	56
Portugal	52	102

Table II. (Source: *World Education Report*, UNESCO, 1998a.)

Given these trends, the arrival of greater numbers of students at the post-secondary level is to be expected (see Table III).

Tertiary Education	1985 (%)	1995 (%)	
Cote d'Ivoire	2.6	4.4	+1.8
Peru	22.4	31.1	+8.7
Bulgaria	18.9	39.4	+12.6
Australia	27.7	71.7	+44.0
Canada	69.9	102.9	+63.0
Norway	29.6	54.5	+24.9

Table III. (Source: *World Education Report*, UNESCO, 1998a).

Two aspects of these data are important. In industrialised countries, the situation has changed significantly since the 1970s when massification was described by Martin Trow as a participation level of around 35% of the student cohort. In the developing world, demand for higher education has grown sharply, despite the pressure on governments to invest more resources in basic education.

Furthermore, if improved access to any level of education is considered to be a matter of equity and witnesses to enhanced social inclusion, then post-secondary education cannot be an exception in this regard. However, one question emerges as paramount: *what type of post-secondary institution should be accessed by what type of student?* Should all students aspire to university education and should entry to such an institution be altered to cater for demand? Should provision be broader to deal with the increased numbers?

It is common for governments to view universities as underutilised in terms of dispensing more varied education and training – especially when the cost of diverse provision is beyond the budget of many states. Meanwhile, universities themselves respond by insisting on specific standards for admission and on quality controls which are appropriate for academic studies. Clearly, ideology and provision will continue to fuel a major debate to which there may be no totally satisfactory solution unless there is a radical rethinking of post-secondary education on national and global scales. There is ample justification for such a move, given the social and labour context of the late 1990s and its expected development into the new millennium.

Towards Diversified Tertiary Education

Responsiveness to demand, diversity and client orientation are keys to the successful adaptation of systems to the changing environment. (OECD, 1998, p. 101)

The Role of Education in the Twenty-first Century

We are often reminded that the third millennium will be characterised as the knowledge society. Already in evidence, this will reach levels of sophistication hitherto inconceivable to all but a few technology gurus. Once again, definitions require review, starting with education itself. As stated, this will encompass knowledge, skills, information, values, communication and the exchange of all these elements. These will be available in both formal and non-formal settings, with technology as a constant and forceful factor, thus broadening still further the scope of educational provision. Learning may be flexible, often self-paced and possibly highly selective – but, above all, the act of learning will be the most valuable of all in terms of equipping the student for a changing world.

This is a daunting prospect to all nations and especially for the developing countries where exclusion from progress by means of broader and innovative educational provision will surely result in aggravated levels of poverty and deprivation.

The knowledge society will require a new emphasis on the role of the learner, whose needs will drive policy decisions. Importantly, the knowledge society extends to the labour market, which has undergone its own profound transformation. This is witnessed by the changes in employment patterns in recent years (see Table IV).

1990	Agriculture (%)	Industry (%)	Services (%)
Developing countries	61	16	23
Industrialised countries	10	33	57
World	49	20	31

Table IV. (Source: UNDP: *Human Development Report*, 1997.)

The key factor, however, is the steady rise in the service sector for all countries (see Table V).

Service sector	1980 (%)	1990 (%)
Developing countries	14	23
Industrialised countries	38	57
World	22	31

Table V. (Source: UNDP: *Human Development Report*, 1997.)

Such trends oblige countries to adopt new policies to educate and train their citizens quite differently for the knowledge-based contexts of both work and community life. Never before has education occupied such an elevated position in the global development process. The expectations of education as a social investment are expressed in eloquent words by the Report of the International Commission on Education for the XXI Century:

> *While education is an ongoing process of improving*
> *knowledge and skills, it is also – perhaps primarily – an*
> *exceptional means of bringing about personal development*
> *and building relationships amongst individuals, groups and*
> *nations. (UNESCO, 1996, p. 12)*

The Foundations for Diversification

In an enquiry into the mission of higher education in a changing environment, a short discussion of diversification is in order. For many countries, rich or poor, diversified higher – or tertiary – education has emerged as the only practical path for their optimal development.

The guiding principles might be as follows:

- enhanced social investment for all nations;
- improved access on the basis of equity;
- assuring a socially inclusive and coherent learning context;
- ensuring maximum flexibility in the learning process;
- resourcing to guarantee optimal educational opportunity; and
- more effective and efficient higher education provision.

Differentiation of institutional mission or of teaching and learning should be viewed in terms of a nation's capacity to respond to its own development priorities. To do this, a wide variety of educated and trained people will be necessary. In addition, trends indicate that learner profiles are changing rapidly – for example, in OECD countries, older students, frequently female and already in the workforce, are now numerous and are expected to increase. In contrast, the developing world faces an urgent need to adapt universities to the practical challenges of development and to strengthen non-university provision in general.

Such issues suggest that a horizontal view of provision should be encouraged so as to validate all types of education and training at any period of the learner's life and in any type of institution or system. This means that academic higher education, traditionally viewed as the superior form of provision, will take its place alongside more skill-based learning provision. For this reason, a number of countries are experimenting with a qualifications framework – a sort of matrix which situates and links all types of education and training and encourages interaction amongst these. This might be considered to be lifelong education in practice where provision is facilitated and validated for the optimal benefit of the student at any age and in any learning mode.

These principles will be disputed, especially by the academic community. Further debate will ensue as experts in all types of provision present the pros and cons of such a vision of tertiary education. It may also be that those students who are able to pursue a first or advanced degree according to the traditional time frame and in a classic university-type context will emerge as a privileged group. Whether this results or not, each and every government is obliged to focus on the needs of its citizenry as a whole so as to reduce the risk of social exclusion.

Against this background, the polemic surrounding policy and institutional imperatives can be expected to continue.

Transforming Universities

A crucial question in this discussion is to define the proper place and function of universities. Must they change? What of their traditional mission should remain? What will their future profiles be?

At this point, scholarship merits strong defence. On one hand, it is true that intellectual excellence needs to rank as one of many competences, rather than as the best of these. However, on the other hand, the university must constantly review its role and practices to ensure that it can continue to do what is has always done best, namely:

- act as servant and critic to society;
- uphold the values of a given community and those of a just society on a universal scale;
- advance knowledge through research;
- assure research-based teaching;
- offer crucial socialising experiences to students of all ages through intellectual enquiry and peer interaction;
- develop social leadership; and
- foster international understanding and tolerance.

While other institutions in a tertiary education system may have one or several of these attributes, a university must possess them all.

A related question is that of *graduate education*, which is itself undergoing major change as students reflect on their investment in long-term advanced study. If the massification problem (and that of increased demand) preoccupies governments, the issue of the purpose, variety and cost of graduate education is a concern for higher education institutions. Increasingly, masters' degrees can be classified as those which further knowledge (so as to permit graduates to proceed to PhDs and so to academic and research careers) and those which provide practical expertise (for example, the MBA, teaching degrees and specialised masters' courses). Even the doctoral qualification is under scrutiny as tenured posts in research universities become scarcer and employers prefer a blend of expertise and experience in their recruits. In short, institutions offering graduate degrees are now obliged to diversify the range of these so as to provide students with the education and training required in the non-academic sector.

Thus, in general, universities consider that they are under excessive scrutiny today. They are pressured by governments and their ever-expanding plethora of evaluation mechanisms to improve quality. They are pressured by students to meet new learning needs which require more flexible learning approaches. They are told to be entrepreneurial by forging innovative identities and taking their change into the global market place. Change is certainly high on their agenda but its success depends greatly on:

- creative institutional governance supported by effective central management structures;
- a socially responsive mission which is perceived as bringing knowledge and know-how to the community at large;
- diversified funding bases to optimise the benefits of the expertise and services available in universities; and
- a collegial approach to managing the change process.

In such a scenario, the long-term goal of excellence never ceases to be valid – but, rather than being achieved by individuals only, it becomes the common objective because of its clear benefits for the stakeholders. The old and the new approaches need not be opposed. Indeed, 'The strong desire to raise the standards that the university sets for itself is the best indicator of institutional strength' (Borrero Cabal, 1993, p. 215). Furthermore, the American scholar, Burton Clark (1998), reminds us that the culture of higher education can accommodate the risks of entrepreneurship, provided that the sources of institutional resourcing and support are broad-based.

These observations would suggest that the basic product should not alter but that its marketing should be fine-tuned to the spirit of the age. Transformation should thus be enhancing to the institution, which should be ready for change through auto-assessment and possible resetting of priorities. Certainly, a weakened university would constitute a great loss to any country – politically, culturally and socially. Hence, this must be avoided at all cost.

Promoting the Concept of Diversification

This issue has been high on the agenda of the major agencies, which have launched initiatives in this sector over recent years. Once diversification is defined, it must be implemented successfully. This depends on quite radical conceptual and attitudinal shift on the part of the stakeholders concerned.

In this regard, major international agencies have a key role to play. Recent initiatives are as follows.

UNESCO. In 1995 UNESCO published its *Policy Paper for Change and Development in Higher Education*. Based on a worldwide reflection of the main issues involved, this study emphasised the need to diversify institutional structures, as well as programmes and forms of study.

The paper complemented the twinning and linking arrangements of the UNITWIN/UNESCO *Chairs Programme*, which seeks to promote academic solidarity and interinstitutional cooperation via the exchange of professors and advanced students in disciplines directly pertinent to the development process, as well as in the field of modernised institutional development. The programme is focused on innovations in curriculum design at postgraduate level, in staff development and in governance and management.

The World Conference on Higher Education took place in Paris 1998. Entitled *Higher Education in the XXI Century: vision and action*, this aimed to set down the major orientations for reform based on the principles of merit-based access, enhanced systemic and institutional effectiveness and efficiency, and closer linkages between higher education and the world of work.

As the global agency for education, UNESCO is acutely aware that solutions to problems must be always be country- or region-specific in order to take account of the sociocultural and economic factors in play. However, debate at the international level enriches the quest for successful strategies and permits a wide range of experiences to be compared.

In recent years, the United Nations system, including UNESCO, has sponsored a number of international meetings on subjects allied to the discussion on higher education, *inter alia*: basic education, the role of information technology in education, women and development, technical and vocational education, lifelong learning and cultural diversity. Through such debates, the contribution of higher education to other areas of the system can be better articulated. The end result is a mosaic in which education finds a central position.

The World Bank. The extensive review of post-secondary education across varied regions and national contexts resulted in the report entitled *The Lessons of Experience*, published in 1994. This sought to present examples of good practice to demonstrate differentiated mission, cost-sharing schemes, new interfaces with national authorities and, as a constant objective, increased quality and pertinence in teaching and learning.

As is well known, this report has been controversial, and some countries have feared that bank lending would be contingent upon the acceptance of certain paradigms of change. However, it may also have been ahead of its time in its prescient view of the complex issues to be resolved in the years to come. More recently, and while still insisting on the complexity of the problems involved, the World Bank has reconfirmed the fundamental importance of the higher education sector for the developing world.

The OECD. Post-secondary education has been analysed by this agency in a number of studies: *Towards Mass Higher Education* (1974), *Universities under Scrutiny* (1985) *and Alternatives to Universities* (1991), *University Research in Transition* (1998).

The latest review, *Redefining Tertiary Education* (1998), focuses on the management of massified demand through a reconceptualisation of different types of education and training, as well as of their contribution to broad based social development.

Despite their specific perspectives, these analyses have important common ground: an insistence on the importance of post-secondary learning, a recognition of the right of people to participate in this and the necessity to establish its status as both a public and private good.

The Potential of Partnerships

Meeting the new demands facing higher education will rely on the ability of the interested stakeholders to forge cooperative alliances. These linkages commence with dialogue to ascertain the needs of the various areas of the sector, including the requirements of the learners, and to ensure that outcomes are optimal in terms of their quality and relevance.

From dialogue, alliances then move into other modalities. For example:

- cost-sharing arrangements with students, with the private sector and with alumni as a way of complementing state funding, which is remaining limited;
- joint research ventures;
- study–work arrangements for students and professors alike;
- international exchanges to foster academic solidarity and the sharing of knowledge and know-how.
- interaction with the community, at local, national or regional levels, to contribute to the strengthening of capacities necessary for development.

Partnerships already enjoy a long tradition in certain contexts and are manifested in various ways, such as the 'town/gown relationship' and the presence of staff and students in institutional governance bodies. However, overall, and in parts of the developing world in particular, there remains much more to be done in this area so that linkages are transformed into more dynamic commitments to the further development of higher education which best serves society in general and specific needs in particular. To arrive at this type of partnership, all stakeholders must be represented, including students, who are often excluded or marginalised when they dare to criticise systems and institutions.

Partnership implies respect for all voices and viewpoints, as well as responsibility for orienting change on the part of those concerned. As yet, the potential deserves to be better realised since 'There are fruitful avenues to explore if only the doors are opened' (OECD, 1998, p. 51). Last but not least, partnership was described by the 1998 World Conference on Higher Education as the key strategy for the in-depth renewal and reform of this sector.

Conclusions

The world is not an unsolved puzzle waiting for the occasional genius to unlock its secrets. The world, or most of it, is an empty space waiting to be filled. Life, work and organization could become a self-fulfilling prophecy. (Handy, 1996)

Today, the policy debate is characterised by a number of recurring imperatives: increased social justice, strong emphasis on individual capacity-building, on personal contribution to society and on self-reliance for citizens in a changing world. People are expected to take charge of their aspirations and of their lives. Quality education and training are indispensable for them to do this.

In the future, sound policy guidelines will seek to harmonise the many complex aspects surrounding the reform of higher education. Though its definitions require rethinking, its values remain strongly supported and its status as a public good must be retained.

The polemic will continue to be fuelled by one or other of the interest groups involved. However, the long-term vision of higher education must always be in sight. The UNESCO report on *Higher Education in the XXI Century* insists on the need for its diversification in order to better ensure that knowledge will be created, that professional training will be provided, that opportunities for education through life will be given to citizens, and that internationalism will be enhanced by its focus on human solidarity rather than solely on its economic potential. This is the essence of social investment in higher education.

Above all, the reform agenda will benefit from broad dialogue amongst stakeholders, whose shared sense of responsibility and involvement will be the key to the calibre of the renewal. Commitment to equity of participation in higher education and to international solidarity so that all nations reach this goal must underpin policy objectives both to resolve pressing problems and to permit sustained social progress in the long term.

Note

This article expresses the views of the author, which are not necessarily those of UNESCO.

References and Bibliography

Barnett, Ronald (1997) *Realizing the University.* London: Institute of Education, University of London.

Borrero, Cabal Alfonso (1993) *The University as an Institution Today.* Paris: UNESCO/IDRC.

Burgess, Robert (Ed.) (1998) *Beyond the First Degree.* Buckingham: Society for Research into Higher Education/Open University Press.

Clark, Burton (1998) *Creating Entrepreneurial Universities: organizational pathways of transformation.* IAU/Elsevier.

Commonwealth of Australia (1998) *Learning for Life. Review of Higher Education Financing and Policy.*

Handy, Charles (1996) *Beyond Certainty.* London: Arrow.

Holden Ronning, Anne & Kearney, Mary-Louise (Eds) (1998) *Graduate Prospects in a Changing Society.* UNESCO/IOHE.

Organisation for Economic Cooperation and Development (OECD) (1974) *Towards Mass Higher Education.* Paris: OECD.

Organisation for Economic Cooperation and Development (OECD) (1985) *Universities under Scrutiny.* Paris: OECD.

Organisation for Economic Cooperation and Development (OECD) (1991) *Alternatives to Universities.* Paris: OECD.

Organisation for Economic Cooperation and Development (OECD) (1995) *The Jobs Study.* Paris: OECD.

Organisation for Economic Cooperation and Development (OECD) (1998a) *Redefining Tertiary Education.* Paris: OECD.

Organisation for Economic Cooperation and Development (OECD) (1998b) *University Research in Transition.* Paris: OECD.

Organisation for Economic Cooperation and Development (OECD) *High Quality Education and Training for All.* Paris: OECD.

United Nations Development Programme (UNDP) (1997) *Human Development Report, 1994.* New York: Oxford University Press.

UNESCO (1995) *Policy Paper for Change and Development in Higher Education.* Paris: UNESCO.

UNESCO (1996) *Learning: the treasure within.* Report of the International Commission on Education for the XXI Century. Paris: UNESCO.

UNESCO (1997) *Fifth International Conference on Adult Education. Final Report.* Paris: UNESCO.

UNESCO (1997) *Our Cultural Diversity.* Report of the International Commission on Culture and Development. Paris: UNESCO.

UNESCO (1998a) *The World Education Report.* Paris: UNESCO.

UNESCO (1998b) *Higher Education in the XXI Century: vision and action.* Paris: UNESCO.

UNESCO (1998c) *World Statistical Outlook on Higher Education, 1980–1995.* Paris: UNESCO.

World Bank (1994) *The Lessons of Experience.* Washington: World Bank.

World Bank (1997) *The State in a Changing World.* Washington: World Bank.

World Bank/UNESCO (2000) *Higher Education in Developing Countries: peril and promise.* Washington: World Bank.

PART TWO

Research, Education and Development

Introduction: research, education and development

ROBIN ALEXANDER

A few months before the turn of the millennium, the United Nations published its 1999 *Human Development Report* (United Nations Development Programme [UNDP], 1999). Its theme was globalisation, and in contrast with the gung-ho attitude adopted by some Western governments, but in line with the warnings of those analysts like Paul Kennedy (1994), Manuel Castells (1998) and David Landes (1998) who take a longer and broader perspective, the report was less interested in utopian visions than in demonstrating just how problematic and double-edged a phenomenon this is.

The United Nations report acknowledges that the increasingly rapid interconnectedness of capital, production, ideas and cultures has the potential to benefit a large proportion of humankind. As yet, however, for all that the European project stays more or less on course, the promise of wider global economic convergence remains as remote as ever. Globalisation maintains established economic trajectories by benefiting a mere 20% of the world's population – located mainly within member states of the Organisation for Economic Cooperation and Development (OECD) and the newly-industrialised countries of south-east Asia – who between them corner 86% of gross domestic product (GDP), 82% of world export markets, 68% of foreign direct investment and 74% of the world's telephone lines (and thus the basic means of communication within a global economy). At the same time, globalisation and the associated information revolution may create new threats to human and national identity and security, marginalise those individuals, groups and nations not in the global economic and communications club, put profit before care, and threaten the agendas of equity, inclusion and human development.

Overarching the UNDP survey is the challenge of what we mean, or should mean, by 'human development' and how, for the purposes of assessing where the world's states and people stand in relation to each other, such development should be measured: whether by gross national product (GNP) alone; or by combining measures such as human longevity, education and *per capita* income as in the Human Development Index (HDI) developed by Amartya Sen and his colleagues; or by reference to a still wider spectrum which encompasses health, education, food and nutrition, income, gender equity, infant mortality, environment, security and human rights.

The *Human Development Report 1999* provides a sobering analysis, and one which is of direct relevance to those working in comparative and international education, for the universalisation of basic education is widely perceived to be a necessary condition – though of course certainly not the only one – of social and economic advancement. Moreover, whereas the comparativist studying France, Germany, the USA or other countries within the economic super-league can retain a comfortable intellectual detachment and concentrate on polishing theory and methodology, for those whose area of interest is, say, south Asia or sub-Saharan Africa, academic engagement is complicated by moral agency.

It is not just the uncomfortable historical legacies of colonialism which demand a particular sensitivity from Western academics working in the field of development in post-colonial countries. It is also the fact that the legacy, and the relationships which go with it, may prove more resilient than they would like to admit as they find themselves drawn into the politics of aid and compete with each other for the opportunity to tell governments of less prosperous countries how to educate their young.

The contributors to Part 2 of this book are alive to the sensibilities which these roles, and the field in general, demand. Michael Crossley, setting the scene for the papers that follow, draws useful parallels between the condition of educational research in the United Kingdom – challenged to conform to a restricted definition of 'relevance' and subject to critique of an increasingly politicised kind – and research in the context of education and development. Like others before (and no doubt after) him, he notes Western economic and political hegemony in the setting of development research and consultancy agendas, and argues the importance of close attention to context as a partial corrective to this.

Cheng Kai-Ming also stresses the centrality of context. In the setting of educational comparisons between West and East, and of development relations between North and South, he detects a tacit assumption that what are taken as key indicators of educational attainment and development have universal currency. Taking the case of China, he challenges this casual universalism by showing how ostensible 'givens' like equity, rights, development and ability are nothing of the sort, and makes a strong case for comparativists to pay much greater attention to the fine detail of culture and cultural values than many do, perhaps because historically they have tended to focus on educational systems and policies rather than educational practices. In this, Cheng reinforces one of the themes from the first volume of *Learning from Comparing,* in which we argued that culturally-embedded study of classroom processes should be given a prominent place in the new comparative education.

Cheng also suggests, contentiously but necessarily, that some of those who find themselves on the international consultancy circuit advising on educational policy in developing countries may have limited experience of the policy context of their own systems and no experience there whatever as policy advisers. This raises salutary questions, which only Cheng touches upon, about who today's experts in education for development really are.

On the other hand, his observations lead neatly into Terry Allsop's account of the changing research agenda of the United Kingdom Department for International Development (DFID), which remains one of the world's larger bilateral donors. Allsop, too, picks up the shifting politics of development research and consultancy, and shows how these point away from donor control to agenda-setting through partnership, collaboratively funded and managed research and long-term capacity building.

Colin Brock & Nadine Cammish draw on their own DFID-funded research to shift the focus of discussion from the control of research to its methodology. They take as their example the problematics of researching female participation in education, one of the indicators of development which features prominently in the 1999 United Nations Development Programme Report referred to earlier. Though Brock & Cammish demonstrate the usefulness of macro-level analysis – in this case cross-national comparison of the factors affecting female participation in education in seven countries – they also press the case made by Crossley and Cheng in this section, and by several of our other contributors in both volumes of *Learning from Comparing,* for intensive and highly localised case studies as the only way meaningfully to access the dynamics of an issue as complex and sensitive as this. Culture, and the problematics of studying it, has proved to be one of the core themes of these two volumes.

Rosemary Preston's chapter was commissioned as a commentary on those of Crossley, Cheng, Allsop and Brock & Cammish. She reflects on the papers as given at the fourth seminar, rather than as published here, but correctly anticipates some of the more prominent concerns of the latter and the sense they convey that as a research field education and development now needs new or modified analytical and empirical parameters to reflect changing consciousness and changing relationships between donor and recipient, researcher and researched.

One such parameter in urgent need of reassessment is the double axis of East–West and North–South, which tends tacitly to inform all these discussions, including those at the fourth seminar. At the seminar, Johanna Crighton argued that such a conveniently geometric approach to development tends to ignore the plight of countries – and children – on the West's doorstep, especially those in the former Soviet Union and south-eastern Europe. The continuing catastrophe of the Balkans at the time of writing gives force to her intervention.

In the initial rationale for the seminar programme from which these papers arose, we said that we would set up encounters which would encourage participants to re-examine the theory, methods and applications of comparative educational research, and the relationship between research producers and users. The chapters in this section touch on all these issues, though probably less on theory than the others, and the imperatives of culture and cultural analysis feature particularly prominently. That social research also raises political and ethical issues is a truism, and they certainly feature here. But to say that is not to consign them to a textbook inventory of 'issues in comparative educational research', there to be forgotten. Far from it: as *Human Development 1999* powerfully demonstrates, in the field of education and development political understanding and moral commitment make a powerful and essential alliance.

References

Castells, M. (1998) *End of Millennium.* Oxford: Blackwell.

Kennedy, P.M. (1994) *Preparing for the Twenty-first Century.* London: Fontana.

Landes, D. (1998) *The Wealth and Poverty of Nations.* London: Little, Brown.

United Nations Development Programme (1999) *Human Development Report 1999.* New York: Oxford University Press.

Research, Education and Development: setting the scene

MICHAEL CROSSLEY

This introductory article begins with a contemporary and critical perspective. Educational research is currently being challenged on many different fronts for not contributing effectively enough to the improvement of educational policy and practice. Researchers such as Kennedy (1997) in the USA, and Hargreaves (1996), along with bodies such as the Economic and Social Research Council (ESRC) in the United Kingdom, call for more cumulative and authoritative research. External agencies, including government representatives, echo similar themes and press for more useful and accessible studies that are relevant to the needs of policy-makers. Decision-makers at all levels are thus seeking more visible returns from research, and better value for money as budgets tighten and accountability is emphasised.

This is a familiar story in developing countries where greater degrees of austerity have long influenced the scope, nature and quality of educational research (Lewin, 1987). In many such contexts the human and material capacity for educational research is in an early phase of development, but, of the work that has been done, much has been dominated by:

1. influential international agendas and priorities;
2. external development agency funding;
3. Western or agency personnel; and
4. a policy orientation closely tied to the development, implementation or evaluation of internationally inspired reform initiatives.

Jones (1992, 1997), for example, points to the widespread influence of the World Bank upon the international education research agenda – and the Bank's inevitable concern to identify the most cost-effective strategies for educational intervention (World Bank, 1995).

There is therefore much that we can learn from the experience of the South (Little, 1988; Buchert, 1998) and from the education and development literature; and it is with reference to this broad perspective that key intellectual and organisational implications for the future of comparative and international research in education are considered here.

Firstly, while the focus on cumulative, policy-oriented research has much to offer in terms of authoritative knowledge and project relevance, in the light of the points made earlier, it has attracted substantial criticism in developing countries for overly dominating the research agenda (Bennell, 1996; Lauglo, 1996). Much research has also too readily adopted Western theoretical frameworks and positivistic research paradigms (Samoff, 1996) at the expense of alternative perspectives, most notably those emerging *from* the South itself (King, 1991; Buchert, 1998).

Secondly, despite major investment and external support, the success rate of many internationally inspired educational reform initiatives has been disappointing, particularly with respect to their sustainability beyond the period of external funding. This remains a major challenge to all working within the development field.

Thirdly, with recent advances in information and communications technology, the growth of international consultancy work and intensified globalisation, the potential for the rapid export of educational policy and practice has increased (Crossley & Broadfoot, 1992). This emphasises the dangers long recognised by comparativists (Sadler, 1900; Crossley, 1984; Phillips, 1992) of uncritical and inappropriate international transfer from one context to another.

These factors have major implications for the field of comparative and international education because the research of many colleagues interested in development issues is closely associated with work of this nature. Thinking back to our comparisons with the contemporary debate in the United Kingdom, much research in the education and development arena *is* policy-oriented and it *is* directly applied to governmental and aid agency priorities and agendas – but it has its own very real limitations and vocal critics. Here there is much to learn for educational researchers and policy-makers in all contexts, and for the future of the field of comparative and international education itself.

This dilemma also lies at the heart of long-evident tensions within the combined fields of comparative and international education. Many 'internationalists', for example, have traditionally been closely involved with policy, practice and development assistance in developing countries. Those more explicitly known as 'comparativists' have tended to work in other contexts and have emphasised theoretical perspectives, detached critique and the advancement of knowledge. While this is an oversimplified representation, it remains useful as we explore how educational research can more effectively contribute towards the improvement of policy and practice, to related theoretical advances, and to our better understanding of the relationship between education and all dimensions of development.

We have, it is argued, much to gain from a more fundamental *rapprochement* between the international and comparative dimensions of our field. The strengths of the former tradition may indeed relate to its focus on policy issues and action but, especially in times of rapid globalisation, the importance of taking cultural differences more fully into account is increasingly being recognised if educational development, in any context, is to be relevant, worthwhile and sustainable. It is thus to the theoretically informed, critical and contextualised forms of analysis that are more characteristic of the comparative literature that development researchers will increasingly need to look in the future. Similarly, our theoretical advances will be much enhanced if they are more effectively grounded in practice and the field experience characteristic of the international tradition. In short, *context matters*, and such reconceptualised comparative and international research (Crossley, 1999) will be particularly well placed to demonstrate the importance of this in a world where tensions between globalisation and cultural difference underpin all studies of education and national development (Mitter, 1997; Watson, 1998).

In broad scope, the case for reconceptualising comparative and international education encompasses a number of related and fundamental implications for the future of research on education and development. In the face of the rapid advance of globalisation – spurred on by modern information and communications technology – policy-makers and researchers increasingly need to move beyond (but not reject) local and nation state perspectives, if they are fully to understand the social and educational changes they encounter. Global forces play an increasingly influential role in shaping regional, national and local educational developments, and, somewhat paradoxically, understanding such processes is essential if development initiatives are to be effective in meeting local needs and priorities in practice. In a rapidly changing environment such as this, those engaged in development work, at all levels, need to be increasingly conversant with emergent trends in both developed and developing countries. This, in itself, questions the separation of personnel and literatures that, as noted earlier, has often characterised comparative and international research. Moreover, as renewed interest in post-colonial studies illustrates (Tikly, 1999), the limitations of oversimplified, binary and oppositional conceptual frameworks and the predominance of Western analyses of development issues are increasingly untenable. The international politics of educational development, and the legitimising role played by educational research, as highlighted earlier, demand fundamental changes for development studies in the forthcoming 'global century'. Continued use of the very terms developed and developing countries (and their alternatives) is increasingly problematic as economic fortunes rise and fall, as the predominance of economic criteria is challenged and as cultural factors are given increased attention. The limitations of research conducted by outsiders on the South are already well recognised by calls for more studies by insiders (Cheng, 1997), for local research and evaluation capacity building (Crossley, 2000), and for collaborative investigations that acknowledge the significance of international trends in addition to context sensitivity and local insights.

Respect for the differences between and within education systems receives further support from postmodern perspectives, as does the critique of global models and meta-theories. Significantly, however, while a consideration of postmodernism is evident within the comparative literature (Cowen, 1996), little sustained application is, as yet, visible within education and development debates. To some extent this reflects the traditional developed and developing country binary divide – once again pointing to the limitations of intellectual and organisational barriers, and to the need for creative bridge-building across the disciplinary and other divides that separate those engaging in social and educational research, international development and the implementation of policy and practice.

The time is also ripe for fundamental changes in the nature and scope of research on education and development. Western agencies themselves are, for example, taking interest in educational developments in the South (Reynolds & Farrell, 1996), mainstream educationalists are increasingly engaging in comparative and international studies (Alexander, 1996, 1999; Ball, 1998; Bush, 1998), and there is evidence of significantly renewed growth of the intellectual and institutional base of comparative and international education worldwide (Bray, 1998; Schweisfurth, 1999).

Characteristic of these developments are integral efforts to promote multidisciplinary studies, partnerships between the North and the South, collaborations between insiders and outsiders, and more robust linkages between theory, policy and practice. Emergent trends are more explicitly reflected in formal reviews of the field, and of the challenges to be faced at the turn of the new millennium (Crossley & Jarvis, 2000). Methodologically, this includes attention to participatory strategies (Chambers, 1992; World Bank, 1996); innovative forms of qualitative research (Crossley & Vulliamy, 1997); the further refinement of studies of school effectiveness, and 'varifocal' interpretative frameworks (Riddell, 1999); multilevel analyses (Bray & Thomas, 1995); and advances and critiques of large-scale cross-national assessment studies as pioneered by the influential International Association for the Evaluation of Educational Achievement (IEA) (Assessment in Education, 1996). As the 1990s drew to a close, new focuses for attention also emerged in the development arena, including an agency prioritised emphasis upon poverty alleviation (Department for International Development [DfID], 1997), challenges to the economic preoccupations stimulated in the

1980s, and attention to a variety of issues relating to globalisation, culture and identity (Thaman, 1993; Green, 1997; Jones, 1998). While this is not the place to explore such developments in detail, it is clear that both the nature and focus of research on education and development is undergoing fundamental change – and that this extends more broadly to what is an increasingly pertinent, challenging and vibrant field of comparative and international research in education.

As the challenge to grand theory intensifies across the social sciences and the limitations of broad concepts such as 'developing countries' become increasingly apparent, so the division between the work of researchers focusing only upon developed or developing contexts, and their related literatures, becomes more problematic. Comparative and international research in education must therefore continue to renew itself and adapt to meet contemporary and future demands. In doing so, new issues of significance will emerge, but the traditional concerns of comparativists with culture and context will, nevertheless, be reaffirmed. Recent trends towards multilevel analyses, in-depth fieldwork, and studies that engage more directly with local 'social constructions of reality' demonstrate both new avenues for research and differing views of the concept of development itself. Research on education and development, thus, has much to gain from listening more carefully to the voices from the South, from collaborative, comparative research between 'insiders' and 'outsiders', from applied, cumulative and accessible studies, from a bridging of the theory/practice gap and from the changing geopolitical relations that will make this ever more imperative in the future.

References

Alexander, R.J. (1996) *Other Primary Schools and Ours: hazards of international comparison.* Warwick: Centre for Research and Evaluation in Primary Education.

Alexander, R.J. (1999) Culture in Pedagogy, Pedagogy across Cultures, in R. J. Alexander, P. Broadfoot & D. Phillips *Learning from Comparing*, vol. 1, pp. 149–180. Oxford: Symposium Books.

Assessment in Education (1996) *Special Issue: the IEA Studies*, 3.

Ball, S. (Ed.) (1998) Comparative Perspectives in Education Policy, Special Number of *Comparative Education*, 34.

Bennell, P. (1996) Using and Abusing Rates of Return: a critique of the World Bank's 1995 Education Sector Review, *International Journal of Educational Development*, 16, pp. 235–248.

Bray, M. (1998) Comparative Education Research in the Asian Region: implications for the field as a whole, *Comparative Educational Society of Hong Kong*, Bulletin No. 1, pp. 6–10.

Bray, M. & Thomas, R.M. (1995) Levels of Comparison in Educational Studies: different insights from different literatures and the value of multi-level analyses, *Harvard Educational Review*, 65, pp. 472–490.

Buchert, L. (Ed.) (1998) *Educational Reform in the South in the 1990s.* Paris: UNESCO.

Bush, T. (Ed.) (1998) School Management in the People's Republic of China, Special Issue of *Compare*, 28, pp. 131–218.

Chambers, R. (1992) *Rural Appraisal: rapid, relaxed and participatory.* Institute of Development Studies (IDS) Discussion Paper. Brighton: University of Sussex.

Cheng, K.M. (1997) Qualitative Research and Educational Policy Making: approaching the reality, in M. Crossley & G. Vulliamy (Eds) *Qualitative Educational Research in Developing Countries.* New York: Garland.

Cowen, R. (Ed.) (1996) Comparative Education and Post-Modernity, Special Number of *Comparative Education*, 32.

Crossley, M. (1984) Strategies for Curriculum Change and the Question of International Transfer, *Journal of Curriculum Studies*, 16, pp. 75–88.

Crossley, M. (1999) Reconceptualising Comparative and International Education, *Compare*, 29, pp. 249–267.

Crossley, M. (2000) Cross-cultural issues, small states and research capacity building in Belize, *International Journal of Educational Development*, 19.

Crossley, M. & Broadfoot, P. (1992) Comparative and International Research in Education: scope, problems, potential, *British Educational Research Journal*, 18, pp. 99–112.

Crossley, M. & Jarvis, P. (Eds) (2000) Comparative Education for the 21st Century, Special Number of *Comparative Education*, 36.

Crossley, M. & Vulliamy, G. (Eds) (1997) *Qualitative Educational Research in Developing Countries.* New York: Garland.

Department for International Development (DFID) (1997) *Eliminating World Poverty: a challenge for the 21st century.* London: HMSO.

Green, A. (1997) *Education, Globalisation and the Nation State.* London: Macmillan.

Hargreaves, D. (1996) Teaching as a Research Based Profession; possibilities and prospects, *Teacher Training Agency Annual Lecture, 1996.* London: TTA.

Jones, P.W. (1992) *World Bank Financing of Education. Lending, Learning and Development.* London: Routledge.

Jones, P.W. (1997) On World Bank Education Financing. Policies and Strategies for Education: a World Bank Review, *Comparative Education*, 33, pp. 117–129.

Jones, P. (1998) Globalisation and Internationalism: democratic prospects for world education, *Comparative Education*, 34, pp. 143–155.

Kennedy, M.K. (1997) The Connection between Research and Practice, *Educational Researcher*, 26, pp. 4–12.

King, K. (1991) *Aid and Education in the Developing World.* London: Longman.

Lauglo, J. (1996) Banking on Education and the Uses of Research, *International Journal of Educational Development*, 16, pp. 221–233.

Lewin, K.M. (1987) *Education in Austerity: options for planners*. Paris: UNESCO.

Little, A. (1988) *Learning from Developing Countries*. London: University of London, Institute of Education.

Mitter, W. (1997) Challenges to Comparative Education: between retrospective and expectation, *International Review of Education*, 43, pp. 401–412.

Phillips, D. (1992) Borrowing Education Policy, *Oxford Studies in Comparative Education*, 2, pp. 49–55.

Reynolds, D. & Farrell, S. (1996) *Worlds Apart? A Review of International Surveys of Educational Achievement Including England.* London: HMSO.

Riddell, R. (1999) The Need for a Multi-disciplinary Framework for Analysing Educational Reform in Developing Countries, *International Journal of Educational Development*, 19, pp. 207–217.

Sadler, M. (1900) How Far Can We Learn Anything of Practical Value from the Study of Foreign Systems of Education, in J.H. Higginson (Ed.) (1979) *Selections from Michael Sadler*. Liverpool: Dejall & Meyorre.

Samoff, J. (1996) Which Priorities and Strategies for Education? *International Journal of Educational Development*, 16, pp. 249–271.

Schweisfurth, M. (1999) Resilience, Resistance and Responsiveness: comparative and international education at United Kingdom universities, in R. Alexander, P. Broadfoot & D. Phillips (Eds) *Learning from Comparing*, vol. 1. Oxford: Symposium Books.

Thaman, K.H. (1993) Culture and the Curriculum, in M. Crossley (Ed.) Special Issue of *Comparative Education* on *Education in the South Pacific*, 29, pp. 249–260.

Tikly, L. (1999) Post-colonialism and Comparative Education, *International Review of Education*, 49, pp. 603–621.

Watson, K. (1998) Memories, Models and Mapping: the impact of geopolitical changes on comparative studies in education, *Compare*, 28, pp. 5–31.

Word Bank (1995) *Priorities and Strategies for Education. A World Bank Review.* Washington DC: World Bank.

World Bank (1996) *The World Bank Participation Sourcebook.* Washington DC: World Bank.

Education and Development: the neglected mission of cross-cultural studies

CHENG KAI-MING

Introduction

Development studies necessarily focus on systems. Development studies are meaningful only if they pay attention to different systems. Hence, they are comparative by nature. Development studies often tend to explore a general framework that may apply to all nations. However, nations develop on different paths, and often with different destinations. This is perhaps an issue central to comparative studies in education. The issue may be discussed in three dimensions: North–South, East–West and macro–micro. The first uses development as the frame of reference; the second pertains to culture; and the third research.

Development and Education

The debates on development models are largely taken over by developments in reality. Most theoretical models in development assume some kind of uniformity among nations, but nations in the world develop in diverse models. Most theories in development have moved away from pure economic achievements such as gross domestic product (GDP).[1] There is a general recognition that social issues such as the fulfilment of basic needs among the populace, or the level of equity in the distribution of national wealth, should also be the concern of national development. Most Western theories would also include political participation or, in recent years, human rights, as indicators for national development. Such dimensions have made a uniform model even more impossible.

The issue of equity, for example, has aroused much interest in the literature, and there is a demonstrated diversity in the interpretation of equity [2], and the importance of equity in the national agenda. In the final analysis, equity pertains to the distribution of wealth, but different nations have different approaches to allocating resources. Equity is perhaps one approach that is based on individuals as equals in society. In some societies, where individuals are seen as parts of a societal structure (and this is politically incorrect in a Western perspective), and where allocation is based on rules of the game fair to the structure, equity in the Western sense is not a major concern.

The issue of human rights is another example. To start with, the notion of individual rights is again foreign to many societies where rights often come as a complement to responsibilities, and hence absolute rights are not conceivable. In such societies, the concern is often a balance between rights and responsibilities. In these societies, rights are not the starting point of social justice, let alone an indicator of national development.

The preceding two paragraphs might have already disturbed our readers. They are indeed highly controversial. There is no intention here to endorse the alternative views about equity and human rights. However, it is safe to say that such issues are much less controversial in the respective home societies than in any Western forum. The argument here is that apart from economic indicators, many of the interpretations of national development do not subject themselves to right/wrong judgements. If the argument could be pushed further, even the economic indicators are not necessarily universally appropriate, except that the international agenda is so strong that perhaps no nation could move away from economic goals or interpret economic success otherwise.

Moreover, development means different things to different nations. The preferred paths of development also differ among nations. In other words, even with similar goals in mind, different nations follow different routes and aim at different specific objectives. One may just look at the difference in development paths between the USA and Japan, or between Russia and China, between continents such as South America and South Asia, or even between city states such as Singapore and Hong Kong.

The concern of this article, however, is education. If even hard-core economic development can follow different paths, then it would be unfair to expect education, which is much more isolated and culture-specific, to follow internationally uniform paths. However, in reality, few nations promote educational goals other than the global agenda: universal attendance in basic education, vocationalising secondary schools, effective schools, national assessment, management reform in higher education, and so forth.

In China, for example, there are indeed challenges to the national goal of 9-year compulsory education. This is particularly valid in 'less developed' regions where such a target goal is not only difficult to achieve, but is also irrelevant to the local context. In one of the Miao (an ethnic minority) villages I visited in 1989, girls engaged in intensive embroidery since very young, and their talents in embroidery, as exhibited in what they wore, were an essential social capital they had to forgo if they went to school (Cheng, 1997). As another example, vocational education in China also faces challenges. Vocational education is irrelevant in rural regions where there is little industry, but is out of context in metropolitan cities where narrow skills-training is phased out by the rapid growth of the tertiary economic sector.

However, international competition has placed all nations on the same arena. The globalisation that started with the economy has infiltrated all sectors of society. Education is no exception. Developments in information technology have also accelerated such a process of globalisation. To many, globalisation is a process of unification, or the elimination of local cultures. It is based either on the argument that modernisation is but Westernisation (Zwingle, 1999), or that all culture will eventually converge to a global culture (Inkeles, 1997). Although such a view is often challenged (see, for example, Watsons, 1997), by looking at the reality, it is inevitable that the commonalities in societies have attracted more attention then the differences.

It would be too sweeping to say that there is no commonality in education development in different systems. However, all such developments and reforms are appropriate only under certain assumptions, but such assumptions are seldom tested. For example, the modern school system, where students study in classes in schools, where they follow prescribed curricula and pass prescribed examinations, is appropriate to the system of production in the industrial economy. It is perhaps appropriate to industrial societies, where the school system resembles the social pyramid, producing manpower with different levels of skills and abilities, feeding the different tiers of the economy. How such a school system could fit a non-industrial society is a question unanswered.

Hence, for example, on the one hand, many agricultural societies are struggling with the implementation of legislated compulsory education, trying to fight against students who 'drop out' from the system. Such students are reluctant to attend schools for very good reasons. On the other hand, in more developed metropolitan societies, where a 'knowledge-based' economy already prevails and continuous learning is essential, students are reluctant to attend dead-end programmes or undergo narrow training, again for very good reasons.

The effective school movement is another typical example. The movement was initiated in the early or mid-1990s when schools in the USA were not seen as performing. With the intention of improving education, the effective school movement resorted to 'management' as the key to improving schools. Since then, the notion of effective schools has spread throughout the world, attracting the attention of all administrators and policy-makers in almost all societies. Indicator systems and assessment schemes have flourished. Everything involved in running a school has been reduced to 'management'. However, the basic assumption has seldom been challenged. Are good schools the result of good management? Is there anything beyond management that makes a school a good school? If good management is necessary for a school, is it also sufficient? The sad story is that many very good schools have been forced or tempted to abandon their strong tradition and have reduced themselves to well-managed schools. Such strong traditions indeed reflect a much higher level of human relations. Many schools outside the USA were very 'effective' by US standards of the 1970s, but have been forced to submit to managerial means that should be used to cure schools of much lower calibre.

Yet, education has already grown into an institution with its own justification for existence. The education system may develop in a way that pays no attention to what is happening in society at large. In the international arena, there is also the subtle belief that if everybody is doing it then it must be correct. Policies are thus made at the expense of the real development of children.

Education and Culture: China as example

The foregoing discussion should not lead to any suspicion against developing education, for education has its own missions beyond national development. Indeed, the notion that education is for the development of the nation is rather recent. The missions beyond national development, however, are much less universal. In some societies, education serves to develop individuals. In other societies, education is to serve political ideologies (the most common being communism and democracy). Still other societies commit education to religion.

However, such educational missions are often culture-specific. They are deep-rooted in the culture and are not easily understood from another culture. It is in this context that comparative studies of education become more meaningful. Rather than looking at different education systems from a common framework, comparative education could alternatively try to understand the diverse frameworks in which different systems work. In other words, comparative education by nature should be pluralistic.

One would immediately identify an assumption here that cultures are basically plural. Admission of the plurality in culture is much more than admitting the differences and diversity. It requires accommodation of cultures as alternative ways of seeing things and alternative solutions to similar problems, or even different problems. As such, cultures are equal. No culture is better or worse than another culture. It is only that they evolved under very different circumstances and passed along very different historical paths. Schein's statement (1992) could be a very useful working definition for culture in educational studies:

> *Culture is a pattern of shared basic assumptions that the*
> *group learnt as it solved its problems of external adaptation*
> *and internal integration, that has worked well enough to be*
> *considered valid and, therefore, to be taught to new members*
> *as the correct way to perceive, think, and feel in relation to*
> *those problems.*

In this context, I would like to share my understanding, thus far, of the cultural difference between the Chinese culture and the mainstream culture in the West. What I gathered from Western literature are:

- the different assumptions about the relations between individuals and the community;
- the different emphasis between human–human relations and human–nature relations; and
- the different methodologies in approaching reality.

In the literature, there is a generally identifiable tendency in China for individuals to be expected to submit themselves to the needs of the community.[3] Collectivism is perhaps too heavy a word for such a tendency, although it is widely used in the literature. In brief, individuals in a traditional Chinese society are seen as born into a social structure where each individual has a particular role to play. As such, education, as a means of socialisation, is basically to realise such a social structure, and to train individuals to behave as expected by that society. Students are therefore educated in groups (in classes; see, for example, Stevenson & Lee, 1997) and are taught to abide by the norms of the group. Education systems are so designed that individuals study the same curriculum, compete along the same path, sit for the same examination, and are rewarded if they best fulfil the collective goals. Individuals are educated to adapt themselves to the system, rather than the opposite.[4] This is very different from the West, where individual needs are central to educational philosophies, teaching is a matter of individual learning and the system is there to cater for individual needs as far as resources permit.

With such emphasis on social expectations, Chinese society necessarily places more emphasis on human–human relations. This is again different from education in the West, where the emphasis is on human–nature relations and the primary goals of learning are about knowledge and skills (Gardner, 1984). Disciplines, for example, in Chinese education are not a matter of classroom control, or a necessary evil to maintain order in large classes. Disciplines in Chinese education are essential first steps towards socialisation (Redding, 1990). In Mainland China, there are usually three recognised dimensions of education: moral, intellectual and physical. In Hong Kong and Taiwan, two more dimensions are added: group ethics and aesthetics. In all these cases, the moral dimension is regarded as the most important. Students are given grades on their 'conduct' on their report cards, and that refers to their moral behaviour. Moral education, in the Chinese sense, is a matter of social norms rather than a matter of personality development, as is usually the case in the West.[5]

There is also an emerging literature that looks at the methodological aspects of culture (see Liu, 1988; also see Liu, 1990 [in Chinese]). Starting from studies of Chinese medical science, there is a general understanding that the Chinese way of problem-solving often adopts a holistic approach, whereas in the West, an analytic approach is seen as more scientific. In Chinese medicine, the human body is regarded as a holistic system. Diseases are seen as a disturbance to the equilibrium of the system. Healing is therefore intrinsic mobilisation within the system until a new equilibrium is attained. In education, there is a similar (but perhaps implicit) approach where students are trained as a whole person, a *gentleman* in Confucian literature, such that the person is well-rounded and could withstand all weathers. Knowledge and skills are seen as an integral part of comprehensive and holistic personal development. There is even the belief that as long as the person is morally sound, he or she should be able to face all kinds of challenges, social or technical. This is certainly not the case in the West, where a 'good' person is not necessarily able.

Other cultural differences follow. For example, the emphasis on community needs necessarily leads to uniform requirements, hence uniformity and conformity, which are often identified by the West as characteristics of Chinese societies. Such an emphasis on uniformity and conformity is sometimes seen traditionally from the West as a matter of obedience in Chinese societies.

Conformity in education necessarily looks to the efforts rather than the ability of the student. Students are engaged in studying the same curriculum and sit for the same examination, regardless of their individual differences. It is expected that as long as students work hard, they all should be able to achieve what is expected. This is different from the West, where learning achievements are seen as very much affected by the students' abilities. The effort–ability dichotomy has become a major area of study in the literature about culture in education.[6]

An analysis of the ancient system of education in China might provide a very good illustration. In ancient China:

- a scholar was meant to be self-motivated and could be from any family background;

- he (at times she) typically studied the standard curriculum, the *Four Books* and *Five Classics*;
- he typically went through lengthy periods of study under hardship, 'ten years by the cold window [i.e. no heating]';
- he sat in local examinations and, if successful, eventually sat for the civil examination at the imperial court;
- he would typically be expected to write an essay to elaborate his views about governing the nation;
- he would be assessed according to whether or not his views were endorsed by the Emperor;
- if he were successful, he would be appointed into the officialdom;
- the most successful one, the annual champion, could be appointed Prime Minister, married to the princess, and usually launch an elaborate and glorious home-coming.

It is not exaggerating to say that successful scholars are national heroes of ancient China. The theme runs through numerous novels and dramas and is part of national folklore. If we observe carefully, geniuses (who spent little effort) and descendants from rich families (who did not go through hardships) were not always highly regarded. They often played the role of vice in stories. It is also important to note that successful scholars might have come from *any* family. Study, scholarship and examination were the legitimate routes for social mobility, and indeed the only route of social mobility in ancient China.[7]

Therefore, the meaning of education in ancient China was almost exclusively related to incentives for social mobility, was examined for loyalty to society, was based on the firm legitimacy of the examinations, and was committed to producing the elite. Such learning is understandably only extrinsically motivated [8] and indeed is not knowledge-based.

The cultural analysis of educational values in China might explain the high motivation among Chinese parents and students even today. Education is taken for granted as an important test for human life. At the same time, it might also explain the difficulties experienced in curriculum reform, in developing vocational education, in reducing examination pressures, in moving away from unnecessary rote-learning, and so forth. To parents, particularly to parents in the rural areas, all these are irrelevant. Schooling to them is just like studying for the civil examination in ancient times. All that concerns them is that their children could eventually work in the urban cities. What exactly is learnt during such studies is not their concern.[9]

The enrolment ratio in basic education in China is extremely high among developing countries, and is envied by many. People who would like to know the secret of such high enrolments often resort to examining the policy measures, planning and finance. However, the real secret lies in the old tradition, which has its legitimacy in the formal education system, but is not about learning knowledge or skills. An understanding of this secret may disappoint many admirers of the Chinese education tradition.

This does not mean that cross-cultural comparison is meaningless. Quite the opposite, without engaging in cross-cultural comparisons, I would never have understood the essence of education values in the Chinese culture, in which I have lived since birth. Cross-cultural comparisons, or even a serious study of just one other culture, could immediately widen one's horizons. This would help tremendously in understanding one's own culture and fully exploiting the strengths of one's own culture. Only then could one be conscious of the pros and cons of borrowing from another culture, and face the challenges of globalisation.

Research and Education Development

If the foregoing discussion is valid, then the implications for research are enormous. First, in order to face the pressures of 'globalisation', comparative education bears the tremendous mission of identifying what should and can be globalised and what should not or cannot. Most educators and educational researchers either work in a single system, or in a single discipline, whereas the task ahead of us is essentially cross-cultural and multidisciplinary.

Unfortunately, such studies are still rare. The most helpful ones have come from the psychologists. The established literature of cross-cultural psychology, unfortunately, is yet to be noticed by policy-makers in education, or even practitioners in schools. But first of all, it has to receive the attention of comparative educationalists who often play the counsel to policy-makers, albeit often in other countries. Business scholars, political scientists and anthropologists, have also contributed significantly to the understanding of cultures, and most of their findings are very relevant to education, but they are even more remote from the comparative educationalists. If comparative educationalists could pay more attention to such comparisons in culture, they would find totally new dimensions to their academic undertaking. Frankly, the 'discipline' of comparative education may not develop much further if the specificity of cultural values about education is not studied.

At the moment, cultural comparisons are biased towards East Asian culture, very much prompted by the notion of Japan as number one (Vogel, 1979) that prevailed in the high times of the 'East Asian Miracle' (World Bank, 1995). There is an emerging literature about Indian culture, but otherwise there are only scattered studies of, say, Islamic culture and African culture, that bear associations to education. There is considerable room for exploration.

Second, in reality, however, there are few researchers who are ready to commit themselves to cross-cultural comparative education. It is perhaps less a matter of willingness than one of conditions. As I hinted earlier, the vast majority of educational researchers work only in a single system. Those who work across systems often work on macro-dimensions where the cultural implications are less visible. There are, for example, very many grass-root educational researchers. They are seldom exposed to the international literature, and anyway they may not feel such a literature relevant. Most of them do not use an international language. Meanwhile, their contributions to human knowledge are also not known to the international community of researchers. Their research results are almost never translated.

In this context, comparative education researchers, who have the tradition of working across systems, have an almost unique role to play. While researchers in other educational disciplines may also work across cultures, they can do this only on occasions, whereas comparative education researchers are meant to work across cultures.

Third, research methodology is at stake. Comparative education that prevails in the literature is largely functionalist in nature and economic/political in methodology. Cross-cultural studies demand an open mind to native perspectives and the sensitivity not to impose foreign frameworks on the researched. In other words, the methodology has to bear with it some qualitative and ethnographic nature. As such, plain descriptions, which pretend that they are neutral, are no longer sufficient. Quantitative analyses, which are meant to be impartial and 'objective', have to be interpreted culturally (i.e. 'subjectively'), based on qualitative efforts. Methods that are common in qualitative research could be more frequently used in policy-sensitive studies. In-depth case studies, for example, have very strong revealing power and could have extremely strong policy bearings.

Fourth, although the preceding discussion applies generally to all nations, there is a special need for the strengthening of South–South research collaborations. To date, many researchers in comparative education are from the North. Often they are parachuted into a local system, do a blitzkrieg, and come out with a report deliverable to the funding agency. Such 'colonial' or 'missionary' researchers may or may not know much about education in their home system. Few of them participate in educational policy-making in their own countries. With accumulated experience over many quick-wins, they become experts in comparative education. There are, alternatively, real scholars in education who are invited into particular projects to make use of their expertise. These scholars, however, do not always interact with academics in comparative education.

Researchers in the North, nonetheless, will still remain the main thrust in comparative education. Realistically, they will still dominate the literature that is akin to their mother tongue. As such, they could also contribute most significantly in cross-cultural studies, because when compared with their counterparts in the South, they are much more privileged in terms of resources, expertise and networking. However, they may not be able to replace researchers who have a real stake in their own systems. Only these 'native' researchers could be very sensitive to cultural differences and hence benefit most from experiencing such differences. As such, it should be such 'native' researchers who are supported to go into other cultures and research those cultures, rather than someone from the North researching a culture and telling the natives what to do. In this context, South–South exchange becomes particularly meaningful. A researcher in rural China's education, for example, would certainly benefit from studying Indian rural education [10], certainly much more than studying rural education in Virginia, USA.[11]

Fifth, there is an obvious detachment between macro- and micro-studies in education. Macro-studies are important and indeed essential, but many macro-studies stop at the system level, and have lost sight of what such studies are to do with students learning within and outside classrooms. There is nonetheless a growing literature of ethnographic case studies that presents very powerful illustration of the most essential issues in education. Such literature, unfortunately, is seldom used to illuminate policy-making at the macro-level.

Concluding Remarks

Bruner (1996) recently remarked that there are two interpretations of education: 'information processing', which he calls the 'computational' approach, and 'meaning-making', which he calls the 'cultural' approach. Making meaning of lives is what education is about, and that should also be the aim of educational research, so it is inthe realm of comparative education. This is particularly meaningful with the present challenges of globalisation, where traditional cultural values face foreign invasions. Unless we have a better understanding of the cultural specificity in education, many of the strengths accumulated by human wisdom will disappear. In this respect, comparative education could have a very constructive role to play.

Notes

[1] See Fägerlind & Saha (1989) for detailed discussions.

[2] I am indebted to Minxuan Zhang, my doctoral student at the University of Hong Kong, who has done an in-depth review of the notions of equity.

[3] See Hofstede (1980, 1991) and Kim et al (1994) for detailed discussions.

[4] See more detailed analysis of the systems in Cheng (1990).

[5] White (1987) has made similar observations on the Japanese education system.

[6] Readers are strongly recommended to read Stevenson & Stigler (1992) for a research-based discussion of this issue.

[7] For more details, see Miyazaki (1963).

[8] Readers may like to refer to Biggs (1996) for a more comprehensive discussion of this issue. Lynn (1988) has made similar observations in Japan.

[9] More elaborate discussion of this point can be found in Cheng, 1996, ch. 4 and Conclusion.

[10] One of the success stories was carried out by UNICEF in 1990, where Chinese and Indian researchers exchanged visits after completing a review of 40 years of development of basic education in their respective countries. See Ahmed et al (1991).

[11] There was indeed such a case in early 1990s where trainees from Sri Lanka studied in Virginia for rural education!

References

Ahmed, M., Cheng, K.M., Jalaluddin, A.K. & Rmachandran, K. (1991) *Basic Education and National Development: lessons from China and India*. New York: UNICEF.

Biggs, J.B. (1996) Western Misperceptions of the Confucian-heritage Learning Culture, in D.A. Watkins & J.B. Biggs (Eds) *The Chinese Learner: cultural, psychological and contextual influences*, pp. 45–68. Hong Kong/Melbourne: Comparative Education Centre/Australian Council for Educational Research.

Bruner, J. (1996) *The Culture of Education*. Cambridge: Harvard University Press.

Cheng, K.M. (1990) The Culture of Schooling in East Asia, in N. Entwistle (Ed.) *Handbook of Educational Ideas and Practices*, pp. 163–173. London: Routledge.

Cheng, K.M. (1996) *Quality of Basic Education in China: a case study of the province of Zhejiang*. Paris: International Institute for Educational Planning.

Cheng, K.M. (1997) Qualitative Research and Educational Policy-making: approaching reality in developing countries, in M. Crossley & G. Vulliamy (Eds) *Educational Qualitative Research in Developing Countries: current perspectives*, pp. 65–85. New York: Garland.

Fägerlind, I. & Saha, L.J. (1989) *Education and National Development: a comparative perspective*. Oxford: Pergamon.

Gardner, H. (1984) The Development of Competence in Culturally Defined Domains, in R.A. Shweder & R.A. LeVine (Eds) *Culture Theory: essays on minds, self and emotion*, pp. 257–275. Cambridge MA: Harvard University Press.

Hofstede, G. (1980) *Culture's Consequences: international differences in work-related values*. Beverly Hills: Sage.

Hofstede, G. (1991) *Cultures and Organisations: software of mind*. London: McGraw-Hill.

Inkeles, A. (1997) Continuity and Change in Popular Values on the Pacific Rim, in J. Montgomery (Ed.) *Values and Values Diffusion in the Pacific Basin*. Cambridge MA: Pacific Basin Research Center.

Kim, U., Triandis, H.C., Kâgitçibasi, Ç., Choi, S.C. & Yoon, G. (Eds) (1994) *Individualism and Collectivism: theory, methods, and applications*. Thousand Oaks: Sage.

Liu, Changlin (1990) *Zhongguo xitong siwei: Wenhua jiyin toushi* [The Chinese systems thinking: perspectives on cultural genes] Beijing: China Social Science Press (in Chinese).

Liu, Tsun-yan (1988) Address at the Congregation for Honorary Doctorate Degrees, *University of Hong Kong Gazette*, vol. XXXV.

Lynn, R. (1988) *Educational Achievement in Japan: lessons for the West*. London: Macmillan.

Miyazaki, I. (1963) *China's Examination Hell: the civil service examination in imperial China*, trans. C. Schirokauer (1976). New Haven: Yale University Press.

Redding, G. (1990) *The Spirit of Chinese Capitalism*. New York: Walter de Gruyter.

Schein, E.H. (1992) *Organizational Culture and Leadership*, 2nd edn. San Francisco: Jossey–Bass.

Stevenson, H.W. & Stigler, J.W. (1992) *The Learning Gap: why our schools are failing and what we can learn from Japanese and Chinese education*. New York: Summit Books.

Stevenson, H.W. & Lee, S. (1997) The East Asian Version of Whole-class Teaching, in W.K. Cummings & P.G. Altbach (Eds) *The Challenge of Eastern Asian Education: implications for America*. Albany: State University of New York Press.

Vogel, E. (1979) *Japan as Number One: lessons for America*. Cambridge MA: Harvard University Press.

Watsons, J. (Ed.) (1997) *Golden Arches East: McDonald's in East Asia*. Stanford: Stanford University Press.

White, M. (1987) *The Japanese Educational Challenge: a commitment to children*. New York: The Free Press.

Zwingle, E. (1999) Goods Move, People Move, Ideas Move, and Cultures Change, *National Geographic*, 196, pp. 12–33.

The Department for International Development: knowledge generation after the White Paper[1]

TERRY ALLSOP

Introduction

In this article, you will read little or nothing about comparative research methodology in education. As you would expect of one lately charged with managing the education research budget for a large bilateral donor, my preoccupation has been with commissioning research which may have, on some reasonable time-line, policy and practice implications for aspects of education in our partner countries. I reflect ruefully on a much quoted comment by the then youthful David Hargreaves, when he became Chief Inspector of the Inner London Education Authority, that 'he could find no single piece of research which provided him with immediate support in his job', and on the recent prickly debate between the United Kingdom Government's Chief Inspector of Schools and the educational research community, where the two justifications for state funding of research are given as: to improve the quality of access and to raise standards in schools. A quick scan of a randomly chosen issue of the *British Journal of Educational Research* might suggest that there is a kernel of truth in what these hawks are saying.

As a preface to looking more carefully at the emerging focus of educational research within the Department for International Development (DFID), we may reflect briefly on current priorities within research agendas relating specifically to developing countries.

Research Themes for Educational Development

Samoff's recent paper, prepared for the Swedish International Development Agency, titled *Whose Sector Programme? Whose Responsibility? Observations from Recent Education Sector Analyses in Africa* (Samoff, 1997), reminds us (p. 4) of the dominant priorities and related applied research themes within broad sector studies. These are shown in Table I, with my added comment on the methodologies and researchers most likely to be involved.

Research theme	Methodologies/researchers
1. Funding shift from higher education to basic education	Rate-of-return analysis (economists)
2. Increased private sector involvement in delivery	Cost-effectiveness, efficiency (economists)
3. Increased student fees post-primary	Cost-sharing (economists/planners)
4. Decentralisation	Efficiency (economists/planners)
5. Increased girls' education	Social benefits (economists/various)
6. Textbook production and distribution	Quality of instruction (educationists/publishing specialists)
7. In-service teacher education	Quality of instruction (educationists)

Table I. Research themes for educational development.

Samoff points out that these priorities can be detected as largely those of the World Bank, both in its espoused methodologies for education sector work and in its publications. He reasonably adds that these themes 'have little to say about learning' and much to say about systems approaches. Actually, the final item, the in-service education or continuing professional development of teachers, is generally studied as a systems issue. There has been no comprehensive review of the quality of in-service training in Africa since Greenland's 1983 study, and scant attention has been paid to the understandings gleaned in studies in industrialised countries, such as those of Joyce & Showers (1988). This in spite of the fact that many donor agency technical assistance commitments to African countries have been in this field of work.

So there remains much to be done in order to reorient the education research agenda for development, both in relation to addressing those themes which actually make a difference to the quality of learning, and to which research specialisms shall be brought into play. In this context, Samoff remarks pithily, 'Ultimately, whether or not education contributes to development depends less on how many children complete school than on what they do or do not learn' (1997).

Knowledge Generation after the White Paper

In the November 1997 White Paper on international development, titled *Eliminating World Poverty*, the first significant United Kingdom government policy statement in this field for more than 20 years, there is a specific section on research, or knowledge generation, as it is now being designated.

> *One of the main constraints to effective development assistance is an imperfect understanding of social, economic, political and physical environments. We will find local solutions to local problems and involve local people and institutions in the process ... Getting it right means not only investing in effective relationships but in pushing back the boundaries of shared knowledge, understanding the problems which constrain sustainable development and working with national and international partners to develop appropriate, often innovative, solutions which will help to eliminate poverty.*

> *Research is an important weapon in the fight against poverty. Without research, many development interventions would fail or be much less successful; and research has significant multiplier effects – solutions to the causes of poverty in one part of the developing world may well be replaceable in another. The principle of shared knowledge is an important component of the partnerships which are essential to development. The Government sees continued investment in knowledge generation as a key element in achieving its aims and objectives for international development. (White Paper, 1997, panel 18, p. 48)*

There is also a good deal of emphasis, throughout the White Paper, on new ways of working, for example, 'becoming a learning organisation', 'affirming the OECD [Organisation for Economic Cooperation and Development] generated international development targets', 'enhanced partnerships with developing countries', 'stronger contributors to international development forums', all of which relate to our research role. How is this reflected in new directions for knowledge generation/research?

First, a quick review of the present situation. In 1996/97, DFID's centrally-funded research valued just over £60 million, or about 3% of the Department's total budget. In addition, project/programme markers suggest a further £23 million of bilateral country programme funding was committed to research; if aspects of baseline studies and evaluation were to be included, this figure is almost certainly a significant underestimate. By comparison, in 1996 the World Bank spent US$25 million (down from US$30 million in 1992) on centrally-funded research. The World Bank estimates that, over the period 1982–89, its average disbursement of funds for educational projects included a component of about 2.2% for research – but remember that this is *lending* for research.

Within DFID, the knowledge generation programmes have been historically dramatically skewed towards support for the science- and technology-based groups, particularly in the areas of natural resources and engineering. The research programme used to be called TDR – Technology Development and Research. The overall picture is given in the data given in Tables II and III.

Sector	1991/92	1995/96	% share 1995/96
Natural resources	29,378	31,329	55.1
Engineering	8,523	10,546	18.6
Health	6,045	9,256	16.4
Economic and social	4,076	5,400	9.5
Education	147	280	0.5
Total	48,169	56,851	

Table II. Sectoral trends in research expenditure (£'000).

Year	91/92	92/93	93/94	94/95	95/96	96/97	97/98	98/99	99/00
Exp	147	290	367	216	280	350	520	1000	1200

Table III. Education research expenditure (£'000).

For education research within DFID, there is now very real scope for a major increase in our commitment to knowledge generation, in line with the high profile of the social sectors across the organisation.

There has been an interesting debate within DFID in relation to the direction of research within the organisation. At present, the overall control of the research programmes rests with the relevant Chief Adviser. In a review of research programmes in 1997, related to the development of the White Paper, proposals emerged, which were supported by some specialisms, for the creation of a Knowledge Policy Unit (KPU) to be led by a senior research manager, preferably with experience of the management of major research programmes in the public or foundation sectors. The arguments for the appointment of the senior research manager were not taken forward, so there will be little shift in the nexus of control of research programmes. The KPU has been created, with the overall purpose defined as follows:

> *The purpose of the KPU is to enable DFID to increase the*
> *impact of its knowledge generation and dissemination*
> *activities in relation to DFID's aim by providing a focal point*

in DFID for dealing with generic and strategic issues of knowledge management. This is particularly in relation to knowledge generation budgets but also their relationship to other central and bilateral programmes. It will specifically be responsible for dealing with such issues in relation to other Whitehall departments, learned societies, research councils, the European Union and multilateral institutions (where appropriate).

A senior administrator now heads the KPU, supported by a small secretariat. The KPU should have a role in:

- advising on resource allocation;
- dealing with cross-cutting issues;
- improving strategic management of knowledge programmes;
- enhancing monitoring and evaluation of research programmes; and
- improving dissemination of research findings.

These are all important themes to which the KPU may indeed contribute, but my view is that, in the medium term, it is unlikely to influence significantly the overall distribution of resources for research. In the particular case of research in education, and its historical neglect within Overseas Development Administration (ODA)/DFID, this is less than helpful. Despite the recent steady growth in education research funding and resultant output, there is almost an order of magnitude difference between the scale of the education programme and the three biggest research spenders.

I have invested a good deal of energy in the last 3 years in promoting multi/intersectoral research (cross-cutting issues in the current jargon) with a limited return to my efforts. In relation to individual programmes there have been important outputs in areas like agricultural education, health education (HIV/AIDS), training for the informal sector, gender studies, with particularly useful co-sponsorship with the Economic and Social Research programme group. It is less easy to develop joint programmes with natural resources and engineering, as they have institutional commitments on a long timescale and therefore not a great deal of flexibility in planning. Overall, my disappointment is that there is no pot of money for the active development of interface programmes; to get one under way at present requires a disproportionate amount of effort. In the context of the White Paper, with its many restated and new priorities which are cross-cutting, this should be a challenge for knowledge generation programmes rather than a chore. Obvious examples for potential cross-cutting research include human rights and education, poverty eradication and education, and 'participation' and the measurement of progress in the attainment of international development targets.

I was very struck by the review of the literature relating to the economic benefits from basic research reported in the Science Policy Research Unit (SPRU) review of the relationship between publicly-funded basic research and economic performance (Martin & Salter, 1996), which indicates six main forms of outcome:

1. basic research as a source of new useful information;
2. the creation by basic researchers of new instrumentation and new methodologies;
3. skills developed by those engaged in basic research which yield economic benefits when individuals move from basic research carrying codified and tacit knowledge;
4. participation in basic research to gain access to networks of experts and information;
5. the fact that those trained in basic research may be particularly good at solving complex technological problems; and
6. the creation of 'spin-off' companies.

The present education research programme of DFID mainly reflects points 1, 3 and 4, and to a lesser extent 2.

Whilst much of DFID's research output has traditionally been circulated within rather specialised communities, there is now a clear resolution to use the KPU to improve dissemination and visibility. In the education programme, in addition to the main series of education research papers, currently distributing about 20,000 copies per annum, we have a more informal series of shorter papers and are planning to develop a series specifically devoted to outcomes from the higher education links scheme. Collaborating with DFID's Economic and Social Research programme, we have commissioned the ID21 group at the Institute of Development Studies to create a web site with, in the first instance, abstracts of all our research publications. This may be surfed at www.id21.org. Under the same commission, ID21 has recently published an insight review of gender research in education, primarily the outcomes of DFID sponsored education research (Institute of Development Studies, 1999). I anticipate that, in future years, we will utilise this web site to publicise much more DFID-generated educational material. Closer to the ultimate beneficiaries of this research activity, each of the education research programmes sponsors a series of in-country dissemination workshops, so that our total commitment to publication and dissemination takes approximately 15% of the total budget.

Partnerships in Knowledge Generation

The White Paper gives a very high priority to the development of partnerships with developing countries, based essentially on the extent to which a strong businesslike relationship can be sustained in an environment of democracy, financial rectitude and engagement of civil society. It is not anticipated that such partnerships will be defined by formal agreements, but rather through ongoing dialogue and the sharing of policy papers, such as Country Strategy Papers which were formerly developed within DFID but are now created as joint endeavours.

The development of partnerships in knowledge generation will require a reassessment of how business is conducted. At least the following questions need to be addressed in the development of a new Education Knowledge Strategy.

- Whose agenda is driving the research?
- How do we ensure real partnership with local institutions and personnel?
- If this is not immediately possible, how do we invest in the building of local research capacity?

We may anticipate at least the following responses in the short and medium term. First, there will be evidence in submitted proposals of joint planning between United Kingdom and developing country researchers, with a steady shift over time to first articulation of the research priority by the developing country. This should lead, in due course, to an increase in the availability and quality of indigenous research findings and to the use of these findings in education reform (although we should resist the temptation to oversimplify the relationships between research evidence and policy-making).

Secondly, there will be increased emphasis on establishing systems for strengthening developing country educational research capacity, both in ministry of education planning units and in other research-oriented bodies. This should include a commitment to enhancing access for developing country research institutions to knowledge networks. I would anticipate a shift in the focus of the higher education links scheme towards research capacity development, as has been the case in Denmark, where Danish institutions link with developing country partners with a specific research capacity focus. The Social Development Department of DFID has taken an interesting lead in this direction, now that it has for the first time a small research budget in its care; it has chosen to utilise the budget entirely for developing country capacity building. Also within DFID, the Economic and Social Research Programme has laid out new guidelines for partnership in its current strategy; thus:

> *Greater priority will be given to development of partnerships*
> *with institutions in developing countries, usually by means of*
> *a tripartite relationship with British and/or European*
> *institutions.*

And:

> *Limited funds will be made available for the development of research capacity in developing country research institutions, normally as part of a collaborative research project with a UK institution. Greater weight will be given in the assessment of research proposals, to the quality of collaborative arrangements with developing country institutions.*

Thirdly, there is some evidence of serious discourse about programme ownership. This would at least take on questions of commissioning and contracting, and crucially, equitable publication agreements between contributors. This area might be best addressed through the development of a code of conduct or good practice by interested parties.

Finally, we may anticipate an increased percentage of collaboratively funded and jointly managed research programmes. An interesting example is the partnership being developed between DFID, Rockefeller Foundation, UNICEF and the World Bank, with partner researchers in 14 countries, under the general title of 'Learning from Experience: sustainable strategies for girls' education'.

Two countries which already have very considerable educational research capacity, India and South Africa, offer some interesting possibilities. India has both serious research institutes in the social sciences and large numbers of experienced national researchers, yet there are simply too many examples of India being used as a test-bed by external researchers, often with scant regard for proper procedures and behaviour. Gratifyingly, Indian institutions are themselves rapidly becoming more robust in their responses. DFID has recently agreed to support a programme which is specifically working to develop the skills in evaluation of a large number of institution-based Indian researchers, in the context of quality improvements in primary schooling. The resulting researcher network will be one of the key outputs from the programme. From South Africa, clear signals have been transmitted which indicate that South African institutions and researchers must be in the lead, so that researchers from the United Kingdom and elsewhere must recognise this when developing partnerships. In South Africa there is, of course, a significant indigenous research capacity, although mostly situated in the 'historically white' institutions.

As sector-wide approaches to education develop quickly over the next few years, we should expect to see an emerging research theme supporting the development. Given the language of 'partnership' and 'ownership' embodied in the principles of sector-wide approaches, this should provide an interesting opportunity for linking the research functions more closely with the stages of development of the sector-wide programme, so that the findings can be used specifically to plan and adapt practice. Such research will also be managed much more clearly by government and associated institutions, with the resources supplied for it by donor agencies.

How far, and how soon, should these principles apply to research relationships with all developing countries?

Note

[1] The views expressed in this article are those of the author alone. They do not represent the official position of the Department for International Development.

References

Department for International Development (1997) *Eliminating World Poverty*. London: HMSO.

Greenland, J. (Ed.) (1983) *In-service Training of Primary Teachers in Africa*. London: Macmillan.

Institute of Development Studies (IDS) (1999) *Development Research Insights*. Brighton: IDS.

Joyce, B. & Showers, B. (1988) *Student Achievement through Staff Development*. New York: Longman.

Martin, B. & Salter, A. (1996) The Relationship between Publicly Funded Basic Research and Economic Performance, Science Policy Research Unit for HM Treasury.

Samoff, J. (1997) *Whose Sector Programme? Whose Responsibility? Observations from Recent Education Sector Analyses in Africa*. Stockholm: Swedish International Development Cooperation Agency.

Developing a Comparative Approach to the Study of Gender, Education and Development

COLIN BROCK & NADINE CAMMISH

Introduction

In keeping with the rationale of the seminar series, 'Learning from Comparing', on which this book is based, this chapter focuses primarily on approaches to the *study* of gender, education and development rather than on the issue itself, or how gender imbalance in this respect can be rectified in practical terms. We begin by briefly identifying stages apparent in the development of the analysis of the gender issue and move through a discussion of these towards a strategy for adopting a comparative approach. Such an approach would, we argue, be beneficial not only to the enhancement of understanding but also for informing policy-making.

We were involved in the seminar primarily on the basis of our Department for International Development (DFID) sponsored study, 'Factors Affecting Female Participation in Education in Seven Developing Countries' (Brock & Cammish, 1997a), which has significant comparative dimensions. Prior to this project, the emphasis had been mainly on the incidence of female disadvantage and through descriptive analysis. In this way a considerable amount of quantitative data was assembled from various parts of the world, and was effective in raising the profile of the issue. Multilateral and bilateral development agencies began, routinely, to include the gender factor in their project guidelines and requirements, but the adoption of such a stance as a convention came with obvious limitations (Stromquist, 1998). By identifying the key factors affecting female participation in education, an opportunity was created both for comparative analysis, and also for the recognition of the necessity of an interdisciplinary approach to examine interfaces and interconnection between factors.

At the same time, studies were being conducted that focused on issues in relation to gender, education and development, such as literacy (Bown, 1990) and school achievement (Kutnick et al, 1997). Some of our own writings derived from the 'factors' research also considered particular issues such as law (Brock & Cammish, 1994), or country cases: Cameroon (Cammish & Brock 1994) and Vanuatu (Cammish, 1994). Arising from such work came the increasing awareness that the core factor relating to gender imbalance in education is 'culture'. So we took our first steps towards attempting a theoretical position that would accommodate the realisation of the notion of 'cultural capacity' for change as an imperative for the potential contribution of women and girls to the development process (Brock & Cammish, 1997b). This has some resonance with the analysis of Heward (1999) in relation to 'new discourses of gender, education and development', as well as with Stromquist's 'politics of everyday life' (1997) and 'household dynamics' (1999). Such considerations move the analysis into the realm of gender relations and development, with gender and social agency (Betts, 1998) and gender and cooperative conflicts (Sen, 1990) as examples.

Such holistic approaches inform the necessity to examine the factors that influence the effect of gender on realising the potential of education's contribution to development in a more integrative way. First, however, we will outline the aforementioned project on 'Factors Affecting Female Participation in Education' with special reference to its comparative dimensions.

Factors Affecting Female Participation in Education in Six Developing Countries

Our study under this title was conducted under the auspices of, and funded by, the then Overseas Development Agency (ODA) – now DFID – as a result of a competition between proposals invited by that agency from a number of United Kingdom universities. Given that a number of countries were involved, a comparative dimension was inevitable. However, as can always happen with government-sponsored studies, certain influences came to bear upon the selection of bases for comparison.

First, in this case, both the Middle East/North Africa and Latin America were excluded on the grounds that ODA, as it then was, funded very little educational development work in those regions. Secondly, we were required to select a 'better' and a 'worse' case, with respect to female participation in education from within each of the three main areas then recognised as comprising the remainder of the 'developing world': South Asia, sub-Saharan Africa and the tropical island zones.

Thirdly, our initial selection of countries within these parameters was rejected in two cases due to (a) the sudden deterioration between the relations of the government of one such country and the United Kingdom Government, and (b) the availability of aid/reconstruction funds (arising from an environmental disaster) for another country not originally selected. The latter had the result of significantly diminishing the interpretation of one comparison we had wished to include, namely the respective legacies of anglophone and francophone colonial activity. However, although these interventions were unfortunate, they did not invalidate the potential for comparison – rather, they placed some limitations upon it.

The original brief provided by ODA for the selection of factors likely to affect female participation listed only three: social, economic and religious. The first phase of documentary research suggested four additional factors, and two more were added during the first (in effect pilot) field visit. Consequently, the following factors were identified and investigated: geographical, sociocultural, health, economic, religious, legal, political-administrative, educational and initiatives (to address the issue of female disadvantage) in the following countries: Bangladesh, Cameroon, India, Jamaica, Sierra Leone and Vanuatu. A seventh country (the Seychelles) was added at a later date so as to complete the range of tropical island zones, but was not included in the comparative analysis. The executive summary of the project report provides an outline of the outcomes.

The rationale for the project indicates, *inter alia*, its comparative intent:

> *the project was to have a* comparative dimension *to the extent that it would be possible to:*
> (i) synthesise *the outcomes under the same factor headings;*
> (ii) *present the major outcomes in a form that could enable comparison to be facilitated (see matrix chart);*
> (iii) *identify certain* recommendations *that could be relevant at least across the group of countries, but also perhaps beyond to comparable states and regions, though inevitably some recommendations would be country specific. (Brock &
> Cammish, 1997a, p. 10; original emphasis)*

The aforementioned matrix chart is reproduced here as Figure 1. Inevitably it accommodates only a condensed and limited summary, but does permit the following initial comparisons: factors across countries; countries across factors; and countries across countries. The recommendations made to advise the development agency are coded and it can therefore be easily seen across which countries a particular recommendation applies (Brock & Cammish, 1997a, pp. 4–6).

Country	Factor: Geographical	Sociocultural
Bangladesh	Gross disparities in spatial pattern of school provision. Stark rural/urban dichotomy; secondary single sex in towns. Rainy season effects severe physical and economic disruption.	Fundamental cultural bias against females. Patriarchal systems operate against girls' schooling. Means of protection against assault is crucial. Many schools too far from home for girls. The attitude of fathers is very significant indeed.
Cameroon	'Africa in minature', from desert to rain forest. A mosaic of indigenous cultures overlain by a colonial dichotomy: Anglophone and Francophone. Also spatial and religious variation in respect of Christian denominations and Islam.	Not an extreme case, but females still marginalised. Girls needed more at home; links between bride price and schooling. Growing problems of early pregnancy and delinquency in towns. Promotion limited for professional females.
India wih special reference to Gujarat and Orissa	Immense diversity even within Gujarat and Orissa. Massive rural/urban dichotomy; problems of isolation and opening up. Access to schooling incomplete despite overlapping networks. Distance to school still a problem despite progress made.	Patriarchal system prevails in most areas, which gives preference to boys' education. Generally low valuation of female life. Systems of caste, tribe and class all have influence. Local and rural elites are significant, often conservative.
Jamaica	Considerable disparity of provision despite small scale, due to urban/rural juxtaposition, lack of catchments and historical locations of prestigious schools. Complicated migrations in and out of urban areas, also to secondary schools.	Matrifocal system favours females. Girls have positive role models at home and at school. But there is a major problem of teenage pregnancies and a continued male dominance in political and business fields.
Sierra Leone	Christian/Muslim division, also very marked urban/rural dichotomy with capital city Freetown markedly different from the rest of country. Very poor interior road network with incomplete primary system difficult of access.	Traditional female roles still upheld and ceremonially legitimised. Mature rural girls obliged to marry. Much early marriage and teenage pregnancy. Some liaisons with older men to safeguard education and fund it, mainly Freetown area.
Vanuatu	Immense diversity between and within each island. Usual geographical problems of small archipelago states. Some locations face extreme isolation; urban/rural dichotomy is stark. Core/periphery problems for education.	Many cultures and languages plus Anglophone/Francophone dichotomy. Females have lower status than males in all groups. Low aspirations among rural girls but some urban professionals. May miss out on French/English, even Bislama, if they do not attend school.

Figure 1a. Matrix chart to facilitate initial comparison: geographical and sociocultural. Source: (Brock & Cammish, 1997a).

Country	Factor: Health	Economic
Bangladesh	The effect of widespread poverty in contributing to malnutrition is worse for girls, and the physical effects of young pregnancies can be severe. Enhanced food programme would be helpful.	Very low economic profile for the majority cannot overcome the direct and hidden costs of school. Child labour is a key element in family survival. Adult males not yet supportive of females gaining new skills and status.
Cameroon	Sexually precocious youth culture in towns could bring attendant health problems, including the damaging physical effects of young pregnancies.	Rapidly declining situation, but women actively involved in the money economy both urban and rural, which creates tension between school and work in adolescence. External aid to cash crop sector may sometimes undermine the important work of women in the subsistence or locally marketed agricultural sectors, and adversely affect their status.
India with special reference to Gujarat and Orissa	Numerous poverty related conditions, including blindness, severely constrain schooling in rural areas. High female mortality still partly due to infanticide and malnutrition.	Grinding poverty and hunger has both rural and urban variants and a negative effect on girls' schooling. Worsening situation for female work force. Technical development aid may undermine women in that it tends to be directed to men, thereby enhancing the male status and economic position.
Jamaica	Damaging medical effects of early child bearing, but female life expectancy still higher than male. Possibility of stress associated with the crucial Common Entrance examination.	Jamaican women are used to handling money and controlling family budgets. Educated females, including qualified teachers, move into modern sector jobs. Large urban poverty zones.
Sierra Leone	Many health problems linked with extreme poverty and high levels of early sexual activity. Generally low levels of nourishment among girls affects educational performance adversely.	Widespread poverty creates direct and hidden costs which work against girls' schooling especially in rural regions. Both girls and boys involved in petty trading. There are very few income generating jobs for women in rural areas.
Vanuatu	High birth rates and large families in rural areas put pressure on inadequate health provision. Female mortality is higher than male, which is unusual in global terms.	Girls traditionally work on the land; 'gardens' are significant to family economies. Hidden costs of education favour the schooling of boys in the rural societies, but in towns, girls are educated for modern sector jobs.

Figure 1b. Matrix chart to facilitate initial comparison: health and economic. Source: (Brock & Cammish, 1997a).

Country	Factor: Religious	Legal
Bangladesh	Not a direct factor, but invoked by those who oppose the education and development of females. Religious leaders need to espouse the female cause for the general good.	Women are statutory minors, therefore dependent. Illiteracy leaves females impotent to invoke the laws of protection against assault, constraint and early marriage. Dowry problems. Need to strengthen legal support.
Cameroon	Considerable disparity in mission provision; Catholic: Protestant has differential effect for adolescent girls. In theory both Christian and Islamic movements are supportive of female schooling, but in practice development has been slower in the (Islamic) north.	Modern law provides for equal opportunity, but customary law prevails in favour of males. Early marriage is illegal but accepted if both families are agreed.
India wih special reference to Gujarat and Orissa	Indirect effects only, and in any case a multi-religious context. Religious significance of the son in Hindu society may disadvantage girls.	There are long-standing laws against child employment, but often disregarded. In some groups women *are* property, and this low status severely constrains their access to education. Women need more legal support.
Jamaica	Indirect effect in respect of disparate mission legacy and contemporary denominational input. Generally positive for girls, though some criticism of male authority model in Christian churches.	Although schooling not being compulsory is not unique to Jamaica, it may well in this case affect the poor enrolment and attendance rates of boys in the lower socio-economic sectors.
Sierra Leone	Not a direct factor against female education, though some discriminatory customs are blamed on religion, especially Islam. In fact both Islamic and Christian organisations have been supportive of girls' education.	Modern laws are supportive, though not always enforced, but traditional custom is stronger in rural regions and tends to act against female educational opportunity.
Vanuatu	Disparate and varied mission legacy, but generally supportive of girls' schooling. Traditional (kastom) religion not so supportive, and in fact reinforces low female status.	Minimum age of marriage law (18) sometimes disregarded in rural areas where chiefs maintain traditional laws which favour males. Family Law Bill is under consideration

Figure 1c. Matrix chart to facilitate initial comparison: religious and legal.
Source: (Brock & Cammish, 1997a).

Country	Factor: Political-administrative	Educational
Bangladesh	Apparent lack of political will to address the problem, though general policy aims are helpful. The poor and unreliable nature of local administration and support is a crucially weak link.	The system is incomplete, therefore difficult of access to girls; and a consequent shortage of female teachers in rural areas results. Not such a problem in urban areas where middle-class girls are proceeding to university and outscoring men.
Cameroon	Anglophone/Francophone 'divide' still significant, leading to exodus of qualified anglophones. Secondary sector incomplete in some rural areas. It is felt that too much aid goes to (Francophone) higher education, and perhaps not enough to primary.	Extremely varied enrolment and wastage patterns. Very high primary class numbers due to high birth rate. Long school day at odds with family work needs. Technical/vocational sector is very weak.
India wih special reference to Gujarat and Orissa	Federal/state/local hierarchy leads to evaporation of political will to deal with female disadvantage. Power of local elders still significant, but local educational administration is weak.	Provided by a number of systems but provision still disparate and incomplete. Massive urban/rural dichotomy. Very high illiteracy rate among rural women but urban middle-class girls achieving well in universities.
Jamaica	Ministry has an indirect, facilitating/mediating role. Power lies with School Governing Bodies, who it is claimed favour male appointments at senior level. Ministry decentralisation may boost community involvement.	There is an 'educational culture', and strong social class influence. The Common Entrance examination, selecting for high school, dominates the system, and for the majority population, girls gain more places than boys. But sex bias in texts.
Sierra Leone	Political will is weak in meeting educational needs of the majority; system only partly operative. Women's position is weak and The Women's Bureau has inadequate funding. Political problems of indigenous language status.	Underfunded incomplete system. Late payment of teachers adversely affects morale and leads to absenteeism. System of repeating classes increases chances of female dropout. The curriculum could be more relevant.
Vanuatu	Traditionally females are not permitted to speak in public but this is changing. There is said to be regional/island bias in appointments but women face discrimination everywhere. Some pro-female pressure groups.	Primary sector almost complete, plus a growing private nursery feeder system, but geographical factors make secondary participation difficult, especially for girls. Also, the element of selection in the junior secondary sector is adverse, despite the present expansion.

Figure 1d. Matrix chart to facilitate initial comparison: political-administrative and educational. Source: (Brock & Cammish, 1997a).

Country	Factor: Initiatives
Bangladesh	Many good non-formal non-governmental organisation schemes in rural areas, especially BRAC. Also good work at secondary level for girls by Asia Foundation/USAID. Acceptance of female teacher trainees with lower grades than men could be counter-productive.
Cameroon	Ministry is flexible over age of female enrolment. There is a Ministry of Women's Affairs, though underfunded and weak, and numerous schemes for dropout girls. OIC model in Buea (vocational) is effective.
India wih special reference to Gujarat and Orissa	Numerous initiatives involving NGOs in development work for rural women and young children. Also Federal Ministry scheme Operation Blackboard to increase number of rural primary places and female teachers.
Jamaica	Crisis centres for pregnant teenagers are effective but need more support. The YWCA Vocational Education Institute excellent as a second chance for drop-out girls. University of the West Indies has a 'Women in Development' programme.
Sierra Leone	Large birth control programme by IPPF. Various NGO activities in support of rural women. New Basic Education Reform aims to provide work-oriented curriculum. Several women's organisations opening up.
Vanuatu	Much private effort to develop the nursery sector. Vanuatu Council of Women is an active and successful pressure group working for better health, schooling and legal support for women and girls.

Figure 1e. Matrix chart to facilitate initial comparison:
initiatives. Source: (Brock & Cammish, 1997a).

In order to maximise the potential of the project for comparative analysis, the same field strategies, exercises and instruments were designed and used for each consequent country. So in each of the seven cases, in addition to documentary reading comprising of 163 items of locally generated and/or locally available literature, the following were carried out in each location: interviews with senior professionals, interviews with parents, survey with primary teacher trainees, survey with primary pupils. The last named was one of the core exercises in the project and an original feature in this field. The target group was at the top end of the primary school, but given the situation in many developing countries, there was a wide age range. Nonetheless, nearly 80% of the 1193 pupils (50.8% boys and 49.2% girls) were between 11 and 13. We were also careful to sample schools from different but comparable environments in each country: urban, semi-urban and rural.

It is not the purpose here to go into the findings or recommendations. Suffice it to say that the writers, and many respondents, feel that the study did shift the ground forward in gender, education and development research by concentrating on factors, and that the methodology used was appropriate and effective, especially on the comparative front. We concluded that while the findings reinforced the knowledge that the problem of female participation is near universal, 'it is not intractable and that significant and progressive movement has occurred in many areas' (Brock & Cammish, 1997a, p. 28). Despite this observation, it is clear that the closing of the gender gap is not going to occur without at least two major achievements: the acquisition of appropriate literacies by (especially rural) women and girls, and cultural adjustments to accommodate change.

Women, Literacy and Development

This is the subtitle of Lalage Bown's monograph on *Preparing the Future* (1990), commissioned and published by Action Aid. She examined the impact of adult women's literacy acquisition as evidenced in the outcomes of 44 projects across the developing world. The findings again point to a multifactoral solution, showing positive effects in social, economic and personal domains, as summarised in Figure 2.

Lalage Bown concludes that cultural factors are very significant in the creation of 'a large gap between the level of access to education of males and females' (1990, p. 4), and that this gap should be closed not only in response to the demands of equity and natural justice, but also in the interest of recovering better returns in developmental terms than investments in education to date have achieved.

We came to the same conclusion, and have sought to engage the notion of cultural capacity building in seeking a way forward, but before we turn to that, reference must be made to the work of Stephens on Ghana, which illustrates the centrality of the cultural issue to the understanding and resolution of 'the gender problem'.

Key effects of literacy programmes for adult women in developing countries

---

1. *Social effects* include
   - a greater likelihood of literate women making use of child health-care techniques at home, such as Oral Rehydration Therapy;
   - a greater readiness to present children for immunisation;
   - cleaner homes and better child nutrition;
   - an enhanced readiness to send children, including daughters, to school;
   - a greater disposition by literate women to space families.

2. *Economic effects* include:
   - greater capacity to mobilise credit and greater willingness to use banks;
   - readiness to participate in and to establish new forms of economic organisations (e.g. cooperatives, small businesses).

3. *Personal effects* include:
   - a readiness to influence family decisions on such matters as the marriage age of girls;
   - a greater disposition to cooperate in socio-economic organisations;
   - a new capacity for leadership in church and welfare organisations;
   - a readiness to organise against injustice and for positive advocacy on social and economic matters

---

Figure 2. Key effects of literacy programmes for adult women in developing countries. Derived from Lalage Bown (1990).

Culture, Cultural Capacity and Gender

In his recent DFID sponsored study, *Girls and Basic Education: a cultural enquiry* (1998), Stephens explores the cultural factor in the Ghanaian context, comparing and contrasting two regions. The study is concerned with the cultural framework within which development occurs and examines three domains: the home, the school and the economy. Stephens stresses the interrelationship of these domains, showing how culture constitutes an overarching framework within which to examine the interfacing and interaction of social, educational and economic factors.

In the article 'Cultural Capacity Building and the Closing of the Gender Gap' (Brock & Cammish, 1997b), cultural capacity is defined as 'the extent to which and the rate at which a society is capable of absorbing cultural change' (p. 118). To increase and encourage girls' participation in education, not only must schools be made available and accessible and parents be able (economically) to send their daughters to them, but parents must also be willing to do so. Stephens's metaphor of 'the cultural fabric' (1998, p. 35) is useful here: to what extent is it elastic, capable of accommodating new ideas about the role and status of girls? Some societies may be capable of rapid change in response to external stimulation but others, where there is little cultural capacity, cannot be hurried by government intervention, the insistence of donor agencies, or the example of perhaps more highly urbanised areas.

Cultural capacity and its development is embedded in the roles and relationships of males and females within the particular cultural context and change in these is normally a slow process, stretching over generations, unless precipitated by the force of a major outside stimulus.

In seeking a suitable methodology for the testing of the notion of cultural capacity and its potential significance for examining the role of gender in the development process, we have revisited two key publications of the 1980s: Todd's *The Causes of Progress: culture, authority and change* (1987) and Le Vine & White's *Human Conditions: the cultural basis of educational developments* (1986). These would suggest that the issue of *gender relations*, rather than a focus only on resolving problems of female disadvantage in education, is central to creating cultural capacity for change.

Such sources remind us of the prime significance of cultural context, or, as Levine & White put it, 'the complex symbols that move men and women in diverse settings' (1986, p. 119), and they proceed to point out that it would not be meaningful to 'accept any interpretation of the motivating quality of those symbols that is not based on evidence concerning their cultural meanings' (pp. 210–211). They distinguish between the micro-social (e.g. motivation) and macro-social (e.g. mobilisation) imperatives in respect of development, and the tensions between them. The gender issue lies at the heart of these tensions, as illustrated by Stromquist (1999) in her analysis of the 'Impact of Structural Adjustment Programmes in Africa and Latin America'. For, as she points out, 'Poor families are the hardest hit by government cuts in education budgets' (p. 25), and that 'to understand the gender impact it is necessary to consider the internal dynamics of households' (p. 26). This relates to negotiation, and as illustrated by Bown in Figure 2, the acquisition of appropriate literacies by women enhances their confidence and capacity to influence family decisions on matters of education.

As Todd (1987) observes, any changes in the behaviour of a family or a community have to be mediated through the age–sex hierarchy of that community. Awareness of the details and implications of this hierarchy will inform the 'life plan' of both men and women who constitute distinct social groups while also belonging to their own families. According to Todd, a vital conjunction is that between the age of females at marriage and the literacy level of the male partner. As the age of women at marriage rises, a greater degree of equality between the sexes is engendered. This leads Todd to suggest that 'the educational power of a family system may well be determined by the strength of maternal authority' (1987, p. 17), thus suggesting a clear connection between female empowerment and development through the enhancement of cultural capacity. Such an enhancement could enable choices to be made that, as Le Vine & White (1986) indicate, are only meaningful in relation to the ligatures – social linkages and attachments – of any individual. They see these ligatures as being significant in terms of support (interdependence), structure (normative framework) and motivation (personal and collective achievement).

Given the complex, multifactoral situation and the interdisciplinary approaches and techniques needed to address this situation, we need to be interacting with other social scientists in order to explore the issue further. Unfortunately, this interaction seems to be missing. For instance, a survey of the literature on gender, education and development (Brock & Cammish, 1997c) reveals that much of the material focuses on gender or gender and development, with surprisingly few publications within the development context dealing with education as an issue in relation to gender. In preparing *Gender, Education and Development: a partially annotated and selective bibliography*, this was a significant constraint. Books and articles on gender and development are usually edited, and contributed to, by social scientists. Does the lack of material on the education of girls, whether formal or non-formal, which we have noted in these publications, arise accidentally because of intellectual and academic specialisation?

> *Perhaps their analysis of the situation includes the realisation that the role of formal education in the development process is a second order issue, following the satisfaction of certain cultural and infrastructural imperatives? This may well be a fair position to take in respect of the formal mode, but while non-formal dimensions of education and training are more visible in the global and regional literature especially, they are still at the margins of the discussion. It would seem that international and comparative educators still have a great deal to do to effect interaction and dialogue with their social science counterparts involved in issues of gender and development. (Brock & Cammish, 1997c, p. 4)*

Clearly, there is a need for some bridge-building to be attempted here between Becher's *Academic Tribes and Territories* (1989).

Towards a Comparative Methodology

Given the universal significance of gender in relation to education and development, it would seem worthwhile to explore the potential contribution of comparative studies to the further understanding of the issue. One potential approach would be to conduct multiple case studies in a comparative perspective. According to Crossley & Vulliamy (1984), this strategy can be particularly effective at the local scale when 'the complexities of education practices' can be examined and compared cross-nationally. The issue of scale is one of several we now need to address in formulating a research strategy, the others being interdisciplinarity, comparability and generalisability. The methodological problem is illustrated in a three-dimensional model in Figure 3.

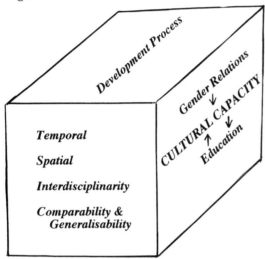

Figure 3. Towards a comparative methodology.

The issue of scale is significant in both spatial and temporal terms. Much of the literature of comparative education indicates a persistent interest in the national frame of reference, but in order to be able to observe the complexities mentioned earlier, a village or community scale would be necessary to deal with social structures, with sample households for micro-investigation of decision-making regarding education. This would be appropriate for the micro-level consideration of motivation for change, but the macro-concerns relating to mobilisation would seem to call for a multilevel approach, as outlined by Bray & Murray Thomas (1995).

Cultural capacity as defined here can be increased as far as girls' education is concerned by a shift in the traditional gender relationships in a particular sociocultural group, whether this be family, village, or larger-scale community. The education of girls can in its turn also help to develop openness to change in the cultural fabric. Research into these processes cannot limit itself, however, to only one point in time: changes in cultural capacity are normally very gradual and so we need to use a temporal scale in our studies. Stephens (1998) has clearly shown the usefulness of a 'life history' approach in studying the impact of the cultural aspects of home, schooling and poverty on girls' and women's education. A development of this approach, which would provide the necessary temporal scale, would be one of *intergenerational studies*. An examination of the 'life histories' of three generations of females – school-age girls, their mothers and their grandmothers, recording the attitudes of the males in their families towards their role and status in their families would enable the researcher to plot on a continuum the changes in experience over the generations. Changes in cultural capacity, if any, would be apparent and their causes could be sought. A participatory model of research on the lines used by Mehran (1997) would seem very appropriate for such an approach.

An intergenerational temporal scale of this kind accords well with the slow, subtle and sometimes almost imperceptible cultural change with which we have to be concerned. How governments, agencies and local organisations tackle innovations to promote girls' participation in education should depend on what point on the continuum particular groups have reached: the degree of cultural capacity and the rate of development in that capacity need to be considered before the particular type or style of innovation or reform is decided.

Attempts to precipitate change in radical ways may be ineffective: the community may be resistant and girls' enrolment and/or attendance remain low and drop-out high. Even worse, such attempts may be too effective and have unsettling and even destabilising effects on the lifestyle and economy of a group which is not ready to accommodate such a degree or rate of change.

The issues of comparability and generalisability are closely connected, and relate to the methodology of multiple case studies mentioned earlier. Within one cultural context such an approach should not be problematic, though of course in many rural areas of developing countries some cultural traits, including language, can be highly localised. The aim here would be to conduct the comparison across cultures, indeed across continents, with multiple cases from each of the main areas: South Asia, sub-Saharan Africa, Latin America and the tropical island zones. This is clearly a massive undertaking and would need to be phased, with a sequence such as the following:

- initial meetings/electronic conferencing to develop a detailed research strategy and methodology;
- pilot phase of testing the methodology in a small selection of cases from each area, comparing outcomes and modifying the method accordingly; and
- the main survey in a larger number of cases over a longer period but using different locations in detail.

There would be many problems to contend with in adopting such an approach, but just two will be mentioned at this stage. The first is to be able to select case study communities where the economic context is sufficiently comparable. Given the majority rural populations where the gender issue is apparently most acute in terms of access, sustainability and improvement, this would be the main economic context. However, given the significant urban/rural dichotomy evident from previous studies in respect of gender and educational opportunity, a parallel survey might be conducted involving urban cases which had connections, through migration and education, with the rural cases.

The combination of highly localised case studies operating at the levels of both household and community interaction in respect of gender relations and education, and the cross-national/cross-continental dimension would enable both the micro and the macro considerations mentioned earlier to be accommodated. One might, therefore, envisage a project involving, say, three countries from each of the main zones already identified, giving 12 in all. Within each of these 12 would be multiple cases, leading to a total of at least 50. Provided the tools for comparative analysis had been prepared with due rigour, both in the theoretical/design phase and in the piloting, then it should be of sufficient scale to facilitate generalisation.

All this would, however, depend on the final issue of interdisciplinarity. For reasons mentioned earlier, it is vitally necessary for the range of social scientists involved in the analysis of gender and development to come together with those from educational studies and pool their skills. The current separation of these camps, apparent from our 'Selected and Annotated Bibliography', is striking. Given the complex of factors, and therefore of disciplines, bearing upon this issue, the team responsible for a project such as this must be interdisciplinary. Not only would this have to be achieved by coming together for the theoretical/design phase but it would also have to involve the training of individual field researchers to be able to accommodate skills and concepts from the range of disciplines. For obvious reasons it would be totally inappropriate to have an interdisciplinary team operating in the field. There would need to be a total agreement at both macro- and micro-levels, from the overall ideology of the project to the detailed field techniques and training of local researchers. For, as Le Vine &White (1986) put it:

> *there is the factor of collaboration between processes*
> *operating at the macro-social level and those operating at the*
> *micro-social level ... In the context of the contemporary*
> *nation-state, neither official policy nor grassroots voluntarism*
> *alone can be relied upon to realise desired potentials; they*
> *must work together, convergently and synergistically. This is*
> *where culture is the critical term, for if policy-makers and*

> *ordinary people share cultural models of life, education and*
> *social performance the possibilities for their collaboration are*
> *enhanced, whereas cultural divisions between them will*
> *inhibit the implementation of policies. The problem of finding*
> *an ideological basis for such collaboration is one of many*
> *problems we have raised for comparative research on*
> *education development.*

Consequently, the first phase suggested in this chapter might be considered as a preparatory project in itself, leading to a practical conference of participants from all 12 countries as well as others that might be a joint initiative between the Economic and Social Research Council and an international facilitator such as UNESCO.

References

Becher, A. (1989) *Academic Tribes and Territories*. Milton Keynes: Open University Press.

Betts, J. (1998) Cooperative Conflicts: literacy and social agency in rural El Salvador, paper presented to the UK Seminar for Latin American Education, Harris Manchester College, Oxford, February, mimeo, p. 25.

Bown, L. (1990) *Preparing the Future: women, literacy and development*. Chard: Action Aid.

Bray, M. & Murray Thomas, R. (1995) Levels of Comparison in Educational Studies: different insights from different literatures and the value of multilevel analysis, *Harvard Education Review*, 65, pp. 472–490.

Brock, C. & Cammish, N.K. (1994) Constraints on female participation in education in developing countries, in G. Strowbridge & W. Tulasiewicz (Eds) *Education and the Law: international perspectives*, pp. 82–93. London: Routledge.

Brock, C. & Cammish, N.K. (1997a) *Factors Affecting Female Participation in Education in Seven Developing Countries*, 2nd edn, Education Research Series no. 9. London: Department for International Development.

Brock, C. & Cammish, N.K. (1997b) Cultural Capacity Building and Closing the Gender Gap, in K. Watson, C. Modgil & S. Modgil (Eds) *Education Dilemmas: debate and diversity*, vol. 4: *Quality in Education*, pp. 118–126. London: Cassell.

Brock, C. & Cammish, N.K. (1997c) *Gender, Education and Development – a partially annotated and selective bibliography*. Education Research Series, no. 19. London: Department for International Development.

Cammish, N.K. (1994) Island Daughters: factors affecting the education of girls in Vanuatu, *Compare*, 24, pp. 139–155.

Cammish, N.K. & Brock, C. (1994) State, Status and *Status Quo*: factors affecting the education of girls in Cameroon, *International Journal of Educational Development*, 14, pp. 233–240.

Crossley, M. & Vulliamy, G. (1984) Case Study Research Method and Comparative Education, *Comparative Education*, 20, pp. 193–207.

Heward, C. (1999) The New Discourses of Gender Education and Development, in C. Heward & S. Bunwaree (Eds) *Gender, Education and Development: Beyond Access to Empowerment*, pp. 1–14. London: Zed Books.

Kutnick, P., Jules, V. & Layne, A. (1997) *Gender and School Achievement in the Caribbean*, Education Research Series no. 21. London: Department for International Development.

LeVine, R.A. & White, M.I. (1986) *Human Conditions: the cultural basis of educational developments*. London: Routledge & Kegan Paul.

Mehran, G. (1997) A Study of Girls' Access to Primary Education in the Islamic Republic of Iran, *Compare*, 27, pp. 263–276.

Sen, A. (1990) Gender and Co-operative Conflicts, in I. Tinker (Ed.) *Persistent Inequalities: women and world development*. Oxford: Oxford University Press.

Stephens, D. (1998) *Girls and Basic Education: a cultural enquiry*, Education Research Series no. 23. London: Department for International Development.

Stromquist, N.P. (1997) *Literacy for Citizenship: gender and grassroots dynamics in Brazil*. New York: State University of New York Press.

Stromquist, N.P. (1998) The Institutionalisation of Gender and its Impact on Education Policy, *Comparative Education*, 34, pp. 85–100.

Stromquist, N.P. (1999) The Impact of Structural Adjustment Programmes in Africa and Latin America, in C. Heward & S. Bunwaree (Eds) *Gender, Education and Development: Beyond Access to Empowerment*, pp. 17–32. London: Zed Books.

Todd, E. (1987) *The Causes of Progress: culture, authority and change*. Oxford: Basil Blackwell.

Learning from Development Research in Educational Contexts

ROSEMARY PRESTON

Positions

At the opening, scene-setting seminar in the series that gave rise to this book, in May 1997, the discussion was of the process and contribution of comparative studies in education: from a liberal functionalist perspective (Broadfoot, 1999); within the context of evolving social theory (Schriewer, 1999); and taking account of how they are being influenced by globalisation and the emergence of the Pacific Rim as the driving force of economic and social development in the years to come (Cowen, 1999). Then and at subsequent meetings in the series, it has been the cross-national which emerges as the defining characteristic of the comparative in the work presented to date. Some of the studies have involved analysis at the level of the state (Robinson, 1999; Steedman, 1999). In several cases, work reported has been at the level of subnational institutions, located in different states (Osborn & Planel, 1999; Tobin, 1999). Some studies have been carried out by multinational research teams, which have included members of the states in which case study research was undertaken (Alexander, 1999; Tobin, 1999). In others (Steedman, 1999), the international dimension has been achieved by a United Kingdom researcher working on data for another country and presumably, although it has not been reported as yet in this series, it would have been legitimate to include studies of Britain undertaken by non-British researchers. Finally, people from countries other than Britain have talked about the situation in their own country, to the largely British seminar audience.

The question of the use, and by implication, abuse, of comparative research has been addressed in several ways, more and less formally. Questions from researchers have related to the political history of the emergence of the field within educational studies; the appropriateness of ascribing national characteristics to institutional case studies; the normative implications for knowledge produced by multinational teams working in a common language on cross-national case study analyses; and the need to account for social and economic background influences at all levels to assure more complete understanding of otherwise descriptive observation of inter- and intra-institutional processes. Speakers from fields of policy and practice have commented on: the seeming irrelevance to them of abstruse theorising; government practice in using or not the findings of research to inform educational policy and development; and the dubious validity of secondary statistics. As an aside, it should also be noted that the research presented to date has been primarily concerned with the formal education of children and young people. There has been little exposition of research into higher, professional or community education and training for people outside this age group, in spite of heavy global investment in each of these areas. There has been no systematic account of incidental learning associated with every activity, designated educational or not. Until now, little account has been taken of the implications of the emphasis on developments in technologically more advanced nations, either for the state of the field or for the politics of its practice.

The fourth seminar (now translated into this section of *Learning from Comparing,* Volume 2) was similar in some respects to the first three, but in the context of educational development in states that are less technologically advanced. Without clarifying the comparators, an assumption seems to have been made that the characteristics of such states affect educational processes within them, in ways that are different from those not so designated. With speakers who assume differences in research strategy and educational processes associated with the local cultures of such states, heterogeneity between them has to inform any research endeavour (Cheng, elsewhere in this volume). Not opposing this position, the assumption of those who compare the performance of educational systems (Brock & Cammish, elsewhere in this volume) may be that there is a common global educational process which allows progress towards its achievement at institutions in different states to be explained. The new structures of collaboration between partners and other stakeholders in the international development aid system, as described by Allsop (elsewhere in this volume), imply similar assumptions that the same modes of systematised education are appropriate to all states, with some modification to account for variations of language and history.

The purpose of this article, initially presented at the end of the fourth seminar, is to contextualise these assumptions in the light of the presentations and locate them in relation to trends in development thinking, practice and research over the last 50 years. It attempts this from a perspective that seeks to account for the distinctive but convergent interests of the different constituencies of a seminar audience which includes researchers, policy-makers, project managers and implementers, and a small number of some-time representatives of those who have come to be known as end-user groups.

Catering to this audience, a starting assumption is that research, policy and practice are complex, inseparable, interrelated processes. For practical reasons, they tend to be disaggregated, undertaken by people who contribute different kinds of expertise. A situational analysis undertaken by one individual or team may inform policy development, action plans, intervention and changed practice which are the responsibility of a series of other individuals or teams. Throughout, yet more individuals or teams may at any stage monitor progress and subsequently evaluate the work. This is the case if the project in question is a research project in its own right (a theoretical study, a situational analysis, or a monitoring or evaluation project, for example) or a more direct intervention (curriculum design, organisational capacity-building or facilitator training), with associated research components. With international development projects, those who intervene in these processes will originate in a range of states, other than those in which the activity occurs.

There is then a range of givens associated with any investigation into policy and practice processes, which have to be acknowledged and which may be of particular relevance to cross-national research. While component activities in relation to any programme or project are typically the responsibility of different people, their sequencing is increasingly thought to be cyclical rather than linear (Overseas Development Adminstration [ODA], 1995a), with any number of subcycles within a single cyclical framework. Lapses of time between stages mean that original situations may have changed, before policy and plans responding to it are formulated, and again before intervention occurs. Similarly, basic theorisation informing policy options may also have changed, as may the principles of their monitoring and evaluation. Just as there are always subjectivities which inform objectively structured enquiry and practice (Silverman, 1997), such disjunctures can never be resolved as long as we are powerless to predict the outcomes of what we do (Ruelle, 1993). This means that it is incumbent on researchers, people of practice and other participants to be as aware as possible of developments in each other's terrains, and of their own subjectivities, so as to optimise the collective outcomes of individual endeavour.

Positioning Education in Development Research and Practice

At any stage of life, educational contexts are those in which learning [1] occurs. Formal or non-formal, they will be planned and organised.[2]

Informal educational contexts are those in which the learning that occurs is incidental. Since incidental learning occurs in all contexts, it is necessarily a feature of learning in designated formal and non-formal educational contexts, supplementary to that specified in syllabi and curricula. The ways in which these contexts and the educational processes within them are described varies with the world-view of the observer and how this is shaped by contemporary trends in thinking and practice. One issue at the fourth seminar was the extent to which researchers of education account for the processes and effects of incidental learning in different national and international contexts, and what they imply for learning in more organised, internationally informed educational environments. At many levels, in different language, this seems to be the thrust of the article by Cheng elsewhere in this volume.

As with 'education', the word 'development' has been appropriated to refer to officially and otherwise planned initiatives which claim to improve and sustain social and economic well-being, at the level of individuals, communities, subnational regions and states. Politically charged, it informs activities through which people in less advantaged states and populations are encouraged to achieve a quality of life approximating that of those more advantaged. Initially based on studies of modernisation in industrial societies, activities included the development of industry, commerce and bureaucracy in newly independent states, as well as the human resource infrastructure (systems of health and education) to support them (Fägerlind & Saha, 1983).

There were many problems. Principal among them were thought to be the limited quality of human resources available to support the social and economic structures of modernising nations and these states' unequal economic relations with the industrial nations that they were seeking to emulate. Then there was the fact that these nations had not remained static, but continued to progress. This made it impossible for most of the majority world to catch up, in an international political environment which was further widening, rather than bridging the gap. The recognition that even when successful in their own terms, the plethora of post-colonial projects, across sectors, was doing little to improve the relative or absolute position of disadvantaged nations and groups within them, led to what is now described as the 1960s/70s *impasse* in development thinking (Hettne, 1990; Schuurman, 1993; Booth, 1994).

In all parts of the world, counter-stream thinkers came to question the failure of rich nations to predict their own failure to protect the vulnerable from destitution (Hettne, 1990). Notwithstanding the benefits of development initiatives to some, they set out to explain the ways in which the political economy of international development served to reproduce the inegalitarian structures of wealth and well-being already in place, even when there had been revolution to redress the balance, not least because it continued to ignore the implications of difference within and between gender, ethnic, class and national groups (Wade, 1997; Arce & Long, 1992).

Maintaining national well-being as the objective, but moving beyond the *impasse*, it has since been claimed that initiatives targeting the needs of specific localities should be the preferred means through which to ensure relevant development (Booth, 1994; Long, 1992). Associated with neo-liberal economic policies, it is now argued by international funding institutions that the decentralisation of management responsibility will better achieve this, regardless of sources of funding and technical procedures (World Bank, 1995; Department for International Development [DFID], 1997). While support continues to be given to local project development initiatives, the limitations of their social impact have seen a further shift in aid management policy. As Allsop describes in this volume, this is now favouring large-scale, cross-sectoral programme investment. The significant feature of this 1990s variant of what appears to be a return to a 1960s development programme model is that: (1) it is likely to be funded by several organisations, multilateral and bilateral; and (2) what are now described as partner governments have direct responsibility for the allocation and management of resources to programme components and for achieving specified outcomes. The growing dependency of international and local voluntary organisations on these sources of funding means that they are increasingly integrated into these programmatic endeavours, although for the present they also continue to support smaller, more random projects (DFID, 2000).

There are multiple explanations for these changes in the international development regime. Significant among them is the way in which adjustment to a global market has incurred worldwide unemployment and levels of poverty, not experienced since before the Second World War (Scott, 1994; United Nations Research Institute for Social Development (UNRISD), 1995) and the recognition of the limitations of earlier conceptualisations of effective assistance (Hobsbawm, 1994). That these have led to significant reductions in the allocation of resources to international social welfare and development assistance (Curtis, 1997) is masked by the new, generously funded sector-wide programmes described earlier, but the truth is that these are located in a much smaller number of low income states than were previously supported. Also masked is the fact that a growing proportion of bi-lateral aid is channelled through regional authorities and, on a smaller scale, through the alternative structures of the humanitarian safety net system, so as to alleviate the most acute symptoms of deprivation of those worst affected and reduce the effects of publicity which are associated with disasters of Malthusian proportions (ODA, 1995b).

Associated with this, the pre-impasse development of mass educational systems occurred, at huge cost, as part of industrial modernisation strategies. Often internationally funded, these were informed by state-level analyses of:

- human capital implications for productivity in the formal sector of economies;
- projected human resource requirements to achieve such productivity; and
- sectoral analyses of the capacity of educational systems to meet these requirements.

While in many states these research-based developments continued through the *impasse*, there was renewed international interest in how to develop educational activities that would further enhance output and well-being through informal economic productivity (Coombs, 1985; Fordham, 1993). For those out of school, vocational training and instruction in small-scale production for local markets were encouraged in many countries. Community-based training for adults in basic health and education has also become an important means of complementing both mainstream and alternative initiatives. Such work is typically administered, directly or indirectly, by specially designated departments within a range of government sectors, which may include industry, education, trade, works and women's affairs. When indirectly overseen, implementation is likely to become the responsibility of the increasing number of international and eventually local voluntary organisations (Archer, 1994; Fowler, 1997). Research into labour market characteristics, intermediate and infrastructural skill needs, combined with local pressure for development investment, is used to justify the development of such schemes.

While all of these activities continue, intended to empower and alleviate poverty in different parts of the world, the language of educational policy at the turn of the twenty-first century emphasises primary schooling for the young. Since the 1990 Jomtien conference, *Education for All* (World Conference on Education for All [WCEFA], 1990; Love, 1992), non-formal basic education for children in marginal communities has become as familiar as it was in the past for similarly situated adults (Freire, 1985; Archer & Costello, 1990). This is supported by a growing literature on education as a human right and as a humanitarian response, without which the attainment of appropriate personal development and citizenship are thought to be problematic (Stromquist, 1997; Retamal & Aedo-Richmond, 1998). In each case, the rationale for these kinds of provision is to compensate for the failure of more mainstream systems to provide them.

This position justifies the concentration of interest on mainstream modes of formal and non-formal education for marginal people within marginal states. It renders invisible the more organic and so marginal forms of education and learning within marginal groups struggling to cope with the effects of poverty, even when the states concerned are among the most poor and such activity might be taken as a basic prerequisite of self-sufficiency. Such selective vision allows avoidance of the issue of whether the target of organised intervention should be the poor directly, or only indirectly, through the building of capacities and understanding of those who will work to assist them (Dia, 1996; Michel, 1996). Historically, the latter approach has been favoured. (A typology of direct and indirect poverty alleviation strategies and their implications for different stakeholding groups is reproduced in Figure 1).

	Poverty reduction strategy		
Categories	Structural	Direct	Indirect
Aims	Create a (neo-liberal) conducive environment at national and international levels	Support clearly defined groups of poor people	Extend scope for action and distribution in favour of the poor
Approach	Policy dialogue/advice Structural reforms of government, economy and administration	Clustering of projects which mainly benefit poor groups Promoting self-help groups	Embedding projects in poverty-oriented sectoral and country programmes, where beneficiaries may not be clearly identified or even poor
Examples	TA on: public expenditure reforms, social policy and structural adjustment programmes	Water supplies and waste treatment, public works, poor women's self-help groups	Advisory services on improving tax system and use of revenue for fairer, poverty-oriented policies
Areas of promotion	Projects in all sectors (agriculture, health, environment, education)	Infrastructural development	Private sector development

Figure 1. Source: Weidnitzer, 1997, p. 22.

Curiously, in all of this, community development, predicated upon incidental learning and organised non-formal training activities, along with professional development in other sectors, health and social development for example, is not said to be educational. This may be, seemingly because it is not associated with the acquisition of knowledge and skills, by inadvertent omission or by intent, because funding lines preclude support to activities said to be educational.

The evolving narratives outlined so far, associated with changes in structures of provision, also relate to changes in the structure and process of associated international development research. With exceptions, it is often inferred that government research (frequently funded with Official Development Assistance), associated with the establishment and maintenance of formal systems of education, is primarily technical and quantified. In contrast, research associated with small-scale, less formal activities, claim to empower the marginal people with whom it is concerned, as much as to inform policy processes. It is thought to favour the participative and other qualitative approaches to data collection, analysis and interpretation that are central to the practice of voluntary organisations which sponsor such work.

These perceptions persist, in spite of a substantial literature on the interdependence of quantitative and qualitative approaches to research. Both statistical information and data obtained from individuals and groups on considered experience are now recognised as a *sine qua non* of end-of-century development practice, from pre-planning to *post hoc* evaluation, in large-scale programme development and small projects alike (Preston, 1997). Research and development funders, from local non-governmental organisations (NGOs) and governments to the World Bank, as well as ensuring that funded schemes conform to current conditionalities of development cooperation, have to justify expenditures and indicate achievements in quantified measure, just as they have to describe end-user roles throughout their project cycles (ODA, 1995). While this practice is held to serve as a mechanism to democratise research and development processes alike, there are concerns about the crudity of the ubiquitous planning tools and their ability to use locally-specific data to produce information for funding organisations that will ensure support for only a narrow range of conceptually similar activities, within and between states (Preston & Arthur, 1997). This concern is with the normalisation of ideas and practice incurred when bilateral and multilateral funder partnerships promote the same global development priorities, leaving the increasing array of intermediary support and local NGOs, grass roots organisations (GROs) and others, down the funding line, no choice but to do so as well, if they wish to survive. Pursuing their own research and development objectives, they have little alternative but to become competitors for aid-funded research and project management work. In an era of challenge to the hegemony of universities in research, their success is attributable to their ability to function at lower costs than university and commercial suppliers, as well as to a belief that they are situated more closely to affected communities. Emergent NGO Support Organisations (NGOSOs) combine research and training capacities as they seek to service local voluntary sector development in poorer states (Fowler, 1997). At the same time, there is concern about the relevance of these organisational support strategies to indigenous social relations (Ostrom et al, 1993).

Such new entrants in the international development research arena may be seen to be located between end-user groups, universities and commercial consultancies. It is to be hypothesised that the knowledge around which they engage augments complementarily that being reconstructed by other players. Similar hypotheses have to be tested, at any stage of a human development project cycle, in respect of short-term consultants employed to investigate its progress. Moving from job to job, at decreasing levels of real pay and limited opportunity for professional development, such practices lend themselves to the reproduction of familiar policy options, for example, deficiency compensation strategies, as the least-risk strategy in achieving stakeholder consensus around policy strategies (Arthur & Preston, 1996). It is in this consensus that, for some analysts, is to be found the principal distinction between policy- and practice-oriented consultancy and more basic international research into social relations and change (Preston, 1996a).

Linking the Analysis of Policy and Practice to Change in General Theory

There is a risk with rapid, practice-oriented research undertaken by contracted researchers or by members of affected communities. It may ignore developments in method and theory, even when they have become well known and have the capacity to render partially redundant, customary deficiency compensation, development/educational strategies. Taking the case of research into poverty alleviation focusing on the poor, rather than indirectly on providers of services to them, it is appropriate to take account of writing on how poor people learn to cope, what this implies for the capacities at their disposal and the strategies to enhance them. Norton et al (1996) and Moser (1996) have both undertaken studies, within the framework of new household economics (Deere, 1990), into the diverse strategies adopted within the sexual division of labour, that enable poor households to subsist, minimising their suffering. Norton's study was of families in Ghana. Moser's was of a single urban family in each of four countries: one in Europe, South America, Africa and Asia. Both writers comment on the points at which children's attendance at school has to be abandoned in the interests of group well-being, although their overall concern is with what might be described as the incidental learning of poverty management. Related to this are Sen's (1992) assumptions that capacity and opportunity should form the basis of politically informed analyses of domestic livelihood strategies and their variations. Combining this understanding with Scott's model (1994) of the polarisation of poverty and privilege in neo-liberal society and its implications for the maintenance of order through increased demand on organisations of civil society would lead to a very different approach to the study of poverty mitigation from that based on education and training within deficiency compensation equations, and their assumptions about individual rather than structural explanations.

In particular, it would lead to research into the range of innovative coping strategies adopted by excluded categories (such as those suggested in Figure 2), to ensure not only survival, but the continuity of the group. This would include analyses appropriate to the study of learning and other educational processes in the global context of contemporary social movements, and include the contribution of learning through information technology to the consolidation of movement identity (Castells, 1997). Over time, based on studies of excluded revolutionary groups, the normalisation of these activities would lead to their formalisation as common practice, across sectors.

A model for development and research to meet the needs of mainstream, marginal and excluded categories

Parameters for action
Fields: social policy, health, gender, trade, education, training, etc.
Policy: privatisation, decentralisation, democratisation, etc.
Process: funding; methods; staffing; planning techniques; institutional support; participation, etc.
Contexts: high population densities; urbanisation; rural poverty; pollution; war; global communications, etc.

Strategies for action

Included groups: Socially and ethnically dominant; employed; educated; fit and able	*Internal options* Sustain capacity for cohesion and prevent further fragmentation Allow process of disintegration to continue	*External options* Attempt to reunite with excluded groups Ensure that the break is maintained
Marginalised and excluded groups: underemployed, unemployed; poor; displaced; minorities; handicapped	Develop capacities to foster cohesion Prevent cohesive development	Attempt to reunite with mainstream Ensure that the break is maintained

Figure 2. Source: Preston, 1996b, p. 27

Changing Geography of Development

So far this article has suggested history, modes of educational provision, related approaches to research and changing conceptual frameworks as parameters for comparative studies of educational dynamics in poorer countries. Geopolitical change means that states construed as developing have also changed. Their number has increased and, with the collapse of the USSR, they have new characteristics. World Bank tables (based on aggregate secondary data within states) have increased their categorisation of states from three to four, with the fourth representing the poorest severely indebted nations (World Bank, 1990). Moving beyond gross domestic product (GDP) per capita as the principal indicator of national well-being, the United Nations Development Programme (UNDP) (1997) has constructed multivariate indices of human development, gender equality and human poverty. The collapse of the USSR and the emergence of the transitional states of Eastern Europe espousing neo-liberal market policies has seen widespread poverty and corruption in these new lower income nations. The collapse of states overcome with debt and ethnic strife adds to the range of contexts against which the development of formal, non-formal and informal learning occurs, as does the hugely extended poverty being experienced in affluent nations.

At the same time, the geopolitical frame of reference has changed as an explanator of these processes. Researchers are grappling with the changing function of states as they adjust to the demands of global financial institutions, multilateralism and supra-national regionalism. As well as comparative studies of the changing structures of aid to education and educational research (King, 1991), there is research into state educational responses to structural adjustment within world regions, based largely on secondary sources (Reimers, 1991; Samoff, 1994). Comparative institutional analyses of global educational agenda setting processes include Mundy's study of school curricula (1997) and Chabbott's (1998) on international conference participation. At a micro-level, there is, in many countries, evidence of the impact of adjustment for school enrolment, retention and motivation as its relevance to a dwindling labour market is in doubt (Ilon, 1994; Watkins, 1995). This is reinforced in the seemingly reduced commitment to education within the poverty eradication strategies of bilateral funders.

Impact Analysis

Analysis of intended and unintended effects through programme and project monitoring and evaluation have long been critical to research into educational development. Much is concerned with project delivery mechanisms and ways in which to enhance their effectiveness. At the same time, evaluations at short and longer intervals after project completion are being more frequently required (Behrmann, 1993; Varghese, 2000). Many take the form of economic analyses of returns to investment (Psacharopolous, 1993; Bennell, 1995). Among work of this kind relating to marginal groups in less developed countries are studies of impact assessment (McKay & Treffgarne, 2000) and a group of graduate destination tracer studies. These include: the analysis by Fordham et al (1998) of working adults in the 1990s who, in the 1960s, were given the chance to attend extramural education in Kenya; research into returned exiles in Namibia after periods of education in some 50 countries (Preston, 1994); similar refugee-related tracer studies by Unterhalter and Maxey (1996) in South Africa; by Brophy et al in the Horn of Africa

(1997) and an overview of methods used in such studies (Preston, 1999). At the same time, within a neo-liberal framework, social impact analysis may be as concerned with the extent to which assistance has been used to develop sustainable commercial educational activities as with its contribution to social capacities (Demery et al, 1993; Becker, 1997).

Ensuring the Complete Picture

The foregoing paragraphs have provided a sketchy overview of some of the complex array of issues that influence the forms and functions of the international community's contribution to education for the improvement of social well-being in poorer parts of the world. If Bray & Thomas (1995) describe the implications of this for educational research, contemporary commitment to cross-disciplinary, cross-sectoral and cross-national comparative and team-based studies exacerbates this complexity. The problem then becomes how to monitor what is being achieved and disseminate information about it in ways that integrate the output of a highly differentiated research labour force. For this to be done comprehensively there should be trust in the validity of contributions made by these different actors to different types of understanding of the same phenomena. There should be less sniping at the abstraction of some and at the unmitigated pragmatism of others. While the growing number of manuals for practitioner research (for example, Marsden & Oakley, 1990) will achieve some comparability of techniques of data collection and analysis at lower and middle ranges of theory, there is a strong case for attempting to map the development of understanding, as it relates to different parts of the world. Only in this way will the fragmentation of knowledge or its duplication be reduced. With reference to Buttel & McMichael (1994) and Mouzelis (1994), this should be within a range of conceptual frameworks and at multiple levels of analysis, which include accounts of the global political dynamics of what is observed. Doing this in ways that ensure research output access to policy-makers, practitioners and users alike, through multiple modes of dissemination, would be one way of maximising participation in its use.

Notes

[1] Where learning refers to the process of acquiring knowledge and skill.

[2] In the literature on education and international development, formal education is that provided through hierarchical systems of schooling, technical and higher education. Non-formal education is that developed outside formal systems to provide basic skills, training in activities that would lead to income generation, skill extension and community

development. Typically, neither initial nor continuing professional development is considered as either formal or non-formal education.

References

Alexander, R.J. (1999) Culture in pedagogy, pedagogy across cultures, in R.J. Alexander, P. Broadfoot & D. Phillips (Eds) *Learning from Comparing*, vol. 1, pp. 149–180. Oxford: Symposium Books.

Arce, A. & Long, N. (1992) The Dynamics of Knowledge: interfaces between bureaucrats and peasants, in N. Long & A. Long (Eds) *Battlefields of Knowledge: the interlocking of theory and practice in social research and development*, pp. 211–246. London: Routledge.

Archer, D. (1994) The Changing Roles of Non-governmental Organisations in the Field of Education (in the Context of Changing Relationships with the State), *International Journal of Educational Development*, 14, pp. 223–232.

Archer, D. & Costello, P. (1990) *Literacy and Power in Latin America*. London: Earthscan.

Arthur, L. & Preston, R. with C. Ngahu, S. Shoaib le Breton & D. Theobald (1996) *Quality and Overseas Consultancy: understanding the issues*. Manchester: British Council.

Becker, H. (1997) *Social Impact Analysis*. London: University College London Press.

Behrmann, J. (1993) Analysing Human Resource Effects: education, in L. Demery, M. Ferroni, C. Grootaert, J. Wong Valle (Eds) *Understanding the Social Effects of Policy Reform*, pp. 114–136. Washington: World Bank.

Bennell, P. (1995) *Using and Abusing Rates of Return. A Critique of the World Bank's Education Sector Review*. Brighton: Institute of Development Studies Working Paper 22.

Booth, D. (1994) Rethinking Social Development: an overview, in D. Booth (Ed.) *Rethinking Social Development: theory, research and practice*, pp. 3–41. Harlow: Longman.

Bray, M. (1996) *Counting the Full Cost: parental and community financing of education*. Washington DC: World Bank, Human Development Department.

Bray, M. & Thomas, M. (1995) Levels of Comparison in Educational Studies: different insights from different literatures and the value of multi-level analyses, *Harvard Education Review*, 65, pp. 472–490.

Broadfoot, P. (1999) Not So Much a Context, More a Way of Life? Comparative Education in the 1990s, in R.J. Alexander, P. Broadfoot & D. Phillips (Eds) *Learning from Comparing*, vol. 1, pp. 121–32. Oxford: Symposium Books.

Brophy, M., Bird, P. & Omona, M. (1997) *Vocational Training for Refugees from the Horn of Africa: an evaluation and review of a DANIDA funded programme for refugees in the UK*, p. 24. London: Africa Educational Trust.

Buttel, F.H. & McMichael, P. (1994) Reconsidering the Explanandum and Scope of Development Studies: toward a comparative sociology of state-economy relations, in D. Booth (Ed.) *Rethinking Social Development: theory, research and practice*, pp. 42–61. Harlow: Longman Booth.

Castells, M. (1997) *The Information Age: economy society and culture, vol. 1. The Power of Identity.* Oxford: Blackwell.

Chabbott, C. (1998) Constructing Educational Consensus: international development professionals and the world conference on education for all. *International Journal of Educational Development*, 18, pp. 207–218.

Coombs, P.H. (1985) *The World Crisis in Education.* New York: Oxford University Press.

Cowen, R. (1999) Late Modernity and the Rules of Chaos: an initial note on transitologies and rims, in R .J. Alexander, P. Broadfoot & D. Phillips (Eds) *Learning from Comparing*, vol. 1, pp. 73–88. Oxford: Symposium Books.

Curtis, M. (1997) *The Reality of Aid: an independent review of development co-operation*, 1997–1998. London: Earthscan/ActionAid/International Council for Voluntary Associations.

Deere, C.D. (1991) *Household and Class Relations: peasants and landlords in Northern Peru.* Berkeley: Oxford University Press.

Department for International Development (DFID) (1997) *Eliminating World Poverty. A Challenge for the 21st Century.* London: HMSO.

DFID (2000) *Education for All: the challenge of universal primary education. Srategies for achieving the international development targets,* consultation document. London.

Dia, M. (1996) *Africa's Management in the 1990s and Beyond: reconciling indigenous and transplanted institutions.* Washington DC: World Bank.

Fägerlind, I. & Saha, L.J. (1983) *Education and National Development: a comparative perspective.* Oxford: Pergamon.

Fordham, P. (1993) Informal, Non-formal and Formal Education Programmes, *Adult Basic Education*, 3, pp. 1–14.

Fordham, P., Fox, J. & Muzaale, P. (1998) *A Chance to Change: access, citizenship and sustainability in open learning.* Leicester: National Institute of Adult Continuing Education.

Fowler, A. (1997) *Striking a Balance: a guide to enhancing the effectiveness of non-governmental organisations in international development.* London: Earthscan.

Freire, P. (1985) *The Politics of Education: culture, power and liberation.* Basingstoke: Macmillan.

Hobsbawm, E. (1994) *The Age of Extremes: the short twentieth century.* London: Abacus.

Hettne, B. (1990) *Development Theory and the Three Worlds.* Harlow: Longman.

Ilon, L. (1994) Structural Adjustment and Education: adapting to a growing global market, *International Journal of Educational Development*, 14, pp. 95–108.

King, K. (1991) *Aid and Education in the Developing World: the role of donor agencies in educational analysis.* London: Longman.

Long, N. (1992) From Paradigm Lost to Paradigm Regained? The Case for an Actor Oriented Sociology of Development, in N. Long & A. Long (Eds)

Battlefields of Knowledge: the interlocking of theory and practice in social research and development, pp. 16–46. London: Routledge.

Love, A. (1992) *Development Co-operation Report 1992*, ch. 3, Meeting basic education needs in developing countries, pp. 53–73. Paris: Organisation for Economic Cooperation and Development, Development Assistance Committee.

Marsden, D. & Oakley, P. (1990) *Evaluating Social Development Projects*. Oxford: Oxfam, Development Guidelines, 5.

McKay, V. & Treffgarne, C. (Eds) (2000) *Evaluating Impact*. London: DFID, Education Research, Serial No. 35.

Michel, J.H. (1996) *Development Co-operation Report 1995*. Paris: Organisation for Economic Cooperation and Development, Development Assistance Committee.

Moser, C.O.N. (1996) *Confronting Crisis: a summary of household responses to poverty and vulnerability in four poor urban communities*. Washington: World Bank, Environmentally Sustainable Development Studies and Monographs, 7.

Mouzelis, N. (1994) The State in Late Development: historical and comparative perspectives, in D. Booth (Ed.) *Rethinking Social Development: theory, research and practice*, pp. 126–151. Harlow: Longman.

Mundy, K. (1997) Educational Multilateralism and World (Dis)order, paper presented to the symposium, Education and Stability, *Comparative Education Review*, 42, pp. 448–478.

Norton, A. et al (1995) *Poverty Assessment in Ghana: using qualitative and participatory research methods*. Washington DC: World Bank, Poverty and Social Policy Department.

Overseas Development Administration (ODA) (1995a) *A Guide to Social Analysis for Projects in Developing Countries*. London: HMSO.

Overseas Development Administration (ODA) (1995b) *Social Policy for Development*. London: Report prepared for ODA's Economic and Social Committee for Overseas Research.

Osborn, M. & Planel, C. (1999) Comparing Children's Learning: attitude and performance in French and English primary schools, in R .J. Alexander, P. Broadfoot & D. Phillips (Ed.) *Learning from Comparing*, vol. 1, pp. 261–294. Oxford: Symposium Books.

Ostrom, E., Schroeder, L. & Wynne, S. (1993) *Institutional Incentives and Sustainable Development: infrastructure, policies in perspective*. Boulder: Westview Press.

Preston, R. (1993) Gender and Relevance: decentralised vocational training in Papua New Guinea, *Oxford Education Review*, 19, pp. 101–115.

Preston, R. (1994) States, Statelessness and Education: post-return integration of Namibians trained abroad, *International Journal of Educational Development*, 14, pp. 299–319.

Preston, R. (1996a) Consultancy, Knowledge and Human Development, in L. Buchert & K. King (Eds) *Consultancy and Research in International*

Education: the new dynamics, pp. 139–152. Bonn: German Foundation for International Development/NDRRAG.

Preston, R. (1996b) *Social Policy and Education: towards a research agenda,* p. 45. London: Overseas Development Administration.

Preston, R. (1997) Integrating Paradigms in Educational Research: issues of quantity and quality in poor countries, in M. Crossley & G. Vulliamy (Eds) *Qualitative Educational Research in Developing Countries,* pp. 31–64. New York: Garland.

Preston, R. (1999) Returns to Investment in Refugee Education: comparing tracer studies, *Journal of International Education,* 10, pp. 38–45.

Preston, R. & Arthur, L. (1997) Knowledge Societies and Planetary Cultures: the changing nature of consultancy in human development, *International Journal of Educational Development,* 17, pp. 3–12.

Psacharopolous, G. (1993) *Returns to Investment in Education: a global update.* Washington: World Bank, Policy Research Working Paper, WPS 1067.

Reimers, F. (1991) *Deuda externa y financiamiento de la educación: su impacto en Latinoamérica.* Paris: UNESCO.

Retamal, G. & Aedo-Richmond, R. (1998) *Education as a Humanitarian Response.* London: Cassell.

Robinson, P. (1999) The Tyranny of League Tables: international comparisons of educational attainment and economic performance, in R.J. Alexander, P. Broadfoot & D. Phillips (Eds) *Learning from Comparing,* vol. 1, pp. 217–236. Oxford: Symposium Books.

Ruelle, D. (1993) *Change and Chaos.* London: Penguin Books.

Samoff, J. (Ed.) (1994) *Coping with Crisis: austerity, adjustment and human resources.* London: Cassell.

Schuurmann, F.J. (1993) Development Theory in the 1990s, in F.J. Schuurman (Ed.) *Beyond the Impasse: new directions in development theory,* pp. 1–48. London: Zed Books.

Scott, J. (1994) *Poverty and Wealth: citizenship, deprivation and privilege.* London: Longman.

Schriewer, J. (1999) Coping with Complexity in Comparative Methodology: issues of social causation and processes of macro-historical globalisation, in R.J. Alexander, P. Broadfoot & D. Phillips (Eds) *Learning from Comparing,* vol. 1, pp. 33–72. Oxford: Symposium Books.

Sen, A. (1992) *Inequality Re-examined.* Oxford: Clarendon Press.

Silverman, D. (1997) The Logics of Qualitative Research, in G. Miller & R. Dingwall (Eds) *Context and Method in Qualitative Research,* pp. 12–26. London: Sage.

Steedman, H. (1999) Measuring the Quality of Educational Outputs: some unresolved problems, in R.J. Alexander, P. Broadfoot & D. Phillips (Eds) *Learning from Comparing,* vol. 1, pp 201–216. Oxford: Symposium Books.

Stromquist, N. (1997) *Literacy for Citizenship: gender, grassroots and dynamics in Brazil.* Albany: State University of New York Press.

Tobin, J.J. (1999) Method and Meaning in Comparative Classroom Ethnography, in R.J. Alexander, P. Broadfoot & D. Phillips (Eds) *Learning from Comparing*, vol. 1, pp. 113–134. Oxford: Symposium Books.

United Nations Development Programme (UNDP) (1997) *Human Development Report*. Oxford: Oxford University Press.

United Nations Research Institute for Social Development (UNRISD) (1995) *States of Disarray: the social effects of globalisation*. Geneva: UNRISD.

Unterhalter, E. & Maxey, K. (1996) *Educating South Africans in Britain and Ireland: a review of thirty three years of sponsorship by the Africa Educational Trust*, p. 90. London: Africa Educational Trust.

Varghese, N.V. (2000) Evaluation versus Impact Studies, in V. McKay & C. Treffgarne (Eds) *Evaluating Impact*. London: DFID, Education Research, Serial No. 35.

Wade, P. (1997) *Race and Culture in Latin America*. London: Pluto Press.

Watkins, K. (1995) *The Oxfam Poverty Report*. Oxford: Oxfam.

Weidnitzer, E. (1997) *German Aid Policies for Poverty Reduction*. London: ODI, Working paper 101, p. 47.

World Bank (1990) *Poverty: world development report, 1990*. Washington DC: World Bank.

World Bank (1992) *Governance and Development*. Washington DC: World Bank.

World Bank (1995) *Priorities and Strategies for Education: a World Bank Review*. Washington DC: World Bank.

World Conference on Education for All (WCEFA) (1990) *Final Report: World Conference on Education for All: meeting basic needs*. New York: UNICEF, Inter-Agency Commission.

Postscript: perspectives from the fourth seminar

MICHELE SCHWEISFURTH

The papers presented at the fourth seminar inspired a series of discussions over the course of the day, raising a number of critical issues surrounding the nature of research into education in developing countries. Out of these discussions emerged the theme of inclusiveness: of building bridges within the research field, within our understanding of the contexts we are researching, and at the level of the global research community. Inside the academic field of development studies, links were sought between macro- and micro-levels of research, between theory and practice, and between educational study and other disciplines, creating new kinds of networks. In conducting international educational research, greater understanding of the contextual relationships between tradition and current practice, between culture and education, and between education and the economy were advocated as important lines of enquiry. And, at the global level, the need for stronger and more equitable research links between rich and poor and North and South was also explored. These inclusive ideals are not simple to achieve, however, and some of the constraints to establishing these links were also debated in the course of the discussion.

The research fields of comparative and international education are plagued by what Robin Alexander called 'the real or non-existent divide' between pure and applied research, which hampers both discussion among researchers and the impact of research findings. Michael Crossley characterised comparative educationalists as 'detached social scientists' and the international side as 'applied research', and in his words, 'we've a great deal to gain from the stronger blending of the two dimensions of our field', a bridge between the two being 'one way to get culture more firmly into the debate' by combining the comparativists' concern with theoretical issues around context with internationalists' grounding in policy and practice. Brian Pratt also encouraged 'trust in the validity of contributions at different levels' and 'less sniping' about research being either 'too abstract' or 'too practical'. Abby Riddell expressed concern at the problems of utilisation of school effectiveness research findings – 'how we actually get into the classrooms the things that actually do work ... not this huge gap between academia and practice'.

Within our own field, the exchange of information across agencies with similar research priorities would facilitate learning, aiding the process of informing policy through cumulative understandings rather than single projects. Kenneth King noted the 'intelligence out there over a 20-year period ... over what people have learned'; more collaboration could make such intelligence accessible and widely used. Several participants also acknowledged the isolation of educational research from other disciplines. As Cheng Kai-Ming pointed out, despite the demands of consultancy terms of reference, 'we are not all-rounders', and we could benefit from collaboration with related expertise. Anthropology and cross-cultural psychology were suggested as having the potential to illuminate cultural factors which may not be accessible using the traditional tools of educational research. Patricia Broadfoot suggested that 'perhaps that broader interdisciplinary perspective could help us out of that very blinkered approach we still seem to have in terms of the discourse we still use talking about development'. Brian Pratt felt that it was not only a question of our bringing in other disciplines, but of projecting outward as well, in order to disseminate and give wider impact to international research in education: 'What is it we are not saying to other social scientists to make them react to what we are saying? ... maybe they're not taking us seriously because we're not taking ourselves seriously'.

Within international research agendas, certain aspects of education receive insufficient attention, and some participants expressed the need for a more inclusive approach here as well. Robin Alexander highlighted the absence of the micro-level focus on teaching and learning among aid agency research priorities, school effectiveness having 'cornered the market' and leaving pedagogical processes as 'the unexamined filling in the input–output sandwich'. And Rosemary Preston pointed out how adult training, so critical to development, is rarely explicitly built into project and research design.

The discussion also emphasised the need for a stronger understanding of correlations within the contexts being investigated. Assumptions about the relationships between education and the economy, for example, are the basis for a great deal of research dominated by 'economic narrative'; assumptions which, as Cheng Kai-Ming noted, are being undermined by the recent economic crises in the 'Asian Tiger' nations. Another complex and very important contextual relationship to be explored is how culture and history are manifested in the education system and practices of the present; how 'different layers of traditions' (Kenneth King) are interwoven. Keith Lewin said that for research purposes culture is often 'treated as residual', while Abby Riddell felt that it 'simply doesn't feature': how can agencies and institutions be encouraged to embrace it as a fundamental aspect of research in education? Michael Brophy gave an example of how policy documents could be formulated with 'all the right words flowing out' while real priorities dictated by local cultural imperatives occupy the reality beyond the documents.

The issue of relationships on a larger scale – the links between researchers in the North and South – was also explored in the course of the discussion. The general feeling was that strong and equitable collaboration was highly desirable – but problematic. Kenneth King spoke of the asymmetries which are 'built into the internationalisation of our expertise ... Northerners study 'the other', [while] those who come north, under our tutelage, also study the same ... the most difficult symmetry of all is the symmetry between the discourse of those who've got the money in the North and the priorities of those who are in the South without it'. Terry Allsop called this asymmetry 'intrinsic' and reminded us of the 'uncomfortable cocktail of innovations' which aid agencies have peddled to poor countries in the past decades. This power imbalance is compounded by increasing constraints on funding. On the one hand, noted Keith Lewin, there is insistence on robust, rigorous, cost-effective products with potential to inform policy; on the other hand, there is the ethical imperative to invest in research partnerships where capacity may not, in some cases, have had the opportunity to develop sufficiently to meet these standards. Michael Brophy's response was to ask, 'Is it not time that we got away from cost–benefit analysis of partnerships ... and ask, not who does it cheaper, or better, but what actually can work?'

The research cultures operating in different countries create their own dynamics when we attempt to bridge the gulf between North and South. The definitions of what constitutes research and what sorts of research are of value were problematised; again, the asymmetries in power mean that a 'Europeanised modality' (Kenneth King) governs aid-funded projects. Considering these conditions, Rosemary Preston questioned some of the costs of cross-cultural collaboration. The process can become an exercise in reductionism in the quest for definitions which are mutually understood among partners: 'What are the processes of compromise as what are cultural factors are negotiated?' Cheng Kai-Ming used the analogy of Chinese versus Western medicine to highlight the fact that there are *alternative* perspectives on research, which are not simply at higher or lower points on the development scale. Yet the West/North continues to export the parameters by which most research is measured internationally: the use of the research assessment exercise at universities in Hong Kong, for example, dictates that academics abide by Western research models. Yet several present expressed the view that this very culture of research at Western academic and aid institutions actually inhibits the potential of studies to have real impact. The outputs demanded, be they Department for International Development log-frames or publications in refereed academic journals, restrict researchers' initiatives to prioritise long-term impact, or quick and accessible dissemination of findings.

The seminar, as Patricia Broadfoot put it, 'has really challenged us to think about what the interface between these two – comparative and development studies – is, particularly how far we need to challenge the current discourse about development education'. The current discourse was certainly challenged in the discussion, and the current gaps and asymmetries were explored, along with the need for more inclusive approaches to help bridge those gaps and balance those asymmetries. Keith Watson ended the discussion on an optimistic note, pointing out that – uncharacteristically – the World Bank had recently met with religious leaders from developing countries; perhaps this is a sign that 'we may be in a major shift towards viewing development in a much more holistic way'.

PART THREE

Education Professionals Compared

Introduction: education professionals compared

MARILYN OSBORN

The focus of this section of the book is on the international comparison of the teachers, headteachers, university academics, inspectors and administrators who are among the many different groups that comprise the broad constituency of 'education professionals'. They are the people who, in one capacity or another, are responsible for implementing the national educational aspirations that inform the organisation and functioning of the education system. In recent years, in the wake of successive policy changes typically aimed at improving the quality of educational provision, scholarly attention has focused increasingly on the personnel that are the key to that quality.

Research studies have explored the way in which policy decisions impact on teachers and hence how they can most effectively be implemented. In two studies at the University of Bristol (STEP: Systems, Teachers and Policy Change and PACE: Primary Assessment, Curriculum and Experience) for example, we have shown how, following recent educational reforms in England and France, teachers have changed their practice while resisting any fundamental change in their values. In both countries there was evidence of teachers clinging to their long-held professional traditions and values despite some superficial changes in their practice until they themselves became convinced of the need for a new approach. In other research studies, issues concerning the development and identification of professional competence have been associated with enquiries concerning how teachers can best be helped to develop their professional skills. Research has also focused on how changes in the policy climate have subjected education professionals to new pressures for demonstrable and direct accountability and simultaneously how changes in the social context have led to new student needs and national priorities.

These and other broad trends are not confined to a particular education system or a particular country but they do take different forms and bear different significance according to the context in question. Thus, it is pertinent to ask what insights comparative studies in particular can contribute concerning the significance of current trends and what advice they can provide for those responsible for policy-making.

Of course, there are dangers in assuming that any of these professional groups is homogeneous in any way even within one country. These concerns are even greater when attempts are made to compare across national contexts since in many cases one may not be comparing like with like, as some of the contributors to this volume demonstrate. These papers highlight the difficulties of comparing in this particular context, the tendency to emphasise diversity rather than to focus on universals, and the problems attached to using the nation state as a unit of comparison as distinct from concepts such as national context or culture. Some fundamental issues about the potential and value of such comparisons are raised.

At the outset of the seminar we focused on some of the central questions about education professionals that comparative studies are well placed to address. These included the following.

- What methodological problems are involved in undertaking comparisons of the work of educational professionals?
- Are these common trends in developing conceptions of professionalism and what insights can comparative studies usefully contribute in this respect?
- What can we learn from comparing different approaches to initial training and professional development?
- How do different education systems seek to promote the quality of professional practice?
- How far is teachers' classroom practice influenced by the different cultural contexts in which they work?
- How can comparative studies of education professionals best contribute to education policy-making?

In the various contributions to this section of the book these questions are addressed in a variety of ways.

Harry Judge's contribution was designed as an introduction to the themes of the seminar, to provide a general context and to address some widely acknowledged problems in comparative studies. His reflections on the three words that formed the title for the whole seminar open up some fundamental questions. How universal is education: does it indeed make sense to treat it as a general phenomenon of civilisation? What about the term 'professionals' and its associated concepts? Is the term 'profession' any longer serviceable, except as a piece of historical sociology? What does it mean to assert that those 'education professionals' might be compared? Is objectivity possible in such comparisons and can comparative studies say anything about values? He charts the rise and fall of the idea of 'the profession' and demonstrates how a professional role might vary dramatically from one national context to another, citing for example, the case of school supervisors. In short, he highlights the difficulties of comparing and contrasting education professionals, but nevertheless argues cogently for the value of the enterprise. In this article he sets the scene for the rest of the papers by asserting that comparative studies should be useful and should be at least as concerned with values and principles as with structures, histories and sociological analysis.

In his stimulating and controversial article Theodor Sandor takes issue with a number of the assumptions that may have been made by comparativists in the past. Taking comparisons of teacher education systems and teacher education policy as his example, he argues that comparative research is often static in its approach rather than emphasising the changing nature of social institutions and phenomena. He is critical of what he sees as the common emphasis of education comparativists on diversity and difference at the expense of understanding the universals in any teaching and learning situation. He also attacks the use of the nation state as a unit of comparison.

He argues for what he calls 'critical' rather than 'affirmative' approaches in comparative methodology, that is approaches which view education and education policy as 'particular but universal' forms of mediation and social control. Such 'critical' approaches emphasise the complex and contradictory reality of social and political processes rather than those 'affirmative' approaches which emphasise diversity and give preference to the normative, administrative and political definitions of the tasks and functions of education systems and education policy by governments. Ultimately, he maintains that the kind of information and knowledge which comparative education could possibly produce about teacher education and education professionals at national, European and global levels depends fully on which of these methodological approaches is adopted.

Lynn Davies's article is concerned with the study of school management in the context of the stringency which is a dominant constraint in the education systems of many countries. Her article argues for the inappropriateness of the application of Western management theory to the study of school effectiveness in cultures which are very different. Western models of leadership, of impartiality and of accountability did not seem to fit many of the countries in which she was interviewing heads about their role. Her article takes up the notion of the 'fragile state' as a useful one when explaining the cultures of fear and deference that permeate education systems in many countries. She then goes on to argue for the potential of chaos and complexity theory in the comparative study of school management and its broader potential for comparative education as a whole. Such theories could, she argues, explain failures of innovation, resistance and 'stuck' schools as well as understanding of the spark that sets off the student riot.

The issues of understanding educational phenomena in their cultural context and the difficulties of comparing 'like with like' are highlighted very clearly in Clive Hopes's contrasting case studies of the external evaluation of school systems in Denmark, the Netherlands, and Germany. He demonstrates that there are many ways of undertaking external evaluation and assessment of schools and shows how each country has devised an approach which 'fits' its own educational culture in order to achieve a satisfactory balance between evaluation and control on the one hand, and assessment and development on the other. His article illuminates the extent to which systems vary in their degree of openness and in the different types and degree of constraints within which they operate. His detailed comparisons of advisers in Denmark, of school inspectors in the Netherlands and of school supervisors in Germany emphasise the extent to which practices within an education system are integrated within a wider cultural system. These case studies highlight the impossibility of transferring unadapted education methods from one country to another. Nevertheless, he argues that where comparative education is linked to the study of management, assessment and evaluation in education, there are considerable benefits for practitioners in this field in terms of professional development and the widening of horizons.

Pam Poppleton's article with Theo Wubbels, which was commissioned after the seminar, focuses on the comparative study of teachers. The research on which Poppleton & Wubbels report considers the impact of current educational policy change on the work lives of teachers in eight countries: Australia, Canada, England, Hungary, Israel, the Netherlands, South Africa and the USA. The study was undertaken with the aim of informing policy by suggesting ways in which educational change can be managed positively to enlist teachers' efforts in the reform, innovation and implementation processes. The article emphasises the point made by Fullan (1982) that 'educational change depends on what teachers think and do – it's as simple as that'.

Poppleton and Wubbels highlight how closely teachers' response to change is related to how the policy change was introduced and implemented. For example, teachers in Hungary and Israel, where changes had been predominantly internal to the school, showed a more positive attitude to participating in future change than teachers in England and the Netherlands, where change had been externally imposed by national governments and where teachers were not included in the development of the policy changes. The authors argue that a dramatic change of attitude occurred amongst teachers in England when they were included in the process of revision of the National Curriculum. Eventually their involvement in the drawing up of curriculum plans for their own schools forced them into collaboration with colleagues from which they derived some satisfaction in spite of the often crippling workload that it created. One of the messages of particular value for policy-makers which emerges from this comparative research is the importance of consulting with and involving teachers in the process of change from the outset.

This collection of articles thus highlights the potential usefulness of comparing and contrasting education professionals, as well as warning of the dangers that lie in inappropriate use of such comparisons. Some fruitful ways forward for comparative education, both conceptually and methodologically, are identified and its potential for the professional development of practitioners and for informing the decisions made by policy-makers is debated and affirmed.

Reference

Fullan, M. (1982) *The Meaning of Educational Change.* Toronto: OISE Press.

Comparing Education Professionals: an introductory essay

HARRY JUDGE

The presentation of a number of studies comparing education professionals needs an introduction, and deserves a fuller one than this. This short essay was nevertheless prepared in an attempt to place well-focused empirical studies in context, and to do so by unpacking some of the difficulties and contradictions that are enclosed in the three key words: professionals, education and comparing. How useful are they in organising a theoretical discussion? Are they obsolescent? Does the concept of *a profession* work well when applied to the diverse workforce engaged in the educational enterprise? Does the term *education* have the same kind of functional precision which has traditionally served well for medicine and law? What does it mean to *compare*, either by placing one profession alongside another, or by examining two or more different national experiences?

Professions

Hovering around the mysterious word 'profession', at least in anglophone societies, is an aroma of superior nobility: the classical exposition of this high doctrine is to be found in the works of Emile Durkheim, where the inherently moral nature of a professional activity is contrasted with the self-serving character of commercial activities dominated by material motives. Professions serve a higher purpose and obey a severe ethical canon, linked to public service. Fitting quite comfortably with that moral emphasis is an interpretation of modern society as characterised by specialisation, the pursuit of efficiency and a functionalist sociology. In this interpretative framework (developed by Max Weber, Talcott Parsons and their disciples), the expert knowledge which a specialised professional needs is characteristically acquired within a university, and the growth of professions during the twentieth century was closely intertwined with the growth in scale and in power of the university, especially in the USA and those countries directly influenced by its example. This perspective, like Durkheim's, carries overtones of worth and of respect: society advances by means of a growing rationalisation, and there were close links between this view of the professions and the ethic of progressivism. The imperatives of quality, expertise and high purpose were blended and applied in the supremely influential report of Abraham Flexner, on the future of medical education, completed in 1910 for the Carnegie Foundation for the Advancement of Teaching (Flexner, 1910; Lagemann, 1983/1999).

This benign view of the professions was never, of course, universally shared. In France, the Revolutionary dislike of professions – as of all forms of corporate privilege as articulated in the nobility, the university or the church – was deeply rooted and echoed across the Atlantic in the populism of President Andrew Jackson. Bernard Shaw memorably pilloried every profession as 'a conspiracy against a laity'. Piously self-serving professionals became part of the stock in trade of satirists. But not until the last four decades of the twentieth century did it become intellectually fashionable to deconstruct the ideology of professions: Robert Wiebe (1967), Burton Bledstein (1976) and Barbara Melosh (1982) were among those who undermined the reassuring assumptions of Flexner. In the USA the once popular images of the infinitely considerate family doctor and the sympathetic lawyer yielded to those of the predatory physician and the ambulance chaser. Professions were attacked with disconcerting unanimity from the left by Ivan Illich (1987) and the right by Milton Friedman (1962). Other, less polemical, scholars such as Etzioni (1969) engaged in the harmless sport of inventing categories of minor professions, subprofessions or semi-professions, and in doing so reflected the serious difficulties of maintaining a relevant and contemporary account of what a profession might, in some essential sense, be. As for education in general and teaching in particular, where the professional aspiration remained anachronistically strong, deep ambiguities were exposed: pleas that teachers should become more professional (code for being more highly regarded and rewarded) sometimes involved a campaign to embed their preparation more deeply in the theoretical world of the university, while on other occasions it represented a contrary effort to make them more practical, less theoretical, better attuned to the everyday tasks of the classroom and therefore prepared in large measure by older and more experienced colleagues (Judge, 1980).

Acute critics, while pointing out the dangers of endorsing too sweeping a condemnation of professionalism as it had been traditionally advocated, commented wryly upon the irony of teachers struggling to get 'into the church just as God was being proclaimed dead' (Metzger, 1987). There seems to have been an odd time lag as earnest reformers urged, in the antique spirit of Abraham Flexner, that teaching should be professionalised. This deeply political initiative, obvious on both sides of the Atlantic, remained glued to the old rhetoric: teachers, like doctors and lawyers, should be professionalised (The Holmes Group, 1986; Carnegie Forum, 1986; Fullan, 1998). A long and determined campaign to create in Britain a General Teaching Council, achieving success in 1998, belongs in the same mainstream. Meanwhile, the rest of the world of work became more complex and varied. Knowledge-based industries and enterprises made little or no use of the arguments about professionalism (and especially of links to universities). Although airline pilots might insist (and passengers be grateful for the distinction) that they were emphatically professional and not amateur, the historically linked arguments about self-discipline, university-managed knowledge, control over admission and expulsion, and the fee-paying relationship to clients did not appear above the horizon.

The twentieth century therefore witnessed both the dramatic rise and the disorganised fall of the idea of 'the profession'. Whether, against that clearly defined background, it makes sense to talk of 'the education professions' is doubtful – doubly so when one rapidly disintegrating term (profession) is linked to another slippery word (education).

Education

The trouble with this word is that it can mean anything or nothing. The critical question for these discussions can be simply put: what are the education professions and who are these professionals who belong to them? It is a question that becomes more intractable as the years pass. In the middle of the nineteenth century the single defining activity would have been closely related to teaching: the educators were those who taught at the university or in the lower schools or, more rarely, as private tutors. The growing complexity of functions and specialisation of tasks – both lying at the heart of the general history of professions – produced a rich variety of new tributaries, especially (as always) in the USA. First among them, in history and in number, were the administrators who applied the doctrines of the new creed of efficiency and professionalisation to the tasks of making schools more efficient and productive (Callahan, 1962; Tyack, 1974). Then there trooped onto the stage counsellors, advisers and inspectors, curriculum developers, school social workers, teacher educators, researchers and – sharply and self-consciously defined as distinct branches – the university teachers and researchers subdivided into their increasingly assertive categories: historians, physicists, sociologists, archaeologists, mathematicians, linguists, chemists. About 'education' there was a unique comprehensiveness, enlarged to a degree not equalled in law, medicine or engineering.

But the expansion of boundaries did not stop even there. Scholars reacted against a narrow identification of education with schooling (at whatever level), and against the formal institutional narratives which had characterised too much of the history of education. They argued persuasively that apprenticeship, the family, libraries, sermons, museums, newspapers were as much part of the educative project of society as were textbooks, teachers and publicly constituted organisations (Bailyn, 1972; Cremin, 1980). The growth of the information society and the accessibility of the Internet now widen still further the boundaries of what might appropriately be defined as education. Even if some restraint is applied to this heady imperialism, the variety of residual or core functions reserved for education as (formalised) schooling remains bewilderingly wide and ambitious. The most modest boundary definitions would now have to include the university professor, the pre-school teacher, the high school principal, the counsellor, the school superintendent and the comparativist. The educator can include everyone from the broadcaster, or even the inexpert parent, to the classroom teacher. Discussions around the theme of 'education professionals compared' should, therefore, as a matter of focused prudence concentrate on those who are hired and paid to work within public systems of schooling for pupils and students within the age-range from about 5 to about 19, and especially on the teachers who, even in the most profligate societies, constitute a majority of the schooling workforce. Even within the apparently narrow confines of 'schooling' strictly defined, dramatically different perceptions exist of what is and should be the professional role of the teacher, and these vary both within and across societies. National stereotypes can too easily mislead and the emphasis on, for example, the teacher as community-builder or therapist and the teacher as instructor can shift within a society such as the British. Nevertheless, it can and should be argued that the teacher in France is much more likely than their American counterpart to emphasise the teacher as instructor and to reject a more socialising and less specialised role. The very word *Educateur* has a resonance within France, which has little or nothing in common with the use and understanding of it in countries which the French themselves (misleadingly and impolitely) refer to as Anglo-Saxon. All this suggests at once the value and the dangers of making comparisons about the role and preparation of education professionals.

Comparisons

The story of comparative education has not been a consistently happy one. Even a superficial review of journals incorporating the word 'comparative' in their titles makes this point painfully obvious. Comparative religion is always comparative in some sense, large or small; so is comparative law; and so is comparative literature. Such a comparison of comparisons highlights certain weaknesses in the field of education. Too many studies labelled as comparative are simply studies of 'elsewhere' – simple accounts, for example, in an anglophone journal of what happens in Japan. Too many are concerned with polemics of one kind or another – making comparisons to elevate a sense of national pride and achievement, or (more frequently) to sharpen criticism of national performance in order to provide a spur for reform. The very titles of some books are an anticipatory essay on this theme (Stevenson & Sigler, 1992; Stearns, 1996). Serious efforts in comparative studies (as attempted in the series to which this volume belongs) should always seek to be comparative in some rigorous sense and should not rest content with the exposition, however sophisticated, of exotic educational behaviours.

Some useful progress might be made if three hygienic principles were more consistently and consciously observed: these three are here identified as limitation, informed detachment and contrast. Comparative studies are more illuminating when they subordinate the general, the holistic or the global to the specific, the focused and the detailed. The application of this principle suggests that a study of child-rearing practices in different societies would yield more insight than a study of (say) the educational philosophy of those same societies (Bronfenbrenner, 1972). Comparative studies of the education professionals are for the same reason likely to yield richer results if they concentrate on specified aspects of particular (sub)professionals: their recruitment, training or career patterns, for example. Equally important is the principle of informed detachment. Comparable studies are best undertaken by a scholar combining inside with outside knowledge. A Dutchman is not necessarily the best equipped person to undertake a study of education in the Netherlands: he may take for granted too many of the locally implicit assumptions and ingrained habits. Equally inadequate, because incomplete and insufficiently informed, would be a discussion of (say) the relationship of private and public schooling in that country by an Australian who had spent no time there, read about the history and culture of that society only in translation, and yet aspired to make meaningful comparisons with a dozen other societies. The two principles of limitation and informed detachment interlock.

They interlock most productively when combined with the third commendable principle: that of contrast, or contractiveness. Too much ink has been spilled in the (relatively short) history of comparative education on making forced comparisons and on detecting underlying trends. Education professions (like any other specific cross-national phenomenon) are as a general rule better understood by being contrasted than by being compared. The advantage of such an emphasis (and it is of course a desirable emphasis rather than an exclusive preference) is that the particularity of national arrangements is more clearly exposed, to the native as much as to the foreigner. A single example may suffice. Educational administration may seem to have common elements in three countries such as France, the USA and England, and doubtless at some levels of high generality it has. But the differences are much more significant in leading towards an understanding of why certain general practices have been adopted in any given society, how such arrangements in fact work, what kind of people assume responsibility for them, and how – if at all – they are prepared. In France the Recteur in each Academy, or educational region, has overall responsibility for all schooling and related services, and until 1968 enjoyed great authority in higher education as well. He or she is by training, inclination and earlier career a tenured and well-established university academic, often exercising wide administrative powers over the non-university world for a limited period, appointed and dismissed by the Minister of Education in Paris. In the USA the School Superintendent is the chief officer of what may be a tiny or a huge educational district, is appointed, and often dismissed, by an elected school board, has no connection to and often little sympathy for the world of higher education, but is effectively required to hold a university degree in educational administration (Tyack & Hansot, 1982). Alongside those two sharply contrasted sets of theory and practice sits the English Chief Education Officer. He, like his American counterpart, is a professional administrator but (until recently at least) most unlikely to have any formal qualification of a university type in educational administration. He is appointed by and accountable to (but unlikely to be dismissed by) a democratically elected body, required to work in close professional partnership with other public servants appointed by that same body, and almost certain to have begun his career with a relatively brief period as a classroom teacher (Tomlinson, 1993). A major study could, and indeed should, be initiated on the meanings of and reasons for all those differences, some subtle and some of spectacular simplicity. Marc Bloch was wise to insist that the purpose of comparing is to contrast.

If the education professions (like any other group or item of analysis) are to be intelligently compared/contrasted, two other dimensions need to be introduced and respected. The first of these relates to changes over time, to what the Annales school of historians has identified as the diachronic dimension. This disciplined requirement is, of course, immediately recalled by any reference to Marc Bloch (Burke, 1990). The structure of all professions, of education itself in any given society, of teaching and administration: all these change across time and there is a profound danger in adopting static and fixed stereotypes, or in supposing that practices, concepts and prejudices do not mutate across the centuries or even decades. Equally important, as indicated at the outset of this essay, is the effort to make connections, comparisons and contrasts with the other professions, aspirant as well as established. A seriously sustained effort in the comparative study of the education professionals would necessarily include not only the generalised history of professions as such – as argued earlier – but also a careful review of the abundant literature on medicine and law as well as of the more exiguous analyses of nursing, journalism, music and business (Johnson, 1978; Melosh, 1982; Stevens, 1983; Sedlak & Williamson, 1983; Ludmerer, 1985; Clifford & Guthrie, 1986).

Coda

It would be wrong to conclude from these introductory remarks that the author of them contrives to be at one and the same time a pessimist and an idealist. In resuming the three key words in the stated theme for discussion, it nonetheless remains true that education is a fiendishly difficult category to define or to handle, that 'profession' is in all probability a word that has outlived its usefulness and that comparison is a rare activity which, even when achieved, is more likely to dissolve into contrasts. The most rigorous interpretation of the rules and principles which have been commended in these pages would suggest (and this would indeed be perfectionist) that an ideal study within the field under review would consist of a contrastive and historical study of the functions of the French Recteur alongside those of the American School Superintendent and the English Chief Education Officer, integrated with a parallel review of the role of judges in those same three countries, conducted jointly by a Spanish and an Australian scholar. While such perfectionism is unlikely to be achieved, it may still draw attention to some very general desiderata. Meanwhile, the studies reported elsewhere in this volume indicate that, even in an unashamedly imperfect world, good work can be achieved.

The position taken in this essay is that of an optimistic sceptic who, while remaining uneasy about positivistic interpretations of the three key words, is nevertheless confident that work can and should be done which will be empirically satisfying and also useful as well as illuminating. The hopes for such an enterprise are closely related to the insistence of Sir Michael Sadler, one of the founders of comparative education, that illumination alone is never enough and that the best scholarly work must also be useful, as the study of history is (or was in his day) believed to be. That must remain a goal for the best comparative studies, to be carefully distinguished from the perverse use of such work for short-term and polemical purposes. Such studies should therefore more often lead to normative conclusions (answering in restrained terms the question of 'What is best?'). In the study of the professions, for example, it may well be that the sociological debates on the characteristics of such human activities which happen to be so dignified is now exhausted. But, as the engaging work of William Sullivan has recently shown, the closing of that particular tradition may offer an opportunity for reasserting the importance of the values which are still commonly regarded as characterising professional activities (Sullivan, 1995). The word 'professional' has (at least) two antonyms: the first may be 'amateur', but the second is certainly 'commercial'. It may be illuminating, useful and ethically refreshing to contrast (and doubtless to compare, as well) the values which underlie the practice and thinking of educational administrators – the Recteur, the Chief Education Officer and the Superintendent, to return to the example offered earlier.

To make the unfashionable claim that comparative studies of the professions should be at least as concerned with values and principles as with structures, histories and sociological analysis is not, of course, to make a simplistic claim that the values of one society are superior to those of another. But neither is it to concede that such values and the activities which they help to shape are all incomparable, that they are all relative. The late Sir Isaiah Berlin did not tire of drawing an all-important distinction between relativism and pluralism. A recognition of difference is not the same as indifference. Many admirable principles, even those as basic as respect for freedom on the one hand and for order on the other, inevitably conflict with one another and need to be painstakingly reconciled in contrastedly different societies at different periods of their history. Such questions as 'which society best prepares its education professionals?' or 'which country has the best arrangements for teaching mathematics?' are not so much unanswerable as unaskable. So would be comparable questions, to turn to a very different field of educational policy, directed at the relationship between religious groups and a public education system. In Canada, the Netherlands, Germany, Pakistan, Australia, South Africa, France, England, Israel and Scotland quite different arrangements are made for the recognition, control and financial support of schools maintained by religious groups and denominations of all kinds. The differences are dramatic and significant, and relate directly to a long and complex history of adjustment and (often) of conflict. It is not the business of the comparativist to pronounce any one of them to be better, in some inappropriately absolutist sense.

But neither should that student eschew any discussion, across very different societies, of the ways in which conflicting principles have been reconciled, and the scholar is not debarred by some spurious rule of neutral objectivity from making a balanced assessment of the nature and appropriateness of that reconciliation (Carter, 1994). History may explain nearly everything, but it cannot excuse everything. Neither should comparative education.

Note

The foregoing text is an edited form of an oral introduction to the seminar sponsored by the Economic and Social Research Council, undertaken jointly by the Universities of Bristol, Oxford and Warwick and (as the last in an important series) conducted at the first and most western of those three universities in March 1999. An article written for the same occasion would have had a very different purpose and a very different structure. The short list which follows is for that reason neither a bibliography nor a list of references. It is meant to serve primarily as a pointer towards the sources of and the background to the comments made in this introduction.

Suggested Readings

Altbach, Philip & Kelly, Gail (Eds) (1986) *New Approaches to Comparative Education.*

Altbach, Philip & Kelly, Gail (Eds) (1992) *Emergent Issues in Education: comparative perspectives.*

Bailyn, Bernard (1972) *Education and the Forming of American Society.*

Bell, Daniel (1976) *The Coming of Post-industrial Society.*

Berlin, Sir Isaiah (1992) *The Crooked Timber of Humanity.*

Bledstein, Barton (1976) *The Culture of Professionalism.*

Bloch, Marc (1974) *Apologie pour l'Histoire.*

Broadfoot, Patricia & Osborn, Marilyn with Gally, Michael & Bûcher, Arlene (1993) *Perceptions of Teaching: primary school teachers in England and France.*

Bronfenbrenner, Urie (1972) *The Two Worlds of Childhood: US and USSR.*

Burke, Peter (1990) *The French Historical Revolution: the Annales School, 1929–89.*

Callahan, Raymond E. (1962) *Education and the Cult of Efficiency.*

Carnegie Forum (1986) *A Nation Prepared: teachers for the 21st century.*

Carter, Stephen L. (1994) *The Culture of Disbelief.*

Clark, B. (Ed.) (1984) *The Academic Profession.*

Clifford, G.J. & Guthrie, J.W. (1988) *Ed School: a brief for professional education.*

Cremin, Lawrence A. (1980) *American Education: the national experience.*

Durkheim, Emile (1983) *Professional Ethics and Civic* Morals, trans. Cornelia Brookfield.

Etzioni, Amitai (1969) *The Semi-Professions.*

Flexner, Abraham (1910) *Medical Education in the United States and Canada.*

Friedman, Milton (1962) *Capitalism and Freedom.*

Fullan, Michael et al (1998) *The Rise and Stall of Teacher Education Reform.*

Gumbert, E.B. (1990) *Fit to Teach: teacher education in comparative perspective.*

Holmes Group (1986) *Tomorrow's Teachers.*

Hoyle, Eric & Megarry, J. (Eds) (1980) *Professional Development of Teachers.*

Hoyle, Eric & John, Peter (1996) *Professional Knowledge and Professional Practice.*

Illich, Ivan (1987) *Disabling Professions.*

Jencks, C. & Riesman, D. (1977) *The Academic Revolution.*

Johnson, William R. (1978) *Schooled Lawyers: a study in the clash of professional cultures.*

Judge, Harry (1980) Professionalism: a study in ambiguity, in Hoyle, Eric (Ed.).

Judge, Harry (1982) *American Graduate Schools of Education: a view from abroad.*

Judge, Harry, Lemosse, Michel, Paine, Lyn & Sedlak, Michael (1994) *The University and the Teachers: France, the United States, England.* Oxford: Symposium Books.

Kirst, Michael W. (1984) *Who Controls our Schools?*

Lagemann, Ellen Condliffe (1983/1999) *Private Power for the Public Good: a history of the Carnegie Foundation for the Advancement of Teaching.*

Ludmerer, Kenneth (1985) *Learning to Heal: the development of American medical education.*

Macintyre, Alasdair (1997) *A Short History of Ethics.*

Melosh, Barbara (1982) *The Physician's Hand.*

Peretti, A. (1982) *La Formation des Personnels de l'Education Nationale.*

Perkin, Harold (1989) *The Rise of Professional Society: England since 1880.*

Rothstein, W. (1987) *American Medical Schools and the Practice of Medicine.*

Sedlak, Michael W. & Williamson, Harold F. (1983) *The Evolution of Management Education.*

Starr, Paul (1982) *The Social Transformation of American Medicine.*

Stearns, Kathryn (1996) *School Reform: lessons from England.*

Stevens, Robert (1983) *Law Schools: legal education in America from the 1850s to the 1980s.*

Stevenson, Harold W. & Sigler, James W. (1992) *The Learning Gap: why our schools are failing and what we can learn from Japanese and Chinese education.*

Sullivan, William J. (1995) *Work and Integrity: the crisis of professionalism in America.*

Tomlinson, John (1993) *The Control of Education.*

Tyack, David (1974) *The One Best System: a history of American urban education.*

Tyack, David & Hansot, Elisabeth (1982) *Managers of Virtue: public school leadership in America 1820–1980.*

Veysey, Lawrence R. (1965) *The Emergence of the American University.*

Weber, Max (1980) The Interpretation of Social Reality, in J.E.T. Eldridge (Ed.)

Wiebe, Robert (1967) *The Search for Order, 1877–1920.*

The Politics of Comparing Teacher Education Systems and Teacher Education Policy

THEODOR SANDER

Introduction: methodological alternatives in comparative education research

This is basically a report on comparative research on developments in teacher education in Europe which has been undertaken since 1991 in the context of various European networks – most of them funded by the European Commission. The references contained in this report are therefore mainly based on the publications and activities of these networks, although this is not meant to imply that the various networks and their members have not benefited from the research and views of other colleagues outside the networks in developing their thinking.

In 1994 the European Commission initiated and funded a pilot action in the field of teacher education within a larger framework of investigating the effects of the European Action Scheme for the Mobility of European Students (ERASMUS) programme on European cooperation and of defining new measures in relation to new needs in view of the transition to the second generation of cooperation programmes (the SOCRATES programme). This was called the SIGMA project, comprising also other fields of university study apart from teacher education. A scientific committee of representatives for the 15 European Union (EU) member states was established, being coordinated by the Universität Osnabrück in Germany on behalf of the Santander Group, an international university consortium. Reports for all member states were used as conference material for a major conference organised in Osnabrück in June 1995. It combined a final meeting of all the subnetworks of the Réseau d'Institutions de Formation d'Enseignants (RIF), an earlier pilot action of the European Commission in teacher education which was begun in 1990 and which comprised several subnetworks, with a general invitation to teacher educators in Europe to discuss fundamental problems of European cooperation under the ERASMUS/SOCRATES programme. RIF subnetwork 4, which included a large number of institutions in eastern and western Europe and which always focused on comparisons of teacher education systems in Europe, survived the end of funding from the European Commission in 1995 and still continues its work until today.

Based on experiences of the RIF and the SIGMA pilot project in teacher education, a group of teacher educators applied for funding from the European Commission for a Thematic Network of Teacher Education in Europe (TNTEE) under the SOCRATES programme. This network started operations in autumn 1996, being coordinated by Umeå Universitet in Sweden. Within a short time TNTEE developed into a large network of teacher education institutions producing various materials in a number of subnetworks working on specific themes (see the website of TNTEE under http://tntee.umu.se where all materials currently available are deposited).

Like any other group or individual researcher working in the field of comparative education, these networks have been continuously faced with the political alternative of affirmative vs critical approaches (see Appendix – Table I for an overview of major characteristics). I wish I could say with confidence that in the networks mentioned earlier we were able to move away from approaches labelled as 'affirmative' towards approaches categorised as 'critical'. But this was not quite the case. Rather, we still found ourselves in a situation of being dissatisfied to some degree with many traditional approaches and in part trying out new ones on specific themes (particularly with student teachers on the occasion of numerous ERASMUS Intensive Programmes), or even of being engaged in more or less amiable academic debates between those deliberately choosing and defending affirmative approaches and those wishing to criticise them.

As for the 'critical approaches' which I have increasingly opted for in recent years and which form the basis of this report, it appears that there is less of a proliferation of colourful variants than on the side of the 'affirmative approaches'. Critical approaches could be classified as representing either a critique of existing (affirmative) theories or a critique of social systems at the level of education. Both procedures might be seen as necessary and useful but the latter is obviously far more important for improving our knowledge and understanding of the functioning of actual (teacher) education systems in reality under concrete historical circumstances.

Major Results of Research Activities
in the Field of Teacher Education

1. Global Level

Affirmative approaches. At the global level, developments in teacher education and teacher education policy were interpreted for decades as forming part of a more general framework of opposition and fierce struggle of allegedly diverse systems, namely socialism/communism and capitalism, each being dominated by a hegemonic power – the (former) Soviet Union and the USA. Comparative education felt compelled to take sides and revealed its genuinely political nature in choosing to defend the 'normality' of the system at home and in denouncing the 'absurdity' of the other system. This attitude continues to be operational, with few changes even after the break-up of the Eastern bloc, when describing its supposed 'transformations' and the alleged 'transition' from planned societies to market societies.

Critical approaches. Developments in teacher education and teacher education policy at the global level are seen as reflecting in very similar ways the internal contradictions of world capital/world capitalism on both sides of the former Iron Curtain, requiring processes of mediation between antagonistic classes in which the nation states have traditionally played a major role. Even if teacher education and teacher education policies were not modelled in identical ways all over the world, they would respond to the same kind of problems and challenges on both the Eastern and the Western sides. They would also fail in similar ways to find adequate and effective solutions for existing problems.

Throughout the post-war period, comparative education in both East and West has followed a highly problematic course, fully identifying with the aims and objectives of Cold War policies as practised by the superpowers and their respective allies, generally accepting warfare (military, industrial, commercial, financial, cultural, ideological, etc.) as the basic mode of existence in the post-war world order, as a reasonable way of defining international relations, and never tiring in producing propaganda about the 'enemy' on the other side of the Iron Curtain (for a detailed analysis see Sander, 1997). The (teacher) education system of the enemy was invariably seen as being class-based, while the system at home was simultaneously regarded as being totally different, either expressing the values of non-existent 'socialism' or of imaginary 'democracy'. At the same time, the (teacher) education system of the enemy was admired and detested for its alleged success in manipulating and indoctrinating the younger generation, whereas the system at home was praised as having no other purpose than promoting individual emancipation through schooling, both ignoring the participation of young people in the ongoing class struggles inside and outside the

163

education sector. Implicitly, the younger generation on the enemy's side was scorned for being so submissive and weak, as it was understood to be so easily manipulated and indoctrinated, but the younger generation at home was denied any right to protest and rebellion as it was simply believed that there was no manipulation or indoctrination to require such responses (Sander, 1991, 1992). This was, therefore, a case of permanent and systematic scientific schizophrenia, if one wanted to borrow a concept from psychology.

In producing comparisons of the two education systems in East and West and their supposed diversity, comparative education barricaded itself behind the walls of a fictitious world in which it constructed the image of the unquestionable superiority and the neat unproblematic functioning of the education system at home. In order to be able to defend this unrealistic interpretation, it became in fact necessary to buy the self-fabricated illusions of the enemy, taking them completely seriously even while in a critical perspective there was certainly not the slightest reason for doing so. Thus, a non-existent pluralism and democracy at home gained the status of a political norm and value to be adhered to and to be defended by stereotyping the enemy's system as based on socialism/communism, monism, totalitarianism and dictatorship. Equally, a non-existent socialism/communism at home gained the status of a political norm to be adhered to and to be defended by stereotyping the enemy's system as representing the most rigorous and heinous variant of a repressive capitalist regime being highly efficient in integrating and subduing the working class. This kind of mutual assurance promised to function reasonably well as long as each side clung to its self-fabricated illusions and the propaganda about the (teacher) education system at home and its wider social context (Sander, 1991, 1996e, 1997a).

Even after the collapse of the Eastern bloc, the ideological heritage of the Cold War continues to play a dominant role in the analysis of 'transition societies' and 'transformation' of education systems on the way 'from planned societies to market societies'. About the nature of these 'transformations' since 1989 there is complete confusion in affirmative variants of comparative education, as 'transitions' would be constructed against the background of false antinomies inherited from Cold War thinking. 'Communism', 'central planning' and 'state property' were seen as being bankrupt and there was only one imaginable solution to the existing problems – replace it by 'democracy', 'market economy' and 'privatisation'. For the education sector, the new key word became 'human resource development'. However, the public debate on educational 'reform' and its supposedly beneficial effects involved in the 'transition' should be clearly distinguished from the actual changes taking place. Certainly, fictitious problems invented by political elites and comparative educationalists, unattainable goals and fictitious political solutions, sold as major democratic advances, are not providing us with any useful elements for understanding such changes (Sander, 1996, 1999a).

Concerning the education sector (including teacher education) and its fundamental characteristics before 1989, both sides agreed on a number of basic assumptions which served to underline the alleged diversity of systems and at the same time the absence of major social antagonisms and basic problems of functioning within each system. If the ideology of diversity effectively may have served purposes of political propaganda, the scientific substance of this ideology was in fact always extremely weak (Sander, 1983, 1997a) The following points need to be made in this respect.

Planning vs market mechanism/consumer-led development? Educational planning in the former Eastern bloc was an important part of the overall planning mechanism, comprising planning of production and productivity, of the labour force and of new recruits from the education system. Voluminous plans were elaborated regularly by a highly inflated corps of planning bureaucrats. In this very superficial sense the education system of the former Eastern bloc was labelled as a planned system. The central and decisive problem is, of course, whether real developments of the education system were in any way regulated through the existing planning mechanisms or not. It has been demonstrated that this was never the case, neither at the level of planning quantitative recruitment of labour for various sectors and branches of the economy, nor at the level of planning for different qualification levels, nor at the level of planning of financial aspects in education. Indeed, it has been argued that regulation of the education system through planning was perfectly impossible under the specific conditions of class struggle prevailing in the former Eastern bloc, and thus educational planning was bound to remain a matter of no more than building castles in the sand.

Centrally directed vs decentralised system? It has been generally assumed that the education system of the former Eastern bloc was strictly controlled from the top through the Party bureaucracy, the Ministry of Education and the Academy of Pedagogical Sciences, critics often comparing modes of control to forms of military command. The political activities of these institutions were invariably seen as following a rational pattern, centres of decision-making were thought of as being well-informed about every important detail (taking a realistic view of problems and their origins), bureaucratic elites were regarded as homogeneous – and society as a passive element that could be shaped, moulded and manipulated at will by the bureaucracy. However, none of these assumptions has stood the test of critical analysis. In fact it has been demonstrated how little the central bureaucracy knew about the reality and the complexities of the education system in particular and the social system in general. Above all, there was never a clear-cut, straightforward relationship between political aims and political actions, the bureaucracy continuously acting against the declared interests of its own plans and programmes. The kind of streamlined unitary command imagined by researchers was not exercised by the Politburo or the Central Committee of the respective ruling party but rather by the harsh realities and constraints of the Eastern bloc's long-term economic decline not quite surprisingly ending in its collapse.

Curricular integration vs separation of general and vocational education? The separation of general and vocational education has always been the cornerstone of a system where knowledge is organised and transmitted in such ways that it facilitates social selection. In fact it was never abolished in the former Eastern bloc. A very instructive case is the experience of polytechnic education, which was at the centre of a major attempt to integrate school and production, learning and work, general and vocational education, theory and practice. One of its basic aims was to overcome the dual system of preparing in different, separate streams of formal education for manual jobs/clerical jobs on one side and for professional jobs/management jobs on the other. The attempt failed completely, since it was neither possible to introduce a polytechnic dimension into *all* subjects (polytechnic education as an additional subject) nor could theoretical and educational aspects of work be sufficiently developed. With more and more emphasis being put on engineering and technology – and increasingly so in the context of the so-called scientific and technological revolution – polytechnic education quickly became integrated into the prevailing culture, which was a culture of social discrimination and selection.

Comprehensive school vs differentiated, vertically structured school system? The non-differentiated comprehensive school is usually regarded as putting into practice the principles of equality and social justice. However, formal equality (indeed, the kind of equality offered by the comprehensive school system is nothing but formal), in treating non-equals as equals, is far from producing such results. Rather, it has to be seen as a perfect instrument for reproducing existing social differences in the student population. Such differences will appear within a class between pupils, between classes at the same level of schooling, between schools, and between regions. Thus, the comprehensive school (or any other system of formal equality) represents a generalised system of maintaining all the differences existing in society in a particular historical situation – with these differences undergoing changes in the long run.

None of the characteristics on which participants in the Cold War agreed at political and academic level seriously lent itself for analysing and understanding the (teacher) education system on the Eastern side. In fact, the antinomies mentioned earlier were completely irrelevant, as the (teacher) education system on the Western side was not described in adequate terms either. Thus, the affirmative views expressed in the antinomies were eliminating the basic fact of fundamental internal conflicts (class conflicts) in both systems and in that sense also hiding the enormous similarities which existed between social systems and specifically (teacher) education systems on the Eastern and Western sides even before 1989. It could generally be stated that the affirmative views never succeeded in identifying any of the factors which actually did shape developments of the education systems on both sides, in perfectly symmetrical and similar ways. Some of the most basic and most relevant factors in both systems are:

- the fundamental role of class antagonism and related systems of mediation;
- the social functions of teacher education in class societies;
- the myths and illusions of professionalism in class societies; and
- the dual system of learning and knowledge in class societies.

The Origins of Internal Conflicts in Eastern and Western Societies – class antagonism and the state

The unity and opposition of civil society and the state has marked the entire history of modern society, on the Eastern side as much as on the Western side. The relationship in itself has not been a constant and stable one but is rather characterised by the gradual encroachment of civil society upon the functions and activities of the state. That process has in fact been speeded up enormously in the post-war period, and particularly so since the crisis of 1973/75. As a result, the logic of mediation is increasingly replaced by the universal and unmitigated validity of the logic of antagonism (for a general critical analysis see Agnoli, 1968, 1975; Holloway & Picciotto, 1978; Negri, 1977, 1978, 1982).

Public education (including teacher education), together with health care and the social security system, has been a cornerstone in the system of mediation as developed in modern society. Although mediation has certainly not worked evenly and smoothly for all social groups, the overall importance and effects of public education for the continuous reproduction and relative stability of society could hardly be overstated. Although the education system itself did not produce differences in social status, it clearly became the major filter through which everyone had to pass in order to reproduce, more or less successfully, social status and the existing social division of labour (see e.g. Willis, 1978; Corrigan, 1979). In this sense the education system was the major distributor of social opportunities. Public education could also be expected to have beneficial effects for the state itself and its functioning (see e.g. Tapper & Salter, 1978). As Adam Smith had already stated in the eighteenth century, an instructed and intelligent people are always more decent and orderly than an ignorant and stupid one, and they are more disposed to respect their superiors and less apt to be misled into any wanton or unnecessary opposition to the measures of government. This would be particularly important in countries where the safety of government depends very much on the favourable judgement which the people may form of its conduct.

The gradual replacement of mediation by antagonism and conflict has serious negative or even destructive effects on the various state functions, among them the important mediating function of public education. Millions of jobs have disappeared at all levels of the economy, which is the very reason for young people to extend the periods spent in education beyond what they would have done under more favourable circumstances. However, rapidly rising participation rates in upper secondary schools and in higher education in a period of labour market crisis inevitably end up destroying whatever links between social status and education might have existed. This is a serious threat to schools and higher education as social institutions because then the question becomes even more pressing as to what could possibly be the uses and value of schooling, formal education and diplomas. In the face of such developments, political interventions of government into this system are more and more overridden and frustrated by tendencies in the development of civil society.

Teacher Education and Class Society: social functions

In order to be able to adequately compare teacher education systems, it is obviously very important to have a precise idea about the role and functions of teacher education within the education system and society in general – and about what its role and functions could definitely not be. This is a more serious problem than it might seem at first sight, as the debate in the 1980s and 1990s has narrowed down on to functions which in my view at best represent a side aspect of teacher education, if they are of any relevance at all. Is the main objective and function of teacher education not, quite simply, to teach prospective teachers how to teach in schools and other educational institutions? This would probably be the question, if not the basic widely shared assumption, among persons inside and outside the field of teacher education. Unfortunately, this assumption does not reflect more than purely normative positions – a perspective abstracting from the wider social context and being dominated by an emphasis on what teacher education ought to do (fully ignoring the question of whether it effectively has the means of doing it) and disregarding what it actually does.

Focusing sharply and exclusively on what teacher education does and not on what it ought to do, the role and functions of teacher education could be described in the following contexts (for a detailed analysis see Sander, 2000c; individual aspects are discussed in Sander, 1994, 1999a), which do not in fact stand in isolation, each of them being separated from the others, but are dynamically linked to each other in a developmental process and tend to reinforce or weaken each other, depending on the circumstances:

- labour market regulation in the face of growing difficulties of the occupational system;
- social reproduction on the basis of the existing division of labour;
- ideological integration, mainly through citizenship education; and
- preparation of teachers for performing the same functions as described earlier at school level.

While the modern school as a public institution, developing with the rise of borgeois society, was characterised by its abstracting from the world of labour (and out of necessity having to do so), university, and with it, teacher education at university level are characterised for their part by a double process of abstraction and opposition to the world of labour. Teacher education does in fact abstract first of all in very practical and not only theoretical ways from the world of the school and the daily problems arising in it, and then also from the world of labour in general (and out of necessity has to do so). This includes abstracting from the existence of classes and ideologies of classes. Otherwise university would have no proper legitimation as being separated from the processes of schooling or from the very experiences of labour/professional practice. In this sense, teacher education represents quite logically a way of reproducing the professions through the negation of professionalism and professionalisation. This is in fact a modern, rational (and not an irrational, basically inefficient) way of reproducing the existing division of labour. Even if the university today has developed significantly in comparison with the beginning of the nineteenth century, its basic orientation has not changed in this respect and will probably only change with the disappearance of the university itself.

Teacher preparation at university or other higher education institutions then has a clear orientation – educate teachers for performing the same tasks and supporting the same functions at school level which are linked to higher education and its role in society, namely labour market regulation, social reproduction and ideological integration. It is of no particular importance for the outcomes and effectiveness of such an education whether this orientation is given prominent place in the teacher education curriculum or not; indeed, whether this orientation is reflected at all in the official curriculum. Rather, there would always have been a tendency that outcomes mainly depended on the functioning and effects of the hidden curriculum of teacher education (see Ginsburg & Clift, 1990; see also Ginsburg, 1988). At the same time, there would have been a complete reliance on the homology of problems and tasks between higher education level and school level. It is this very homology that provided teacher education over many decades with a proper legitimation and with a basis for dealing in relatively effective ways with its fundamental tasks. However, in all likelihood these ties and links are no longer functioning today as smoothly as in the past, for reasons largely beyond the control of teacher education institutions, administrators and teacher educators. In fact, the main reasons for this must be seen as lying in recent developments in class society.

The very idea that teacher education, as taking place at university or at other higher education institutions, should have the aim of preparing students for lesson planning, keeping discipline in the classroom, knowing all about accurate, well-paced explanation in lessons, etc., and the attempt to declare this to be the hallmark of true professionalism could only appear to be extremely misguided, failing to grasp the meaning and role of university and teacher education in history and to understand its actual limits, possibilities and achievements. If such petty matters were indeed all prospective teachers had to learn and know, then there would be absolutely no need for teacher education in a separate educational institution at the level of tertiary education called university; there would not even be a need for any kind of teacher education in any place or institution. One would just throw beginning teachers into the water and ask them to swim – which as a matter of fact they have done with quite satisfactory results for ages.

Teacher Education and Class Society: illusions of professionalism

The emergence of an institutionalised system of teacher education in the context of the rise of bourgeois society during the nineteenth century has helped foster a number of deep-rooted illusions concerning professionalism and professionals (Sander, 1997b, 1999c):

- the illusion of the professional being superior in his/her teaching competence to the non-professional;
- the illusion of the professional as someone who disposes of all the necessary knowledge concerning the learning needs and problems of young people;
- the illusion of the educational sciences as representing a coherent body of rational (and applicable) knowledge which could be passed on in systematic courses to prospective teachers;
- the illusion of teacher professionalism magically resulting from academic studies which are in fact separated completely and radically from the daily reality, problems and routines of teaching in schools;

- the illusion of the professional being capable of educating children for a working life which he/she does not know much about – and in any case not enough; and
- the illusion of the professional as a civil servant standing above the social classes and not being directly involved politically in their antagonism; rather, being faced with nothing but the educational problems and perspectives of individuals, catering for the needs and the development of each and every child's personality and defending the right of children to personal emancipation through school education.

The growth of such illusions was closely linked to the rise of capitalism and to the developing new class antagonism. Class society appeared to produce a range of antagonisms, conflicts and problems, which could not easily, if at all, be dealt with at the level of class relations. Thus, institutional settings for mediation were required, presupposing a social process of abstraction from class and class experience. One of these settings was schools and universities, which became part of 'public service' offered by the state. It involved among others a particular kind of division of labour between pedagogical laymen (parents, grandparents, the village community, etc.) and education professionals.

The 'professionals', allegedly disposing of a specialised knowledge and hence a particular competence, were responsible for compulsory and non-compulsory forms of education. For their actual role in class society it was not even very important whether they had that kind of competency or not, this role being sufficiently stabilised by the links that were established between occupational careers and schooling, as well as by the reproductive/selective functions and disciplinary powers of teachers. However, it has become more evident in recent decades that transitions from school to work are no longer defined as neatly as in former times by different levels of success in school careers. Such differences tend to be of ever lesser significance, with the average time being spent in educational institutions increasing considerably and at the same time opportunities for finding employment in jobs at the upper level of the occupational spectrum decreasing massively (not to speak of youth unemployment in general). In the process, the role and the public image of the 'professional' inevitably must change greatly. It becomes clear that for structural reasons he/she is incapable of solving any of the serious problems arising.

If schools are in fact less and less successful in imparting knowledge, be it only of an elementary kind (keeping in mind that this is nothing but school knowledge), then this makes it much more difficult today to cling to the old illusions about 'professionalism' and the role of 'professionals' in society. The teacher as a 'professional' (allegedly) for education and teaching has become a much-criticised figure and the public does not hesitate to criticise him/her for activities in a field which should be his/her proper professional terrain. Thus, the traditional barriers between professional and non-professional and the concomitant status of teachers, including the respect he/she could expect to be shown are becoming widely inoperational.

Teacher Education and Class Society: dual systems of learning and knowledge

The learning and acquisition of knowledge, skills and attitudes of students is a much more complicated process than most teachers and teacher educators would normally believe (or would in fact be aware of). In a wider perspective, we are faced with the dualism of learning in schools (as state institutions) and learning in various contexts of class society, in particular in the contexts of family socialisation and peer group socialisation (for a case study – East Germany – see Sander, 1983, p. 135ff.) Students would normally understand the difference without problems – knowledge acquired in schools, together with the corresponding certificates and diploma, would be relevant for progressing within the school system and then for career entry within the existing social division of labour. Beyond career entry it would mostly turn out to be of no particular use in occupational contexts or in life as such. Such knowledge would also be very rapidly devalued as soon as unemployment for school leavers becomes a major phenomenon. Considering nothing but the school context, we are faced with the dualism of the official and the hidden curriculum. At this level the available research appears to suggest that there is a strong interference between the two processes, which actually tends to assign much greater importance and effectiveness to the hidden curriculum. Knowledge acquired outside schools, particularly in families, peer groups, etc. has a completely different status – this is the indispensable knowledge needed for finding one's way, getting along and dealing with problems in real life. This knowledge would not be acquired in uniform contexts and we have to clearly distinguish proletarian knowledge/capitalist knowledge as well as knowledge of manual/intellectual labour depending on social contexts in which it is acquired.

The same kind of twofold dualism has always existed in teacher education. Teacher education programmes and courses are characterised by the dualism of an official and a hidden curriculum which represents the framework for learning processes of student teachers in higher education establishments. Looking beyond the higher education sector, student teachers would continuously undergo processes of acquiring knowledge, skills and attitudes relevant not only for life in general but also for teaching. Acquisition would take place before, during and after participating in teacher education programmes.

Summarising the argument so far, critical approaches are aimed at rejecting the idea of the developments in teacher education in the post-war period being basically characterised by conflicts between the superpowers in the context of the Cold War. They would rather insist on the central importance of class antagonism and class conflict on both sides of the Iron Curtain. Teacher education would then be described as being part of a complex system of mediation requiring it to fulfil specific social functions going far beyond tasks of simply teaching young people in various school subjects. The status of teachers within the social division of labour would be characterised as being firmly tied to historical illusions of professionalism and professionalisation going back to the very origins of institutionalising teacher education in modern class society. The learning processes of prospective teachers would be seen as taking place in a dual framework of learning in class society versus learning in educational institutions under the responsibility of the state and at the same time in another dual framework of formal versus informal learning processes.

2. European Level

Affirmative approaches. At European level developments in teacher education and teacher education policy are described as being based on the 'diversity' of national education systems. If ongoing processes of European cooperation and integration at economic and political level are thought to be a positive feature by national governments, this is far from being the case in the field of (teacher) education systems. The 'diversity' of national education systems should be maintained while adding a 'European dimension' as a complementary element. The scope of the European institutions for action in the field of education should be limited by the principle of 'subsidiarity', not allowing them in any way to initiate effective policies of European harmonisation in this particular area. In defending such positions comparative education permits itself to take part in spreading national prejudices and even chauvinism, in close cooperation with representatives of the nation states and in support of their specific narrow political interests.

Critical approaches. At European (and at global) level teacher education systems are regarded as being highly integrated and highly similar, particularly if analysed at the level of informal processes in teacher education. This situation has indeed prevailed for a very long time, long before anyone thought concretely about 'European integration'. It results from specific system characteristics of capitalist societies and their concrete expression in the field of (teacher) education.

In debates on European integration the nation states are regarded as being the most important actors in shaping the respective teacher education systems, having priority over all the other actors. Beyond that, the nation states are seen as efficiently using a number of different policy actions in order to achieve their particular aims and objectives. The main forms of action of the nation states would be the setting of (legal and other) norms, short- and long-term planning, administrative orders and control, the selection of personnel through appropriate general rules and measures, the strategic use of funding, the establishing of institutional structures, i.e. more or less the elements having priority in affirmative variants of comparing (teacher) education systems. It would regularly be assumed that in this way solid foundations are laid for a *national* education system. As a national system an education system would not only be seen as internally homogeneous but above all as clearly different and diverse from that of other nations. (This is the basic assumption in EURYDICE/CEDEFOP, 1991; EURYDICE, 1991, 1995; Buchberger, 1992 and many others, but also in Sander, 1994; and in most of the contributions in Sander & Vez, 1996.) The national education system would in fact represent one of the core elements of what is usually termed a 'national culture' and it would be centrally involved in reproducing 'national identity'.

Ideologies of the 'diversity of national cultures' and in particular of the 'diversity of education systems' are quite openly defended today as having to form the basis of policy at the level of the European Union (see, for example, the Maastricht Treaty, articles 126 and 127). It is true that in past years we have been flooded with glowing reports about European cooperation and integration, about convergence and convergence criteria, about freely moving capital, goods and workers on an integrated European internal market, about European citizenship – but also about the continuity of multi-tiered political systems wherever integration/harmonisation appears not to have been achieved so far or to be completely undesirable. Following the text of the Maastricht Treaty in articles 126 and 127 as well as available official declarations, the latter is the case in the field of education and training. If everything else in Europe will be harmonised one day – from passport photographs to the size of bananas – then a fence still ought to be put around 'national education systems' and no member or functionary of the European Commission or the European Parliament should ever dare to interfere with the prerogatives of national governments in shaping their 'national' education systems. As government members and politicians from the member states are called upon to decide about spheres and processes of European integration (implying that without them and their good intentions and their arduous work this would never happen), they also have the right to decide about spheres of non-integration. It is in this context of 'multi-tiered systems' that the German federal state is often upheld as a model for European integration.

Against this background, the specific role of the European institutions is defined by the principle of 'subsidiarity'. They would not interfere with the prerogatives and responsibilities of the nation states but would rather promote European cooperation in (teacher) education in spheres of common interest, mainly through the instruments of networking, transnational projects, as well as mobility and exchange. While fully respecting the 'national diversity' of education systems, the European institutions would endeavour to add to it a 'European dimension', which over the years has been described in changing terms according to the needs and priorities of the moment. (For a detailed analysis see Beernaert et al, 1993, particularly ch. 3; Sander & Kohlberg, 1993a,b.)

It should be clearly understood that the limited integration process in education as described earlier is based on fiction, not on reality: it does not make sense at all to demand either integration or non-integration of European teacher education systems. Rather, they ought to be regarded as having gradually been integrated long ago – as a result of the triumph of capitalism on a world scale in the last century. If this fact has been obscured in the past by political representatives of the nation states and by the academic ideologues of the 'diversity of nation cultures', then this is due to a very particular and very one-sided approach in comparative education. (For a more detailed analysis see Sander, 1993a,b, 1995a; Sander & Beernaert, 1994; Sander et al, 1995; Lundahl & Sander, 1998.) Traditionally, the analysis of teacher education systems in a comparative perspective is strictly focused on aspects of the legal prescriptions, the administrative structure, the organisational framework and the curricular norms. Quite clearly these are aspects in which diversity prevails (although there is very little reason to believe that the actual functioning of teacher education systems would depend on these aspects). These are also aspects manifestly linked to the interest of the nation state in maintaining political and administrative control of the 'national' teacher education system. Since almost all of those who receive a diploma in teacher education seek employment with the state and since numerically teachers represent the most important category of civil servants, this interest of the nation state is easy to explain.

Adopting a different perspective and asking different questions, we would instead arrive at the firm conclusion that global, European integration of teacher education systems is a matter of the past. Such a result would be obtained from focusing on:

- general links of teacher education with the system of class conflict and mediation;
- social functions of teacher education;
- historical origins of myths of professionalism and professionalisation in teacher education;
- the dual system of knowledge and learning in teacher education;

- the informal constitution of teaching competence in social processes;
- the dominant role of informal learning on the job in teacher education;
- the hidden curriculum of teaching and learning processes in academic teacher education; and
- the informal processes of defining quality standards, evaluation and assessment in teacher education.

With the exception of the last four items, all other aspects have already been dealt with earlier, even if only very briefly. I will now turn to the particular role of informal processes in teacher education and teaching. It is these informal processes that are actually at the root of any theory of the similarity and integration of teacher education systems.

Informal Constitution of Teaching Competence in Social Processes

The existing catalogues of teachers' competencies/professional qualifications as they have been developed in the USA and in the United Kingdom, for example, are all based on the assumption that competencies could be analysed and defined by governments as universally valid norms for assessment and learning, that standards could be taught and acquired in formal education processes and that they would then become part of the personality and skills repertoire of prospective teachers who would be able to draw on such general abilities according to the needs of classroom teaching all through their professional life. It is completely ignored in this perspective that requirements on the qualification of a teacher at his/her workplace are defined by social processes in a continuously changing society (Sander, 1997b, 1999b). In a very narrow sense it is the classroom situation, it is a social interactive process between teachers and students which reveals teachers as being competent or incompetent. However, the classroom view proves to be much too narrow as the classroom situation only reflects prevailing social problems and structural changes in the wider society. It is this general socio-historical situation which makes teachers appear competent or incompetent, which constitutes their level of competence irrespective of any personal knowledge or skills that they might have acquired previously. No catalogue of teachers' 'competencies', neatly laid out as it may be and as being used for assessment on entering the teaching profession, will permit governments to replace or interfere with the social processes of constituting teaching competence. Such catalogues are nothing but a sign of medieval superstition and ignorance.

At this point teacher education institutions are facing a serious problem which they are unable to solve. They are more or less completely separated from the ongoing social processes of defining and constituting competence at the level of schools. There is nothing like coherent efforts of doing systematic research on qualification requirements as set by the changing social reality of schools. Teacher educators are not seriously required to have any competence or knowledge concerning the development of teaching in schools and very many of them have no proper experience at all in school teaching. How, then, could anyone believe that the relevant scientific knowledge on how to develop professional competence could possibly be generated in this context?

Informal Processes of Teacher Development and Learning on the Job

The process in which teachers actually learn to teach specific subjects and themes (keeping in mind that this is not a primary social function of teachers but a secondary, subordinate element), in which teachers acquire some basic competence of teaching young people, takes place beyond the confines of higher education institutions. Whether teacher educators like this or not, for practising teachers themselves there is little doubt that in spite of other influences, on-the-job learning does indeed play a central and even dominant role in their development as teachers. (For a more detailed analysis see Sander, 1996a,b,c; Sander et al, 1995.) This implies that experience (and under favourable circumstances maybe also reflection on that experience) will be the main method of acquiring pedagogical competencies. Changes, even from the same sort of experience, will not occur in a uniform manner but depending on personal qualities, intentions, prior experiences, social origin, general workplace conditions, etc. It is, however, important to stress that on-the-job learning presupposes highly specific school and classroom contexts and specific impacts of such contexts. The kind of generalised knowledge and competence independent of contexts, as the one initial teacher education usually focuses upon, will never be achieved through on-the-job learning (and not through academic learning either). Any change of context will inevitably implicate the teacher in new learning processes. On the other hand, problems arising on the job will never lend themselves to treatment on the basis of the generalised knowledge and competence independent of contexts which represents the core of teacher education ideology. Seen in this particular perspective, the process of teachers learning to teach has always been an informal, lifelong learning process, and nothing else. Within this process, catalogues of competencies as prescribed by governments for teacher education are just irrelevant for professional development.

Certainly there is no reason to idealise the informal experiential process of lifelong learning. Undoubtedly teacher development could not be expected to occur as a simple process of continuous and automatic improvement, ending only with retirement. The possibility of a teacher changing in a negative sense is not just a hypothetical question. The possibility of a teacher ending up in a situation of burnout and bitterness is always there. The possibility of a teacher misinterpreting his/her own experience and not understanding him/herself the complexities of his/her development could never be excluded. But there are more important reasons for not being overoptimistic about the results of experiential on-the-job-learning of teachers. All problems connected to informal lifelong learning processes of teachers are focused in the relations between teachers and pupils, although they definitely do not all originate in that relationship. Antagonisms, conflicts and pressures generated and operating in society at large are omnipresent in the classroom, whether teachers and pupils know this or not. This is why teachers are typically working under circumstances and conditions which are far beyond their influence, and the existing social division of labour has a tendency to prevent them from gaining insight into this particular situation.

Hidden Curriculum of Teaching and Learning Processes in Initial Teacher Education

The dominant tradition of teacher education certainly does not motivate students for active, self-determined, self-organised learning – and is probably not even intended to do so. Very often it takes place in hierarchical settings requiring the students to listen passively and suppress all questions and problems they might have. Hardly anyone would claim that this is a very promising and effective arrangement for successful learning. Looking more closely into the arrangement and basic problems of teaching and learning situations in teacher education, it is extremely difficult to avoid the conclusion that they are planned (or at least functioning in a way) to prevent and sabotage learning, not to promote and facilitate it. There are several factors which could be seen as having a very negative effect (see Sander, 1996b,c).

(a) Teacher educators as poor role models for student teachers. Teacher educators seem to be characterised by the same kind of basic attitude as has been found to be typical for teachers as well: They appear not to gear their planning to the way in which students are likely to actually deal with curriculum content but rather on the sequencing of such content. That is, in general they appear to be more concerned with the technical aspects of information transfer than with the sense students make of the information. The focus of instruction is some abstract target skill or knowledge itself, not the process that facilitates the acquisition of these. On top of this, the quality of teaching methods in universities and other higher education institutions is widely thought to be poor and passed on to students as such. Processes of teaching and learning in teacher education appear to be highly ritualised, requiring students to adapt to a range of the strangest rituals. In other words, the learner characteristics,

learning processes and theories of learning are very widely ignored in teacher education courses. Student teachers tend to be particularly critical of this fact, often having a low esteem for the pedagogical competence of teaching staff.

(b) Hierarchical relations between teacher educators and students. Independent of the system or model of teacher education, interaction between teacher educators and students is very often characterised by hierarchical relations. This includes a basic orientation of teaching–learning processes on passive learning, although in an abstract sense the inefficiency and the counterproductive effects of such an orientation are no secret to teacher educators. It is just one particular aspect of this situation that as a rule students are not (sufficiently) familiarised with the results of current research nor given opportunities for participating actively in research activities. Very often a kind of knowledge is transmitted to them which is unrelated to the respective state of the art in educational research and to basic results of past research. It has been concluded from this that teacher education is certainly not very practical but equally far removed from being theoretical.

(c) Emphasis on socialisation through disciplinary studies. Everywhere in Europe teacher education courses, be this for teaching in primary schools or in secondary schools, are characterised by a clear emphasis on disciplinary studies. This kind of emphasis is all the more strange as it could hardly be claimed that such disciplinary studies are to be seen as an indispensable element in the process of teachers learning to teach. Teacher education always grappled with the dualism of academic disciplines/school subjects, persistently ignoring the fact that the two sides represent completely different traditions, being absolutely independent of each other. As for the academic disciplines, they have developed in ways which tend to obscure their social origins, their political functions and their practical meaning. This appears to be the very advantage and the very motive of their being emphasised in processes of socialisation in higher education establishments.

(d) Obsession with testing and assessment of students. In almost all European countries teacher education is clearly characterised by an extreme obsession with testing and assessment of students. The available knowledge accumulated in the educational sciences about the limits and disadvantages (if not complete uselessness) of the prevailing techniques of evaluation and assessment at school level is generally ignored by teacher educators once it comes to tests and examinations at higher education level. Strategies for the evaluation of teacher education and students' learning processes thus are patently inadequate. They also reflect and reproduce the existing separation and the gap between school teaching and teacher education since the criteria of success are usually defined in terms of academic standards and achievement but not in

terms of the quality of professional practice. A more important aspect of the obsession with assessment consists in its promoting a highly superficial attitude of students and teacher educators towards course content and learning processes. This is bound to have negative effects on the learning processes of students.

The prevailing situation at the level of teaching and learning processes in teacher education could hardly be stranger: Political contexts and functions of teacher education are believed to be meaningless, course content and structure do not really matter, learners and their specific processes of learning are regarded with contempt, the idiocies of testing and examinations are defended tooth and nail or at least silently accepted as a necessary evil, professional competence is seen as somehow falling from heaven ... The simultaneous existence of an official and a hidden curriculum, of formal and informal learning processes, represents one of the fundamental problems of teacher education in any kind of system. The official curriculum tends to be based on an ideology of national or regional culture, thus disregarding the facts of historical processes of integration as expressed at the level of the hidden curriculum. Co-existence between the official and the hidden curriculum is by no means peaceful and the results of teacher education will depend heavily on the degree of interference from the side of the hidden curriculum.

Informal Processes of Defining Quality Standards, Evaluation and Assessment

Evaluation is not really a new phenomenon in teacher education, nor is it in the area of higher education in general. All higher education institutions, all university faculties and departments have always had (sometimes quite elaborate) informal mechanisms of permanent internal evaluation and assessment (for a more detailed analysis see Sander, 2000c). Depending on the degree of these informal mechanisms being operative, and on the way they were handled, faculties and departments were in a position to develop not only internal standards of quality but also more or less informal procedures of putting group pressure on staff members who were believed not to properly fulfil their duties – or of distributing rewards to those who were evaluated positively. Certainly, it could not be excluded that under local circumstances standards of research and teaching might be quite idiosyncratic or even absurd. And certainly, there was no guarantee that standards resulted from a democratic process of debate and decisions among colleagues, and they might well be based on the autocratic power of individuals or 'leading circles' within the larger framework of a faculty or department. However, there could be no doubt about the relevance of these mechanisms within small group situations of university institutions and their (varying) effects on the definition of the quality of research and teaching.

The traditional role of students in assessing the teaching of staff members represents an important aspect of informal processes of evaluation and assessment. In a more liberal and open system of study organisation (as, for example, in Germany), students would usually express the results of their assessment by voting with their feet. The share of compulsory courses is extremely low for student teachers at the level of university studies as the first phase of preparation (this is different in the second phase of predominantly school-based training in the Ausbildungs- und Studienseminare). Beyond the few compulsory elements students are completely free to choose from the existing courses on offer – although there is now an increasing tendency to destroy this freedom through reforms of the study organisation. Students are also completely free to choose specific members of staff in the case of parallel course offers. Students are mostly not obliged to attend a course for the duration of a full semester if they do not like the course or the teacher or both. They do take the liberty to attend from time to time wherever that is possible, if they believe that this is a rational way of dealing with a particular course. There are non-compulsory courses with compulsory attendance for those who want a certificate at the end but again the number of certificates student teachers have to acquire is very low by international standards. Most importantly, students are free to extend their studies beyond the limits of minimum duration set by examination regulations.

Within such a system, an unpopular or an incompetent or a (sometimes/regularly) not very well-prepared staff member would normally very soon be stranded, with decreasing numbers of attending students. Quite often, students, at least some of them, would not just stay away or change to other courses, if they disliked a particular staff member or the way he/she ran a course, but would not hesitate to complain about it. Except in very large departments and faculties, such events would normally not remain hidden from other staff members but would form part of the normal gossip, and it could very well be assumed that the popularity, the efforts and the degree of success of a teacher educator would be wellknown to the rest of the department, not to speak of the entire student population, which has its own functioning mechanisms of spreading news and rumours. It is on this basis that group pressure again comes into play.

While these are normal procedures within a more liberal and open system, students would also have ways of expressing the results of their personal evaluation of courses and competencies of teacher educators in a more strictly regulated system (as, for example, in the United Kingdom).

It is apparent that the formal mechanisms for the evaluation and assessment of students' achievement were always more elaborate and more intense than in the case of teacher educators. However, behind the smokescreen of formal occasions, general procedures and established standards for assessment, the evaluation of students was always clearly determined by informal processes and informal norms. Any teacher educator will be sufficiently familiar with these informal processes, even if he/she does not reflect much about them. Their impact is particularly strong on the occasion of written and oral examinations taken at the end of study or at an intermediate stage during studies, but basically it would be universal wherever evaluation of students takes place. The kind of distortions resulting from a teacher educator's expectations, personal likes and dislikes, the halo effect, insufficient information about the student, one-sided task definitions, etc. are all too well known and do not have to be explained again in this context. Such distortions are continuously being developed inside informal processes in teacher education and they are quite unavoidable elements in them, which could never really be eliminated.

It is my conclusion from the brief analysis undertaken here that the functioning and outcomes of teacher education in any system are largely determined by the informal processes of learning, not the formal processes and objectives. Considering some of the major informal processes taking place in teacher education (constitution of teaching competence, on-the-job learning, learning in the context of the hidden curriculum of initial teacher education, definition of quality standards, evaluation and assessment), it is an obvious fact that informal processes are ignored in affirmative variants of comparative education – for good reason. At the level of informal processes there is nothing like the 'diversity' of 'national' teacher education systems and thus nothing really lending itself to support the kind of national prejudices which usually form the substance of affirmative approaches and dreaming about policies of 'European integration' or introducing a 'European dimension'. Instead, an analysis of informal processes of learning in teacher education suggests a very high degree of similarity, if not identity, of teacher education systems in Europe and even at global level. It should be remembered that both formal and informal processes form part of a complex system of mediation in class societies.

3. Nation State Level

Affirmative approaches. At national level developments in teacher education are seen as being basically initiated by relevant policies of state institutions, which are believed to be independent of class antagonism, its movements and effects. This is particularly true in the case of recent theories of neoliberal governance and new public management. The internal contradictions of capitalist development at the level of the nation states and their effects on the contradictory unity of civil society and the state are simply ignored. They are replaced by ideologies of 'national identity' and 'national culture' as something which is reproduced continuously and successfully through adequate policies of the nation state and its agencies. In defending such positions comparative education actively participates in spreading the self-fabricated illusions of the state and its representatives concerning the supposed power of the state and the efficient use of policy instruments.

Critical approaches. Developments of government policies concerning teacher education at national level would be interpreted as responding to specific problems and challenges generated in class struggles and to a lesser degree in the functioning of the public sector itself. At the same time policies are analysed as not really following a straightforward and rational means–ends model but rather as generating counterproductive effects in the shape of various forms of opposition and refusal among students but also among teacher educators. Fundamentally, policies of the nation states are therefore described as self-defeating and self-destructive.

In the post-war period affirmative approaches in comparative education have provided support and legitimation for Cold War policies of the superpowers and they have provided support and legitimation for the development of national prejudices deriving from the ideology of the 'diversity' of national education systems in a European and global context. In a national context, affirmative approaches have provided support for ideologies of the nation state as acting independently from the antagonism of classes and even being able to direct the movement of classes according to its own priorities and needs. This ideology of the nation state in its most recent form contains a number of important elements:

(a) Power and influence of the state exercised independently of class antagonism? Among all actors having a stake in formulating and producing educational policies, the state is viewed by its representatives and in affirmative theories of policy-making at national level as occupying a privileged position. Traditionally research has constructed, although more implicitly than explicitly, hierarchies of influence and power, assuming a sort of omnipotence of governments in planning and directing what is seen as a more or less dynamic and positive development of society. Interestingly enough, this is an assumption which has always been shared by researchers in eastern and western Europe. At the same time, it has been part of this assumption to regard actors at the level of teacher education establishments as a passive element, as objects and not as subjects of politics. Clearly, the assumption as such is perfectly in line with the prevailing self-image of

governments, parties and politicians regarding themselves as being fully independent from the movements and tendencies generated by the antagonism of classes.

This is a point of view which has been defended ever since the dual system of capital and the state opposing each other was constituted with the rise of capitalist society in modern times. Considering long-term historical development of the state budget and the historical development of policies in the education sector, it is difficult to share this view (for a more detailed discussion see Sander, 1997a). Rather, it appears that in every single phase developments have been shaped by class struggle and its concrete results. (General conclusion: state institutions are held together – or gradually destroyed – by class struggle and at the same time they are not very powerful in defining and implementing policies of their own.)

(b) Decisive role of the political will and consciousness of actors at nation state level? Representatives of the state and those advocating affirmative approaches in comparative education would insist on policies of the state reflecting a specific political will and specific political choices which are made consciously and deliberately. The basic tenets involved might be formulated as follows.

- The state/government has absolute *primacy over civil society*. This implies that social reproduction through educational systems can be regulated completely or almost completely through the *state/government, its interventions and its regulative policies*.
- The reality of educational systems is completely or fundamentally determined by *normative acts* of the state/government (legal provisions, administrative planning and norms, political intentions and decisions at the level of Parliament or at the level of party politics, etc.)
- The functioning of educational systems depends completely or fundamentally on their *organisational structure* as defined in general by state/government institutions.
- The state/government disposes of *reliable information on the problems* that arise in educational systems and on the proper means to solve these problems. Interventions usually have the intended effects, not counterproductive or contrary ones.

Case studies of specific governmental activities and concrete analysis of the overall effects of policy-making in the education sector do not confirm such views (e.g. Sander, 1983, analysing the former German Democratic Republic). As much as these assumptions are part of state ideology, they are also part of the current illusions prevailing in theoretical thinking and political action in the field of education policy. It is quite normal that policies produce nothing but counterproductive effects and very often actors would not be aware of them. (General conclusion: policy-making state institutions do not simply do what they want and very often do not know what they do.)

(c) Rise of 'neoliberalism' as reflecting fundamental political changes? Supporters and critics of 'neoliberal governance' have both been eager, for different reasons, to describe the policy shifts in question as a radical break with the past. At school level the break would be identified as a politically motivated turn away from (social democratic) ideals of the past – the provision of excellent educational opportunities for all children – towards the authoritarian introduction of differentiation, hierarchy and so new divisions within the publicly provided school system. At teacher education level, the break would be described as a politically motivated move, replacing a humanist, democratic, child-centred vision of teaching and teacher education with new general standards of effectiveness and flexibility as well as hierarchical concepts of society in general and teaching and teachers in particular.

However, using the label of 'neoliberal policies' tends to obscure the meaning of the policies in question, which were gradually introduced in the 1980s and 1990s in many countries. Generally, the idea of radical political alternatives in education policies in the post-war period is not supported by the facts (Sander, 1996d, 1999a). Considering the various party systems, we are rather faced with what critical observers have termed the pluralist version of a one-party state dominating in the Eastern as well as in the Western part of the world. Thus, it must be concluded, changes in parliamentary majorities would hardly ever result in fundamental political change, and the assumption of a radical break brought about through neoliberal reforms in recent decades must be rejected. (General conclusion: policy-making state institutions are not the object of struggles between opposing parties for power.)

(d) New managerialism as a means of increasing rationality and effectiveness? One of the major driving forces in policy reform in the education sector in recent years has been the alleged need to increase 'effectiveness' in order to be competitive in the global economy. Another has involved the drive to cut taxes particularly for the rich and increase support for the business sector, thus creating a need to make the public sector in general more efficient. To this end New Public Management (NPM) has been introduced in most OECD (Organisation for Economic Cooperation and Development) countries, which has involved modelling the management, reporting and accounting approaches in the public sector, including the education sector, along the lines of 'best' commercial practice. This has also implied the establishment of quasi markets, including the introduction of competition for lower costs and the 'best' products/services in every area of the public sector.

185

The problem with such interpretation is that the search for a realistic picture of managerialism is replaced with legends about managerialism as spread by managers themselves (see the controversial debate in Sander, 1999b). In fact I have not yet seen a single piece of analysis of the ideology of NPM where the claims and assumptions about the neat, smooth functioning of capitalist managerialism have been seriously investigated and questioned. This, however, appears to be very much necessary for a number of reasons. First, it is an obvious fact that none of the huge monopoly firms in whatever branch of production and circulation (be this arms production, telecommunication, road, rail and air transport, chemicals or whatever) could survive today without massive direct or indirect support from the state budget. Second, it is also quite evident that, even with more and more massive support from the state, big business is unable to achieve any kind of stability. In fact, there is only one area in which capitalist production of profit has definitely and continuously proved to be efficient – and that is the destruction of the bases for its own further development. This is demonstrated clearly by the long-term decline of national and sectoral growth rates of production and productivity. Third, whatever detailed reports we have on the efficiency of capitalist business firms mostly testifies to the irrationalism and inefficiency of production and circulation and the incompetence of managers in finding ways to change this situation. Some researchers in the field of sociology have even concluded that production could only be upheld through workers ignoring most of the instructions of management and using their own experiential know-how of the production process. It is a complete mystery why some tend to believe that transferring such a highly problematic system to the education sector could have anything but disastrous results. (General conclusion: policy-making state institutions could not be made more efficient by copying the inefficient model of managing the capitalist business firm.)

All of these assumptions and concepts concerning the role and functions of the nation state in defining and implementing policies in the field of (teacher) education, in recent years increasingly linked to the myths of 'neoliberal reforms' and 'managerialism in education', would be rejected in a critical perspective. Instead, policies of the nation state are interpreted as forming part of a complex system of mediation between antagonistic classes, and as such, responding to specific problems and challenges arising in class society as well as at the level of the state institutions. Whereas in abstract terms mediation might result in either integration or disintegration, recent decades are seen rather as being characterised by policies generating various forms of opposition and refusal among students but also among teacher educators. The following themes would all be regarded as lending themselves particularly well to gaining insight into such developments in the field of teacher education:

- policies of emphasising formal processes of lifelong learning;
- policies of establishing formal catalogues of teachers' professional qualifications;
- policies of introducing formal systems of quality criteria and quality improvement measures; and
- policies of reorganising formal procedures of evaluation.

Policies of Emphasising Formal Processes of Lifelong Learning in Teacher Education

At least for a number of decades the myth of teacher professionalism sufficed for winning a minimum of respect and recognition for teachers' work. If the debate in recent years has turned towards discussing the introduction of a formal system of lifelong learning (see contributions in Sander & Vez, 1996), then the existing system must be regarded as having failed or as not achieving fully the results to be expected – and in the same sense the myth of teacher professionalism must have lost its former functions and meaning in many ways. Indeed, it could be argued that there are very many good reasons justifying this mostly implicit assumption, almost all of them linked to historical developments in teacher education and in school teaching. They are closely related to transformations of class society since the mid-1970s; much less (if at all) to fictional matters like 'neoliberalism', 'post-Fordism' or 'New Right policies'. Briefly said, the present situation is characterised by a growing refusal of learning in the context of compulsory schooling and beyond and by more and more signs of teacher burnout/teacher educator burnout; by the inability (impossibility) for teacher education to continue pretending that it actually provides students with the necessary professional competence; by a growing tendency in the educational sciences to formulate nonsensical theories about education and the process of teaching and learning; and by the increasing irrelevance of educational research for the needs of teachers and policy-makers.

Undoubtedly such tendencies require greater efforts on the side of the state/government in order to successfully roll back developments in the last two or three decades and to regain control of the education sector as a central piece in its policy of mediation between classes. However, the objective of more efficient mediation and political control might in fact be unattainable. The margins for changing the system of teacher education in the sense of increased political control appear to be very narrow. This certainly does not imply at all that a formal system of lifelong learning for teachers could never be installed. It rather implies that the policies of lifelong learning now being implemented in many countries will produce some serious counterproductive effects (for a more detailed account see Sander, 1996c).

Such effects were already visible under conditions prevailing in teacher education before the introduction of lifelong learning concepts, with the emphasis being on pre-service education. With the workplace of teacher educators and the situation for student teachers having changed quite dramatically in more recent times, it is no wonder that in the last two decades a vast area of conflict has opened up between student teachers and higher education institutions/teacher educators. It is very much evident that basically it is the claims of teacher educators to professionalism and the alleged values of academic professionalisation which are at stake in these conflicts. Against this background it is almost logical that teacher educators' reactions and interpretations of the conflict tend to take on a highly negative and derogatory character. Thus, student teachers tend to be stigmatised by teacher educators who believe they are encountering many learners who are not easily engaged in serious intellectual growth with the aim of improving schools and professional practice. Not only are the academic interests and abilities of the student majority described as being low when compared with the university/college-educated population as a whole, but the learners' affective propensities are regarded as being equally problematic. The 'research evidence' teacher educators would draw upon also seems to suggest that both prospective and practising teachers maintain low expectations for the professional knowledge aspects of their education. The desire of student teachers for serious and continued learning for improvement purposes is thought to be low in the light of rapid declines in extrinsic and intrinsic rewards for the occupation of teaching itself. Student teachers are believed to generally regard the job of teaching as relatively easy and to have an exaggerated confidence in their teaching abilities.

Nothing of what many teacher educators tend to think and say about prospective teachers sounds very flattering. But the seemingly objective descriptions (even if backed by massive 'empirical' research and decades of 'experience') clearly echo the kind of stigmatising concepts used by teachers and educational researchers when talking about the lack of academic ability, linguistic competence, high achievement motives and deferred gratification patterns on the side of working-class children (particularly manual workers). They indicate an evolving state of alienation and confrontation between students and teacher educators, between students and academic education as well as students and 'professional work' in schools. We could expect that the intensification of educational efforts through formal processes of lifelong learning will further aggravate the situation, as they have nothing to offer for solving the existing problems in teacher education.

*Policies of Establishing Formal Catalogues
of Teachers' Professional Qualifications*

Current debates on the situation of teacher education in the late 1990s revolve around many aspects and problems – but definitely not around the basic question of whether teacher education still succeeds in maintaining its fundamental social functions, as briefly sketched earlier. Rather, recent debates on teacher education focus on key words like 'professionalisation', 'competencies', 'qualifications', 'accountability', etc. There is a strong tendency, even echoed among teacher educators, to demand that university and in particular pre-service teacher education should be more strictly oriented on 'professional practice', 'professionalism', 'professionalisation', 'professional competence' in quite a narrow sense – and to pretend that this would produce positive results in coping with present-day problems in schools. For example, a list of standards to be attained by student teachers at the end of pre-service education which was published recently in the United Kingdom contains, among others, the following items:

> *Those to be awarded Qualified Teacher Status must, when assessed, demonstrate that they use teaching methods which sustain the momentum of pupils' work and keep all pupils engaged through:*
> *• stimulating intellectual curiosity, communicating enthusiasm for the subject being taught, fostering pupils' enthusiasm and maintaining pupils' motivation;*
> *• matching the approaches used to the subject matter and the pupils being taught;*
> *• structuring information well, including outlining content and aims, signalling transitions and summarising key points as the lesson progresses;*
> *• clear presentation of content around a set of key ideas, using appropriate subject-specific vocabulary and well-chosen illustrations and examples;*
> *• clear instruction and demonstration, and accurate well-paced explanation;*
> *• effective questioning which matches the pace and direction of the lesson and ensures that pupils take part;*
> *• careful attention to pupils' errors and misconceptions, and helping to remedy them;*
> *• listening carefully to pupils, analysing their responses and responding constructively in order to take pupils' learning forward;*
> *• selecting and making good use of textbooks, IT and other learning resources which enable teaching objectives to be met;*
> *• providing opportunities for pupils to consolidate their*

knowledge and maximising opportunities, both in the classroom and through setting well-focused homework, to reinforce and develop what has been learnt;

♦ exploiting opportunities to improve pupils' basic skills in literacy, numeracy and IT, and the individual and collaborative study skills needed for effective learning, including information retrieval from libraries, texts and other sources;

♦ exploiting opportunities to contribute to the quality of pupils' wider educational development, including their personal, spiritual, moral, social and cultural development;

♦ setting high expectations for all pupils notwithstanding individual differences, including gender, and cultural and linguistic backgrounds;

♦ providing opportunities to develop pupils' wider understanding by relating their learning to real and work-related examples.

(Department for Education and Employment [1997] Teaching: high status, high standards. Circular 10/97, p. 10ff.)

For any critical observer this (and the rest of the catalogue contained in circular 10/97) is nothing but a mass of vague and hollow phrases which definitely could not serve in any way as an orientation for beginning teachers in understanding and learning how to organise their work in the classroom or how to structure processes within teacher education courses with the aim of gaining the required competence. The need for interpreting the respective requirements in their complete vagueness (what is 'good use of textbooks', what is 'effective questioning', what is 'well-paced explanation' outside highly specific contexts and beyond personal interpretations? – more circulars by narrow-minded technocrats needed to explain this!) makes it perfectly impossible to regard them as appropriate standards which could be used in any rational way for assessing specific classroom behaviour of students. Requirements could be deliberately interpreted in widely differing and even opposite ways. Whatever behaviour students demonstrate in practice, it could be regarded at will as corresponding with the standards or as not corresponding, as there are absolutely no criteria for knowing whether specific behaviour of specific students in specific situations does correspond with the standards.

On top of this, it is completely unclear how such competencies could be acquired at all in pre-service teacher education, be this at university or in schools. It is only too obvious that university does not have the means of promoting the acquisition of competencies in this very narrow sense and it is definitely not its role to deal with such matters. Therefore teacher educators should be very reluctant to promise results which could never be achieved. At the same time, it is absolutely clear that schools are not more effective in this respect. The often heard claim that students would be better prepared for their job if more elements of practice, practical experience, school experience, practicum, etc. were introduced into the study programmes of prospective teachers, has no foundations whatsoever. This is just thoughtless propaganda. Practical experience in a particular school will never provide more than a few highly contextualised skills, which might be completely useless (and even a hindrance) in other school contexts.

Such problems of a very fundamental nature, linked with far-reaching promises concerning the positive uses of catalogues of (national) professional qualifications, are bound to further complicate relations between student teachers and teacher educators/mentors in schools. Once students find out about the arbitrary political nature of the exercise, their frustrations might grow very rapidly. There is actually no reason for assuming that they will not find out.

Policies of Introducing Formal Systems
of Quality Criteria and Quality Improvement Measures

Quality and efficiency are in fact loaded words implying preferences, values and standards which are rarely discussed openly and which are instead shrouded in words betraying the same spurious scientific neutrality which once accompanied the practice and theory of Taylorism. The potentially conflicting values and standards are usually hidden in the construction of seemingly objective 'performance indicators' and 'quality criteria', attempting to depoliticise what in effect is a highly political problem involving very particular choices.

Three aspects of this political problem of introducing formal systems of 'quality management' in (teacher) education appear to be particularly important. The first conclusion from the current debate on quality in education would be that it is neither the quality of the product nor the quality of the process which are at stake but just the production costs. Mostly, a primitive managerialist perspective is taken in order to enhance quality, pretending to emulate management strategies of business firms but at the same time being unable to define precisely the process and the product and consequently to say a single reasonable word about quality. At the same time, quality management ignores the fact that for different levels and groups involved (the entire system, the state/government, education institutions, parents, pupils) the concept of quality most certainly implies very different meanings. Present developments in quality management as promoted by the nation states/governments appear to ignore them all and substitute for them a technical and completely meaningless concept related to superficial ideas about the functioning of individual institutions and aimed at driving costs down by all means.

The managerialist business unit approach chosen for the purpose implies that the causes and origins of what is assumed to be a quality problem have to be rigorously ignored (Sander, 1995b,c). Instead it has to be assumed that problems originate at the level of specific institutions because they have to be dealt with at the level of individual institutions. Although this might be an attractive move for governments in the process of shifting responsibility for the malfunctioning of the (teacher) education system to educational establishments and teachers/teacher educators, it does presuppose an extremely primitive model of the relations of the education sector with the rest of society. It is evident for the critical observer that very many of the current problems in schools and other educational institutions are nothing but an expression of changes in class relations, changes on the technical side of production systems of capital, changes in the labour market situation, etc. For governments, any pretence of being able to intervene effectively in these wider social processes has now become totally absurd.

The second conclusion from the current debate on quality in education concerns the uselessness and inappropriateness of quality measurement and assessment for gaining insight into the development of quality. In fact, quality assessment strategies confirm views that have already been expressed under the first conclusion concerning the irrelevance of product quality and process quality. It is evident that the best way of learning about the true meaning and implications of quality consists in working back to it from the side of measurement and assessment. Fundamental problems with more ambitious forms of assessment have remained unsolved and this is particularly true for experimental designs, attempting to detect and assess causal links between teaching organisation, teaching behaviour and teaching efficiency (in terms of students' achievement, examination results, etc.) Since quality cannot be measured directly, indicator models with numerous assumptions about causal links have to be used. It has been forcefully argued that, with the present insights into learning processes, such models will either be empirically void or easily refuted as irrelevant. More modest approaches like strategies of programme evaluation, taking specific definitions of quality, specific aims and objectives of quality improvement and their translation into practice by collective actors (teaching staff) for granted, end up with the same problems as experimental research. Therefore highly simple and highly problematic instruments tend to be widely used in practice, e.g. examination results, which are perfectly known to be related to social class and social stratification but not to ability, intelligence or whatever. Without much hesitation, current strategies of quality assessment could be rejected as providing nothing but completely arbitrary and meaningless insights about quality – in whichever sense.

The third conclusion refers to the attempts to introduce strategies for quality improvement and enhancement. As in the case of quality assessment, strategies for enhancing quality implicitly inform us about the basic ideas of those promoting them with regard to the nature of quality and the relevant performance indicators. Undoubtedly standards in education could still be raised in many places, be this at the level of schools or at the level of higher education. However, it is difficult to see the relationship between the strategies and means being currently proposed for quality enhancement on one side and quality on the other. Rather, they appear to be devised in a way to enhance social control by governments through a new system of punishment and reward being now added to the existing disciplinary mechanisms and replacing them wherever they might be seen as having failed.

Performance indicators, quality assessment and quality improvement strategies as they are introduced by governments and educational establishments are desperate attempts at battling uphill against the ongoing informal social process of defining powerful historical versions of quality in education and of the overall quality and usefulness of education. This process depends ultimately on the development of class relations, not on what this or that government, this or that educational establishment, this or that researcher might wish to establish as quality criteria and to devise as a programme of quality enhancement.

Policies of Reorganising Formal Procedures of Evaluation in Teacher Education

For many decades evaluation of teacher education largely consisted in a combination of informal evaluation processes and specific forms of administrative control through the allocation of funds and reporting requirements. It was governments which increasingly demanded in recent years that the old system be replaced by a new one, also introducing a number of important new elements (see e.g. the reports in Sander, 2000a). The new elements include above all:

- the attempt to extend the limits of central, hierarchical control by introducing a systematic and seemingly coherent framework for evaluation which is intended to comprise the totality of achievements and conditions for achievement of teacher education institutions;
- the combination of external and internal evaluation and assessment which obliges teacher education establishments and their members to accept the systematic collection of relevant data and regular comprehensive reporting as a permanent task;
- new obligations of teacher educators in the field of regular self-evaluation and/or in the field of organising their being evaluated by students through distributing questionnaires at regular intervals;

- the systematic use of evaluation results for establishing hierarchies of teacher education institutions, with possible consequences for being allocated capacities for student intake; and
- direct or indirect links between evaluation results, accreditation and funding of teacher education institutions.

Such initiatives do not stand in isolation but form part of a much wider context of higher education reform, which is shifting more and more problems to institutions but reserving the right of decision-making and control in all fundamental aspects for government. The key words in higher education reform are 'autonomy', 'global budgets' (lump sums) and 'professionalisation' as well as 'individual profiles' and 'competition' between institutions, and study reforms on the basis of 'modules' and 'credit points', all this allegedly contributing to a greater 'efficiency' of institutions. Although some elements of the old administrative system of evaluation and reporting are usually retained in this context, the new political initiatives clearly reflect the transition to a policy intending to reverse developments in higher education in the last decades or, if this proves to be impossible, at least to drastically reduce costs.

It could be expected that the debate about evaluation and quality assessment in teacher education will become more heated in coming years. Evaluation is such a vague and meaningless procedure if it is not tied firmly to a very precise understanding of the social functions and role of teacher education. It could not be seen as an accident that few attempts are made to arrive at such a precise understanding and the vagueness of the evaluation concept appears to be its very advantage for governments in using it for increasingly massive attacks on the education sector. In my view there are three fundamental aspects to be taken into account concerning evaluation processes as they are now rapidly being introduced into teacher education all over Europe (Sander, 2000b).

(a) Evaluation attempts to eliminate its political context, i.e. its instrumental value and functions for austerity policies and hierarchical control in the education sector (including teacher education), and instead prefers to present itself as a simple rational mechanism of quality assessment and control according to a technical model (as, for example, in car production) which could not possibly be refuted by any rational person.

(b) Evaluation claims to provide indicators for the achievements and quality of teacher education but never enters into a proper debate about the social functions of teacher education and instead proceeds from assumptions about aims and objectives of teacher education as a frame of reference for assessment, which quite clearly teacher education institutions do not and cannot achieve.

(c) Evaluation tends to employ methods for assessing the achievements and quality of teacher education which presuppose the readiness to radically ignore the wealth of critical reflection on methodological problems which have been produced in the so-called empirical sciences, and alternative scientific orientations in the past five decades or so, be this in the field of sociology, psychology, ethnology, the educational sciences or whatever branch of scientific reasoning one might think of.

If the political context is left aside quite intentionally, if functions are ascribed to teacher education which it never had and could never fulfil and if methods are applied which are at best pre-scientific – could we really expect that evaluation, systematic as it might be, is going to provide the kind of insights needed in order to understand the specific achievements and failures of teacher education establishments or teacher education systems? Rather, we are more justified in assuming that the entirely arbitrary character of the evaluation procedures will provoke increasing opposition, be this in open or hidden form, to the concepts and practices involved.

From this discussion of some of the major themes appearing in political initiatives of governments in recent times (formal processes of lifelong learning, formal catalogues of teachers' professional qualifications, formal systems of quality management, formal procedures of evaluation) it must be concluded that policies are not planned and implemented according to principles of rationality and effectiveness but rather according to a model of irrationalism and ineffectiveness. The effects produced by policies in the field of teacher education (be this at national, European or global level) are regularly and systematically diverging from what was intended and counterproductive effects would rather be the norm, not the exception. There are two kinds of explanations for this. First, in each case dominant informal processes would interfere with the formal processes, much to the detriment of the latter. Such informal processes have already been described. Second, efforts of mediation as promoted through activities of the state would be annihilated by the development of the antagonism of classes and its effects in the field of (teacher) education and at the same time by the increasing need for the state itself to reduce costs and limit services.

Conclusions

Affirmative approaches. The world system (for this concept see Ginsburg, 1991; Ginsburg et al, 1990) is analysed as a multi-tiered system with separate political institutions, responsibilities and mechanisms of functioning. Analysis clearly distinguishes the global, European, national, regional/local levels. The key concept within such approaches is that of the 'diversity' of 'national' or 'regional' teacher education systems.

Critical approaches. The world system is analysed in terms of an emerging single world culture forming a particular aspect of the development of world capitalism/the world market. Thus, the transitional character of European, national and regional levels is emphasised. The key concept is that of the class nature of teacher education systems at global level, linking developments in teacher education to historical processes of the development of class antagonism.

While not making an attempt to summarise the details of this report, there are still some general points to be made.

(a) The kind of information and knowledge comparative education could possibly produce about teacher education and education professionals at national, European and global levels depends fully on the respective methodological approach chosen. While there is certainly a wide range of possible choices, it is absolutely vital to distinguish clearly between affirmative and critical approaches, as they will yield completely different results.

(b) Comparative education never ceased to have close links with politics, in fact producing mostly nothing but unashamed political propaganda supporting Cold War policies of the superpowers, nationalist prejudices resulting from the concept of the 'diversity' of national cultures and self-fabricated illusions of the nation states/national governments concerning their independence from the system of class antagonism. Indeed, it has to be admitted that in comparative education there is absolutely no possibility of being neutral, detached, objective – although there is definitely no particular need to offer nothing but political propaganda without the slightest information value.

(c) Based on highly specific political and methodological options, the key word in affirmative approaches of comparative education is 'diversity' of education systems, education processes, education policies, status and functions of education professionals, etc. However, 'diversity' is nothing but an artefact of specific methodological options and choices. It should also be noted that both 'diversity' and 'similarity' of (teacher) education systems are entirely static concepts – comparative education ought rather to focus on dynamic long-term and short-term changes of overall social contexts and conflicts in class societies and their impact on the development of teacher education as well as of teacher education policies.

(d) Different results will be obtained in comparative education if the emphasis is on critical research methodologies which implies focusing:

- on internal contradictions of capital and its expressions at the level of social functions of teacher education; illusions of professionalism; the hidden curriculum of teaching and learning processes; the dual system of knowledge and learning;

- on informal processes of teaching and learning in teacher education, in particular at the level of teacher development and learning on the job; the hidden curriculum in initial teacher education; quality criteria and evaluation;

- on opposition to education and professional work as generated by capital relations and by the activities of the state, e.g. through implementing policies which emphasise formal processes of lifelong learning; establish formal catalogues of teachers' professional qualifications; introduce formal systems of quality management; and reorganise formal procedures of evaluation and assessment.

(e) Certainly there are many opportunities to learn from comparing the situation and development of teacher education and education professionals at national, European and global levels, with results ultimately depending again on the particular approach chosen in comparative education. However, there are indeed many ways of missing this opportunity, as could easily be concluded from a quick glance at the history of comparative education in the post-war period.

Bibliography

Agnoli, J. (1968) Die Transformation der Demokratie, in J. Agnoli & P. Brückner, *Die Transformation der Demokratie*. Frankfurt a.M.: Europäische Verlags-Anstalt.

Agnoli, J. (1975) *Überlegungen zum bürgerlichen Staat*. Berlin: Verlag Klaus Wagenbach.

Beernaert, Y., van Dijck, H. & Sander, T. (1993) *The European Dimension of Teacher Education*. Brussels-Nijmegen-Osnabrück: RIF Subnetwork 4.

Corrigan, P. (1979) *Schooling the Smash Street Kids*. London: Macmillan Press.

Department for Education and Employment (1997) *Teaching: high status, high standards. Circular 10/97*. London: Department for Education and Employment.

Ginsburg, M. (1988) *Contradictions in Teacher Education and Society: a critical analysis*. London: Falmer Press.

Ginsburg, M. (Ed.) (1991) *Understanding Educational Reform in Global Context: economy, ideology and the state*. New York: Garland.

Ginsburg, M. & Clift, R. (1990) The Hidden Curriculum of Preservice Teacher Education, in W.R. Houston (Ed.) *Handbook of Research on Teacher Education*, pp. 450–465. New York: Macmillan.

Ginsburg, M., Cooper, S., Raghu, R. & Zegarra, H. (1990) National and World System Level Explanations of Educational Reform, *Comparative Education Review*, 34, pp. 474–499.

Ginsburg, M.B. & Lindsay, B. (Eds) (1995) *The Political Dimension in Teacher Education: comparative perspectives on policy formation, socialization and society*. London: Falmer Press.

Holloway, J. & Picciotto, S. (Eds) (1978) *State and Capital: a Marxist debate*. London: Edward and Arnold.

Lundah, L. & Sander, T. (Eds) (1998) *Vocational Education and Training in Germany and Sweden. Strategies of Control and Movements of Resistance and Opposition*. Umeå: Umeå University.

Negri, A. (1977) *La forma stato. Per la critica dell'economia politica della Costituzione*. Milano: Feltrinelli.

Negri, A. (1978) *Il dominio e il sabotaggio. Sul metodo marxista della trasformazione sociale*. Milano: Feltrinelli.

Negri, A. (1982) *Macchina tempo. Rompicapi Liberazione Costituzione*. Milano: Feltrinelli.

Sander, T. (1983) *Bildungsplanung als Illusion. Empirische Untersuchungen zur Unplanbarkeit des Bildungswesens in der DDR*. Münster: WURF Verlag.

Sander, T. (1991) Zur Diskussion zwischen WissenschaftlerInnen aus dem östlichen und westlichen Teil Deutschlands, in T. Sander (Ed.) *Auf dem Wege zur deutschen Bildungseinheit?* pp. 103–111. Osnabrück: Universität Osnabrück – Fachbereich Erziehungs- und Kulturwissenschaften.

Sander, T. (1992) Zur Lage der Nation. Ein gründlich mißlungener Materialienband über Bildung und Erziehung in der BRD und in der (ehemaligen) DDR, *Pädagogisches Forum*, 1, pp. 18–22.

Sander, T. (1993a) Introducing Comparative Information on Educational Systems into European Dimension Modules, *ATEE News*, 40, pp. 21–25.

Sander, T. (1993b) Vergleichende Erziehungswissenschaft oder: Die Pflege nationalistischer Vorurteile, in T. Sander & W.D. Kohlberg (Eds) *Lehrerbildung in Europa – Europäische Lehrerbildung*, pp. 70–77. Osnabrück: Universität Osnabrück – Fachbereich Erziehungs- und Kulturwissenschaften.

Sander, T. (Ed.) (1994) *Current Changes and Challenges in European Teacher Education*. Brussels: RIF Subnetwork 4.

Sander, T. (1995a) [Comparative Perspectives] Do Scottish and German teacher education systems differ? in J. O'Brien (Ed.) *Current Changes and Challenges in European Teacher Education:* Scotland, pp. 66–71. Brussels: COMPARE-TE European Network.

Sander, T. (1995b) Quality Improvement and Austerity Measures in Teacher Education: lessons from Germany, *European Journal of Teacher Education*, 18, pp. 97–113.

Sander, T. (1995c) La destruction progressive de la qualité dans la formation des enseignants, in *Place et rôle du conseil pédagogique dans la construction des compétences professionnelles des enseignants*. Actes du séminaire organisé par l'IUFM de Bretagne et University of Exeter – School of Education, pp. 125–133. Rennes: IUFM de Bretagne.

Sander, T. (1996a) Comparative Perspectives: is modernisation of Turkish and German teacher education systems possible? in E.H. Altun (Ed.) *Current*

Changes and Challenges in European Teacher Education: Turkey, pp. 53–59. Brussels: COMPARE-TE European Network.

Sander, T. (1996b) Dynamics of Teacher Education in Germany in the Context of Social Change, in T. Sander, F. Buchberger, A.E. Greaves & D. Kallós (Eds) *Teacher-Education in Europe: evaluation and perspectives*, 2nd edn, pp. 163–204. Osnabrück: Thematic Network for Teacher Education in Europe.

Sander, T. (1996c) Introduction: problems and origins of the debate on promoting life-long learning strategies for teachers, in T. Sander & J.M. Vez (Eds) *Life-Long Learning in European Teacher-Education*, pp. 9–38. Osnabrück: COMPARE-TE European Network.

Sander, T. (1996d) Market Ideology, Autonomy and Competition between Institutions in the Field of Education, in T. Sander & J.M. Vez (Eds) *Life-Long Learning in European Teacher-Education*, pp. 264–281. Osnabrück: COMPARE-TE European Network.

Sander, T. (1996e) Curriculum Change and Didactics/Curriculum Theory in Germany in a 20-year Perspective, in I. Nilsson (Ed.) *European Curriculum Theory and Research in a Twenty Year Perspective*, Monographs on Teacher Education and Research, Umeå University, vol. 2, pp. 35–72. Umeå: Umeå University.

Sander, T. (1997a) Cold War and the Politics of Comparative Education: the case of divided Germany. Contribution to the American Educational Research Association Conference in Chicago, March (published on the website of TNTEE: http://tntee.umu.se/ and available as microfiche ED 421 379 from ERIC).

Sander, T. (1997b) Comparative Perspectives: professionalisation, citizenship education or what? in J.M. Vez & L. Montero (Eds) *Current Changes and Challenges in European Teacher Education:* Galicia, pp. 205–221. Santiago de Compostela/Osnabrück: COMPARE-TE European Network.

Sander, T. (1999a) The Production of Effective Teachers for Effective Schools through Neoliberal Reforms? Recent Trends in the Development of Teacher Education in Germany, in T. Sander (Ed.) *New Flexibilities in Teacher Education?* Contributions to the symposium of TNTEE Subnetwork A at the European Conference of Educational Research, Frankfurt, September, pp. 33–46. Umeå: TNTEE Publications.

Sander, T. (Ed.) (1999b) *New Flexibilities in Teacher Education?* Contributions to the symposium of TNTEE Subnetwork A at the European Conference of Educational Research, Frankfurt, September. Umeå: TNTEE Publications.

Sander, T. (1999c) Professionalisierung von Lehrern – ein berufskonstituierender Mythos, in C. Solzbacher & C. Freitag (Eds) *Wege zur Mündigkeit – Herausforderungen pädagogischer Professionalisierung*, pp. 18–25. Osnabrück: Rasch Verlag.

Sander, T. (Ed.) (2000a) *Teacher Education in Europe in the late 1990s: evaluation and quality*. Umeå: TNTEE Publications.

Sander, T. (2000b) European Teacher Education in the late 1990s – updating the SIGMA report, in T. Sander (Ed.) *Teacher Education Europe: evaluation and perspectives*, pp. 7–15. Umeå: TNTEE Publications.

Sander, T. (2000c) Recent Trends in Teacher Education in Germany, in T. Sander (Ed.) *Teacher Education Europe: evaluation and perspectives*. Umeå: TNTEE Publications.

Sander, T. & Beernaert, Y. (1994) Introduction: the European dimension of teacher education systems, in T. Sander (Ed.) *Current Changes and Challenges in European Teacher Education*, pp. 9–36. Brussels: RIF Subnetwork 4.

Sander, T., Buchberger, F., Greaves, A.E. & Kallós, D. (1995) Synthesis – SIGMA Project: *Teacher Education in Europe: evaluation and perspectives*, September (published on the website of TNTEE: http://tntee.umu.se).

Sander, T., Buchberger, F., Greaves, A.E. & Kallós, D. (Eds) (1996) *Teacher-Education in Europe: evaluation and perspectives*, 2nd edn. Osnabrück: Thematic Network for Teacher Education in Europe.

Sander, T. & Kohlberg, W.D. (Eds) (1993a) *Lehrerbildung in Europa – Europäische Lehrerbildung*. Osnabrück: Universität Osnabrück – Fachbereich Erziehungs- und Kulturwissenschaften.

Sander, T.& Kohlberg, W.D. (Eds) (1993b) *Die Europäische Dimension der Erziehung*. Zusammenarbeit zwischen Schule, Hochschule, Ausbildungs- und Studienseminar. Osnabrück: Universität Osnabrück – Fachbereich Erziehungs- und Kulturwissenschaften.

Sander, T. & Vez, J.M. (Eds) (1996) *Life-Long Learning in European Teacher-Education*. Osnabrück: COMPARE-TE European Network.

Tapper, T. & Salter, B. (1978) *Education and the Political Order: changing patterns of class control*. London: Macmillan Press.

Willis, P. (1978) *Learning to Labour: how working class kids get working class jobs*. Farnborough: Saxon House.

APPENDIX. Table I. Alternative approaches in comparative methodology.

	Affirmative approaches	Critical approaches
Definition of the subject to be studied	Education systems as reflecting the diversity of cultures (and education policy as having the task to maintain it)	Education and education policy as particular but universal forms of mediation and social control – and of generating opposition to mechanisms of control
Selection of sources of information on the subject	Preference given to the normative legal basis and the normative administrative and political definitions of the tasks and functions of education systems and education policy by governments	Emphasis on the complex and contradictory reality of social and political processes in the field of education and education policy
Methodological options in producing research results	Reading and quoting from texts (simple text reproduction and summary, not even hermeneutical interpretation)	Analysing social processes, including all stakeholders, their actions, attitudes and ideologies, their specific interests, strategies and power relations
Strategies of interpreting research results	Tendency of producing self-fulfilling prophecies confirming the myths of 'diversity' and 'difference'	Focus on understanding fundamental problems in the historical development of social systems through analysing the education sector education and education policy
Basic objectives/ functions of research	Production of affirmative ideologies (Cold War ideologies, European dimension ideologies, nationalist ideologies, regionalist ideologies, etc.)	Radical critique of social systems (the history and impact of class system in education and education policy)

Chaos and Complexity in the Study of School Management

LYNN DAVIES

Introduction

The edge of chaos is where information gets its foot in the door in the physical world, where it gets the upper hand over energy. Being at the transition point between order and chaos not only buys you exquisite control – small input/big change – but it also buys you the possibility that information processing can become an important part of the dynamics of the system. (Lewin, 1993, p. 51)

The origin of this article is work on school effectiveness in contexts of stringency (Harber & Davies, 1997) – which arose out of concerns about the uneasy application of Western management theory to different cultures. Models of leadership, of impartiality, of accountability did not seem to fit many of the countries we knew, where we were interviewing heads about their 'role'. This was partly perhaps because we ourselves were using taken-for-granted 'role theory' of some dubious relevance. We know from contingency theory that headteachers and schools obviously operate in response to a number of different influences and contingencies; but schools in developing countries seemed to have particular sets of tensions and contradictions not always found in Western management literature. We analysed them by going back to Riggs's notion of 'prismatic society' (1964). This theory was developed to understand the conflict between the highly differentiated and relatively autonomous Western modes of organisation imposed at the time of colonialism and the less differentiated indigenous models of organisation, where concerns of family, clan and kin are not easily distinguishable from organisational roles and job descriptions. The analogy is of a fused white light passing through a prism and emerging diffracted as a series of colours. Within the prism there is a point where the diffraction process begins but is not complete. Riggs suggested that developing countries are prismatic in that they contain elements of the traditional fused type of society and the structurally differentiated or 'modern' society. Kinship and religious networks intertwine with the separation of powers demanded by Western administrative theory and models of the democratic state. Riggs termed such societies 'polyfunctional', as the existence of older values will mean that concerns and roles will be dealt with in different and unexpected ways. Translated into education, this typifies the head who publicly espouses objective recruitment or student admission but privately appoints within the family network, or is pushed by local politicians to accept children from high-ranking families. It typifies the student who simultaneously revises for examinations and makes sacrifices to the Gods in order to pass (which of course we all do in one way or another). It typifies the teacher who does their day job but who also has a farm, a number of cattle, or a thriving travel business, and where the activities of each are not necessarily compartmentalised.

Fuller took up a similar theme in his notion of the 'fragile state', a state which lacks deeply rooted legitimacy, and where government must attempt to enhance its shallow authority by appearing 'modern'. This includes promising mass opportunity and building schools with the appearance of a modern and efficient, meritocratic organisation.

> *The district education officer (DEO) faced a painful*
> *predicament when the sobbing teacher called. The teacher's*
> *uncle had just died, some 40 kilometres away, far to the south*
> *of Zomba. But the DEO's only Land Rover was in the*
> *government repair shop, having vanished into that automotive*
> *black hole from which few vehicles emerge (at least in less*
> *than six months' time). The DEO, acting under a peculiar mix*
> *of state regulation and government tradition, was obliged to*
> *move the body to the preferred burial ground. (Distribution of*
> *teacher salaries and textbooks must wait under such a*
> *situation.) As the education ministry's representative, the DEO*
> *must respect this entitlement and protect the government's*
> *credibility. (Fuller, 1991, p. 89)*

The notion of 'fragility' is a useful one in explaining cultures of fear and deference which permeate education systems in many countries. The 'predicaments' of officials, and therefore the lack of predictability in their actions, link well to their positioning in Riggs's prismatic society. However, one of the problems of Riggs's model is that it is two-dimensional, and we now need a more sophisticated schema to explain, predict and improve school organisational life. (String theory apparently conceptualises the universe in 11 dimensions!) This is where I now turn to the potential of chaos and complexity theory.

Chaos and Complexity

I was introduced to chaos and complexity theory by one of my research students, the principal of a college in Peshawar in North-west Pakistan. In attempting to 'turn his school round', he was grappling with all the factorial models of school effectiveness and school improvement, and finding difficulties with these classical reductionist models (Brooke-Smith, 1999). The very point of such models is to reduce to simplicities the complexities of organisational life, so that there can be a singular focus on unitary dimensions such as 'high expectations' or 'home–school links' or 'safe and orderly environment'. Such simplicities did not match the slippery, messy realities of the culture in his college – itself the product of a number of competing histories of Christian missionaries, North West Frontier Province (NWFP) ideologies, patriarchy, examination pressure and powerful local political interests. Robin turned to the emerging science of chaos and complexity both to explain his world and to improve it. We are in the process of dialogue about this, exchanging texts and struggling with the concepts. What follows, therefore, is an early attempt on my part to think about the potential of chaos and complexity theory for comparative educational management.

Like weather systems, there is the realisation that educational organisations may be so complex that they are inherently unpredictable, and their range of developmental possibilities almost incalculable. Chaos theory is characterised by the recognition that one small event can have huge effects elsewhere – the conventional analogy being a butterfly flapping its wings on one side of the world causing a hurricane on the other. Explanatory variables are exquisitely sensitive to very small differences or initial conditions. Such effects are not completely random, but are the product of a highly complex chain of events and non-linear dynamics. There are scientific and social scientific laws of behaviour to explain broad trends, but they cannot predict the behaviour of individuals. The analogy here is the sand pile: when you pour sand on to a surface through a funnel, it will act according to physical principles to form a conical shape. However, at certain times small 'avalanches' will appear, where cascades of sand form and rush to the bottom. That there will be avalanches, and that in the end the sand pile stays the same shape is predictable, but not the path of an individual grain of sand.

This is not a Foucault-like postmodernism, where everything is relative, and the social world is linguistically constructed. The aim of complexity theory is to make sense of a world that exists objectively regardless of our language games, and has a degree of autonomy outside the people who live in it (Price, 1997). Nonetheless, complexity theory offers a more optimistic view of agency than Foucault, where people have difficulty breaking free of totalitarianisms of the modern era, the discursive formations which govern our lives. Subjectivity is not a creation of language, but objectively real, an emergent property of biological and social life. The key to this is the notion of 'self-organising systems'.

At the same time as chaos is the acceptance that life is robust, it is continuously overbalancing and correcting itself, as we do, unconsciously, when walking on two legs. Complex systems like brains and schools need to balance order with disorder, stasis with turbulence, stability with fluidity. This balance point has been termed 'the edge of chaos'. In social organisation, people who are trying to satisfy mutual needs unconsciously organise themselves into an economy through myriad acts of buying and selling – this happens without anyone being in charge or consciously planning it (Waldrop, 1992). In the same way, atoms search for minimum energy by forming complex bonds with others, making molecules. Complexity is a property of a variety of interactions, and the possibility to align themselves into many different configurations. You could have a large number of components, but if there were no possibility to interact, align or organise themselves differently, then this would not be a complex system.

What happens is something called 'emergence' – a combination of elements brings about something that was not there before. Complex adaptive systems do not just have high interaction, but generate outcomes which are not linearly related to initial conditions, and have non-obvious or surprising consequences. Emergence is not measurable, by definition, not causally related in any simple way to individual parts. Culture emerges on a separate level of organisation or abstraction from the individuals, organisations or beliefs that constitute it. But it also emerges *in* each individual through socialisation, interaction and experience. This is why it is so difficult to pin down something called a 'school culture', let alone make recommendations about its ideal transfer from one institution to another.

There is a sort of Darwinian evolution about this; but there is a difference. Darwinian selection is slow, the product of random mutations very gradually gaining ground. In the emergence arising from complex adaptive systems, this can be relatively sudden, a 'spontaneous order'. Apparently, features such as the eye are difficult to explain through random mutation. Systems do not usually evolve themselves into nothingness, but typically add new features on. The mechanism for selection is 'communicative success'. Some types are more flexible than others, and allow for better adjustment to environmental realities. This sounds like the 'survival of the fittest', in social terms, the promotion of the strong or privileged. Yet the point about a self-organising system is that it seeks balance. This leads to the concept of 'rupture': systems branch and bifurcate, but after three bifurcations, most systems will have exploded into far-from-stable non-linearity. For example, we know that the rich get richer; but if income differences become twice, then four times, then eight, then sixteen times greater between rich and poor, chaos, in the form of non-normative behaviour (i.e. riots) is much more likely. The system has to adjust again. Here we see the link to catastrophe theory, where there is abrupt change. This has been applied to war, revolution, prison riots, settlement patterns, as well as curriculum change. Whether one thinks the National Curriculum is a catastrophe is interesting, but it certainly represented an abrupt departure for education in England and Wales.

Between different systems are 'boundaries' and 'boundary conditions', with different types of feedback and feed forward between them. For example, the family produces children; a retail system is devised dependent on the family wanting children's clothes. In turn, a manufacturing industry supplies the retail system. The family could exist without the children's clothes retailer, but not the other way round. One could not have an Office for Standards in Education (OFSTED) without schools to inspect. There is therefore a 'threshold' between the two systems, where change clearly affects the next level, where there is asymmetric dependency. Behaviour depends, therefore, on feedback: does the family still want to buy these clothes? Will a school allow OFSTED in? In non-linear dynamics, there is feedback in which internal or external changes to a system produce an amplifying effect. A yawn, epidemic or lifestyle can spread through a population. Courtney Brown's analysis of US environmental policy includes data on a heap of variables such as environmental degradation, political structure, citizen attitudes and electoral outcomes. It shows how political and policy choices in the USA can produce environmental damage across the globe. Such analyses also show how arms escalation also produces increased tension and the likelihood of war (Eve et al, 1997).

What scientists try to do using these concepts and theories is 'modelling' – as with computers, drawing up complex models of effect and probability. Some phenomena are unstable – the spread of AIDS, the failure of Betamax. Others remain stable – for example, the correlation between educational attainment and income level, between education and birth rate. What is being looked for in terms of policy and policy-making, when moving into using complexity theory, is to identify the point at which a multiplier effect happens. This is the search for the 'gentle action' which has the same multiplier effect positively – for example, to try to solve the problem of crime, to find a sort of policy butterfly. My own interest in democracy and democratic processes in schools would recognise the inherent chaos and complexity in this, as the debate, consultation and multiple participation in decision-making make outcomes inherently unpredictable. Yet there is also interest in sufficient turbulence to bring a system to 'the edge of chaos', and the search for a gentle action which would lead to emergence and a new, better way of organising.

Finally, most complex systems exhibit what mathematicians call attractors, states to which the system eventually settles, depending on the properties of the system (Lewin, 1993). 'Strange attractors' (strange because they are not always explicable to us) are the system's bounded 'preference' for an organisation of micro-states (atoms? people?) into a specific range of macro-states. Research and models have been drawn up, not just in mathematics, but in children's friendships, teenage pregnancies and the 'collapse' of the Soviet Union. It still seems chaotic, but patterns emerge, even if these patterns, while recognisable as patterns, are themselves unpredictable. In a sense, the Soviet Union is still there. None of the populations was destroyed; the towns are still there. Perhaps it did not collapse, but entered a new phase, like ice becomes water.

> *It might be more appropriate to suggest that 'energy' was at last being poured into the Soviet Union in the form of information (as a result of telecommunications and markets). Perhaps they are undergoing a dynamical trial and error in which the process seeks an evolutionary best fit to an environment that would have been unimaginable at the time of the 1917 revolution. (Eve, 1997, p. 272)*

A dynamic system has multiple attractors; cultural evolution would have attractors equivalent to bands, tribes, chiefdoms and states. An education system is itself a strange attractor, but contains within it other attractors, periods of stasis punctuated with periods of change, like sea creatures caught in a whirlpool. We are so accustomed to education systems as permanent features of our society that it takes an effort to remember that they have been (and may remain) a very temporary constellation. They have been with us a shorter time than Coca Cola (invented in 1857), and may indeed be a 'hiccup in history'. Complexity theory enables us to see education systems as particular sets of strange attractors coming together to enable adaptation to new turbulences in society (although we should return to the implied functionalism of such an approach).

Educational Applications

Chaos and complexity start out as models in mathematics and physics; they have started to be applied to social systems and economics. It is interesting to see the application to education and to relatively complex systems such as schools and colleges. Particularly in trying to change or improve a system, one seeks the 'emergence' achieved through positive, non-linear feedback. The obvious example is the human brain, which constantly organises and reorganises billions of neural connections and pathways in order to learn profitably from complex and sometimes confusing experiences. A school cannot reorganise its connections with anything like this speed and sophistication, but it can certainly improve its feedback processes. Basic questions begin with communication: who is communicating with whom, about what; where is information flowing, where is it stored, where is it used, made available, forgotten or destroyed when no longer useful? We are recognising the imperatives of the 'information age' in our information and communications technology (ICT) teaching, and in the use of computers in educational administration, but I would claim that we are still very far behind in the search for qualitative information in educational institutions. We keep records of student results, but not all schools seek and analyse information from students about their everyday school experience and their learning in any systematic manner. The more authoritarian (and less adaptive) a school, the less likely it is to seek student feedback on teaching and learning.

How can a school develop its communication processes, adapt swiftly and positively to change, and organise itself? Three characteristics of complex systems, as pioneered by Holland (1975), can be applied here. The first is *networking*. A system comprises a number of 'agents' working together – in a school this is all the participants. It is important to note that the control of complex adaptive systems is often very dispersed and decentralised. Brains have no master neurone and economies have a frustrating tendency to defy attempts at centralised control. The feedback loops in a school would not all be operating directly to some central point, to the head's office. The ability to use information in order to adapt has to be shared out and dispersed, as with power-sharing. Bentley (1998) argues that the predominant metaphor for the information age is the 'organism' – recognising complexity and interrelatedness as opposed to order and control. He suggests that the successful firms of the 1990s have moved from a vertical to a horizontal division of labour – from hierarchies to networks, from rigid role definitions to flexible webs of collaboration based on individual and group expertise and knowledge. The implications for educational institutions are for fluid and varied ways of both producing and sharing information. This would be information as currently found in syllabi and curriculum, information about the participants themselves and information about the running of the organisation. The imperative of the information age is the democratisation of schools and of learning.

One interesting gap in information in most schools is students knowing about how teachers interact and learn. While teachers may see themselves as a collectivity, having meetings and development days, students rarely observe teachers as a group. They see teachers only one at a time, and have little idea of their alliances and preferred modes of interaction. Still less do they see teachers learning. In an information-rich school, the networks and information exchanges would be highly transparent.

A second characteristic of complex adaptive systems is a number of *levels*, and a constant rearrangement and revision in the light of information. While levels seem clear in a school (pupils, teachers, departments, senior management), these may not correspond to the notion of levels in the scientific world, and it is unlikely that constant rearrangement will find favour or be efficient. The most that can be recommended is to treat all levels as provisional rather than fixed in concrete. The important feature to remember is that of asymmetrical dependency. Just as the retail shop could not function without the family needing clothes, teachers and departments could not function without someone to teach and persons to manage. This may seem an obvious point, but it is interesting how management can come to take on a life of its own, without seeing the need constantly to get feedback on its functioning from the next level. A key component of complex systems is flexibility, and here the use of rotational, elected positions also provides greater adaptability than fixed appointments (Harber & Davies, 1997). Elected members, as in any democracy, have to be alert to feedback signals from their constituents, if they wish to continue in power. Identification of the 'default hierarchies', the weak general rules which operate as internal codes and models, reveals whether they are practical and valuable in an organisation attempting self-criticality. How can new 'default hierarchies' be generated? Who are the agents in this, who are the 'strange attractors' that reshape and recombine the micro-organisms?

A third characteristic is the capacity to *predict the future*. An effective school therefore anticipates changes in the economy, in the government, in England and Wales in the Teacher Training Agency (although even the TTA itself appears to have no internal feedback loops to tell it where it is going). Complex systems themselves apparently constantly make predictions based on their various internal models of the world. These are not passive models, but can come to life and 'execute' in order to produce behaviour in the system. Obviously, efficient organisations try consciously to predict by making a business or marketing plan. Models are also often 'inside the head', as when a shopper tries to imagine how a new couch might look in the living room, or when a timid employee tries to imagine the consequences of telling off his boss (Waldrop, 1992, p. 177). Anything that we call a 'skill' or 'expertise' is an implicit model – or more precisely a huge set of operating procedures that have been inscribed on the nervous system and refined by years of experience.

But, as Waldrop asks, where do the models come from? Who programmes the programmer? Ultimately the answer is no one. This was Darwin's great insight, that an agent can improve on its internal models without any paranormal guidance at all. It simply tries the models out and sees how they work in the real world, and – if it survives the experience – adjusts the model to do better next time. This is the basis of cognition and learning, and hence the hallmark of the 'learning organisation'. Clearly, 'trying the models out' involves an element of risk, and the fearful or highly stable organisation will not reach emergence, not strike the balance between balance and turbulence.

Robin Brooke-Smith very effectively developed the concept of 'mutation':

> *The school perhaps is stable and mature with highly*
> *traditional leaders and deeply conservative stakeholders. All*
> *the agents have become well adapted to each other. There is*
> *little pressure for systemic change or development. However*
> *the agents cannot forever remain static, because of the slow*
> *drip of time and eventually one or more agents may*
> *experience a 'mutation'. Perhaps an ageing head retires and a*
> *new person brings in a cascade of ideas, people and practices.*
> *Maybe a firm is in the same static condition, but there is a*
> *major technological breakthrough. (1999, p. 10)*

New principals such as Robin would no doubt see themselves as a 'mutation', leading to what the Danish physicist, Per Bak, has called 'self-organised criticality'. In Edwardes college, when this mutant head arrived, there were hardly any feedback loops at all, and communication systems had to be built from scratch. It was 'as though we had a computer without proper connections or software'. Wittingly and unwittingly, work for change was based on the three key characteristics of complex adaptive systems: first, building a network of agents with dispersed control; secondly, agents organised in interlocking hierarchies that are constantly being rearranged and shuffled; and thirdly, creating a system that learns by interacting with its environment and predicting the future. The school is building up its routine information collection (record systems, benchmarking, questionnaires to students, parents and staff, consultative committees, use of information in training days, pastoral and tutor group discussion, peer observation of teaching, casual discourse, chats). This may sound obvious in the age of accountability in market-driven systems such as the United Kingdom, but lack – and fear – of such information flows may be a feature of schools in fragile states.

Similarly, in Birmingham we are currently working with the Ministry of Education in Peru on a Department for International Development funded project to enhance the Ministry's capacity, and find that while there is much energy to instigate projects, and a clear organisational structure set out in organograms, there is less emphasis on routine information flows. One department or project team has little idea what another is doing; minutes are not kept of meetings; progress is not disseminated across the organisation. There is an official attempt at flexibility, keeping many of the staff on short-term contracts, but this flexibility is perhaps in the wrong arena, as one needs organisational adaptation rather than individual uncertainty. Departments become fixed in acronyms (PLANMED, ACAA) and even the participants may not remember what they stand for. Once hierarchies are established, and there is a permanent appointed head of a department, it becomes more difficult to ask the uncomfortable question of whether a department is needed, or could be merged, or disbanded.

The implication of chaos and complexity theory would seem to fit with a notion I have developed before, that of a school as a research park, and the principal as senior researcher (Davies, 1994). The role of the head is less directly to 'manage' and more to facilitate the information flows, the feedback loops, the research that will enable the organisation to survive and emerge. Students in this model are seen as researchers, not just of knowledge and skills for their own learning, but of the institution itself. Teachers actively search out as well as intuitively use feedback from student-researchers, using formal and informal evaluations of their teaching, collecting and analysing students' targets for learning and their evaluations of whether these targets have been achieved. Pupil evaluations of teachers are now routinely built into staff appraisal in countries such as Austria. Saying that teachers and students are researchers does not mean the traditional university idea of 'doing a piece of research' (although that may be part of their learning), but is more akin to the notion of the 'reflective practitioner' who seeks both positive and negative feedback and is willing to change and adapt as a result. It is moving out of one's 'comfort zone' to engage in new interactions, attempt new modes of operating.

Institutions need to develop memories. History and tradition are far more powerful determinants of how a society is organised than economic or political 'forces' that nineteenth-century social theory reduced to social 'laws' (Turner, 1997). Behaviour is determined by memory of past interactions, with a 'feed forward' to control the next set of interactions. This is not to say that organisations should remain the same, or should claim the right to act in certain ways because of 'culture' or 'tradition', but that there should be a constant process of analysing whether or why things worked in the past and what else might be needed in the light of predictions about the future.

A particularly appropriate aspect of this from complexity theory is that of 'rules'. Complex adaptive systems hone the efficiency of their rules as they adapt towards the edge of chaos. 'The population of rules is seen to move toward a region on the space of all rules that marks the boundary between chaotic and non-chaotic rules' (Packard, quoted in Lewin, 1993). The edge of chaos is where maximum fitness of purpose emerges, and in schools a re-examination of the traditional school rules (uniform? no talking?) would enable greater fitness to the current age and to the locality. The growing use of conventions on human rights and children's rights as principles for behaviour by teachers and students, to replace more surface traditional prohibitions, could be an example of a better fit and sophistication. Schools can 'benchmark' themselves not just in achievement terms but also against sets of values.

Conclusion

The question that arises from all of this is whether chaos and complexity theory when applied to education is just a valuable metaphor, or whether it has real explanatory and prescriptive power. It is a hugely intricate field, with a growing literature and whole websites devoted to it. But for social institutions, is it just a useful way of confirming existing wish lists about democracy, networking, or the information age? Is it simply a return to a functionalist view of society as gradually making progress towards some higher order of evolution? I think it does have more potential than nice analogies and parallel universes. It explains war and maladaptation as well as the intricate balances in ant colonies. (Incidentally, ants are at a greater degree of social evolution than humans, and are more skilled at non-violent conflict resolution.) If it can explain the collapse of civilisations, it can certainly help explain 'failing schools'.

The most tantalising – but currently salutary – aspect of a foray into complexity theory is the realisation of how little we know about communication and the transmission of information in complex adaptive systems. The brain is not just 'a computer made of meat'. There is certainly a place for intuition. There is a place for feelings, and chemistry.

> *Survival has to do with gathering information about the environment, and responding appropriately ... bacteria do that, by responding to the presence or absence of certain chemicals and by moving. Trees communicate chemically too. Computation is a fundamental property of complex adaptive systems ... any complex adaptive system can compute; that's the key point. You don't have to have a brain to process information in the way I'm talking about it.*
> *(Lewin, 1993, p. 138)*

We communicate through music, for example, but have little idea of how the information actually flows. 'Think of musical melodies; they are messages that we feel we understand, yet we are quite incapable of saying what they mean. The existence of music is a permanent intellectual scandal, but it is just one scandal among many others' (Ruelle, 1993, p. 135). If we go back to our prismatic societies, it could be that these, rather than being a 'problem', are simply using a more complex information system which incorporates both 'rational' and 'subjective' feedback.

What does all this tell us about comparative school effectiveness research? First, there is the confirmation that externally imposed solutions do not work. For emergence to happen, the organisation has to be self-adapting, self-critical and self-balancing. The only time where external effects impinge is in the sense of the organisation learning from 'environmental' factors: either the imminent presence of OFSTED which would cause closure and therefore has to be entered into the equation as a threat to stability, or as a deliberate attempt at learning from other systems which would be part of a feedback loop to kick-start a process of experimentation. It is not clear from the biological or mathematical analyses how far complex systems actually peer at other systems in order consciously to adapt their own, and how far there is just a continuous process of trial and error to find the optimum adaptability and emergence. Does the brain have anything else comparable to look at? It would seem that in human organisation, and given the way we can use brain and language to refine our consciousness, it could not do harm to benefit from the research of others, even if this is not how animal or plant evolution works. But complex systems have to internalise new ideas and actively incorporate them, or the precarious balance between stability and turbulence recedes.

Little & McLaughlin (1993) observe from their research on teachers' work that context matters, and locally shared interpretations of practice triumph over abstract principles; also that the greater the appreciation for context specificity, the less categorical statements appear to be a sound basis for policy. They recognise that by emphasising the complexity of within-school contexts, they risk the impression that complexity is chaotic, and that schools need more regulation, not less. But patterned complexity feeds the emphasis towards a management style that is unfamiliar and unpractised, demanding risk-taking and constant learning.

In terms of aid policy, then, chaos and complexity theory have much to teach us about the failure of externally imposed conditionalities and Western ideas. Each system is unique in its potential interactions, and uniform prescriptions about effectiveness and efficiency will have unforeseen consequences, depending on how agents within a system realign to meet this new environmental threat – or opportunity. Returning to our research on effective schools in contexts of stringency, we contrasted the schools – and their principals and teachers – who accepted financial or cultural constraints with fatalism with those who used creative accounting, vired funds, milked the community and sensitively adapted to the exigencies of the local environment. Similarly, we contrasted fearful systems where democracy was mere rhetoric with education systems such as Colombia that took the decision to instigate whole system reform and experiment with devolution of decision-making about educational outcomes to schools, teachers and students.

Comparative education would have something to gain from the application of chaos and complexity theory. It could explain failures of innovation, resistance and 'stuck' schools as well as understanding the spark that sets off the student riot. The notion of attractors would explain the surface similarity of schools and classrooms across the world, while recognising that each system settles into a unique pattern. The policy and consultancy implications are not to impose prescription, but to encourage self-criticality; to help develop the questions, not to answer them; to aid a school's own information processing and response to its environment, not supply the information. It is to help an institution move towards the edge of chaos.

References

Bentley, T. (1998) *Learning beyond the Classroom: education for a changing world*. London: Routledge.

Brooke-Smith, R. (1999) Complexity and Information Feedback Systems in Schools and Colleges: some lessons from Pakistan, paper presented at the International Congress for School Effectiveness and Improvement (ICSEI) 1999 Conference, San Antonio, Texas, January.

Davies, L. (1994) *Beyond Authoritarian School Management: the challenge for transparency*. Nottingham: Education Now.

Eve, R. (1997) Afterword: So Where are We Now? in R. Eve, S. Horsfall & M. Lee (Eds) *Chaos, Complexity and Social Theory*. Thousand Oaks: Sage.

Eve, R., Horsfall, S. & Lee, M. (Eds) *Chaos, Complexity and Social Theory*. Thousand Oaks: Sage.

Fuller, B. (1991) *Growing Up Modern: the Western state builds Third World schools*. London: Routledge.

Harber, C. & Davies, L. (1997) *School Management and Effectiveness in Developing Countries*. London: Cassell.

Holland, J. (1975) *Adaptation in Natural and Artificial Systems*. Ann Arbor: University of Michigan Press.

Lewin, R. (1993) *Complexity: life on the edge of chaos*. London: Phoenix.

Little, J. & McLaughlin, M. (Eds) (1993) *Teachers' Work: individuals, colleagues and contexts*. New York: Teachers' College Press.

Riggs, F. (1964) *Administration in Developing Countries: the theory of prismatic society*. Boston: Houghton Mifflin.

Price, B. (1997) The Myth of Postmodern Science, in R. Eve, S. Horsfall & M. Lee (Eds) *Chaos, Complexity and Social Theory*. Thousand Oaks: Sage.

Turner, F. (1997) Foreword, in R. Eve, S. Horsfall & M. Lee (Eds) *Chaos, Complexity and Social Theory*. Thousand Oaks: Sage.

Waldrop, M. (1992) *Complexity: the emerging science at the edge of order and chaos*. London: Penguin.

System Supervisors and Evaluators Compared

CLIVE HOPES

Introduction: objectives

In this article some of the findings of the project 'The Assessment, Evaluation and Assurance of Quality in Schools in the European Union', which was carried out in selected member states in 1995 and 1996, are discussed. It was originally presented and discussed in a seminar at the University of Bristol on the topic of 'Education Professionals Compared', which was the last of a series of Economic and Social Research Council (ESRC) Research Seminars. Three countries – Denmark, Germany and the Netherlands – were chosen to compare various professionals engaged in system assessment and evaluation.

The project had its origins in previous work carried out from 1989 until 1991 on the related theme of 'School Inspectorates in the Member States of the European Community'. The latter study was published in a series of country analyses (Hopes, 1991). Both projects were directed and coordinated from the *Deutsches Institut für Internationale Pädagogische Forschung* in Frankfurt-am-Main and were carried out with the cooperation of the Chief Inspectors of Schools in the several member states. These initiatives were supported by subventions from the Commission of the European Union. The intention behind this second project was to bring together advisers, inspectors and school supervisors to discuss, analyse and document their field of work at an international level.

The project was also motivated by the need to demonstrate the complexities of trying to understand foreign systems, particularly at levels beyond structures, the curriculum and teaching. During my work in other projects it became clear to me that too many international comparisons seemed to be made only through culture-bound eyes of the observer. It seemed that many persons assume that most countries have inspectorates which work roughly the same as in their own country.

Another objective of the seminars was to develop reading materials for use in professional development programmes for assessors and evaluators as a contribution towards modifying attitudes by reflecting on practices in other systems. During the seminars there was an obvious advantage of having peer pressure applied to foreign colleagues. Their familiarity with some of the problems involved served as a brake on those who might otherwise have thought they had an ideal system to sell.

It was not a comparative education study, but the basic information gathered should be of assistance to those wishing to do more research at a deeper level and avoid the dangers of interpreting what they see only through the filter of their own educational culture. The final Report and Supplement, presented to the European Commission in 1996, have been merged into a book (Hopes, 1997 [English]; 1998 [German]).

Terminology, Definitions and Delimitation

Terminology

When working in international groups, it is not only the language barrier that can hinder understanding. Certain words are unclear or ambiguous even in just one language. From the outset of the project the words 'assessment' and 'evaluation' in English were given a strict interpretation, which enabled the group to use each word in one special sense.

Definitions

Assessment. An assessment means an estimate, an approximation or an opinion in general terms of a situation in a system (system assessment) or of a person (personnel assessment). Some consultants in the project used the words 'audit' and 'appraisal'. These terms were described in the context of their texts, but, in general, these words can usually be expressed respectively in terms of either an assessment or an evaluation.

Evaluation. Evaluation was defined by reference to the definition of the verb 'to evaluate', being 'to find the numerical expression for, to reckon up, to ascertain the amount of, to express in terms of the known'. Evaluation, the action of evaluating, became, for the purpose of our discussions, a concept which would place absolute values on a judgement. For example, 'good', 'bad', 'passed', 'failed', and marks such as '1' to '5' or 'A' to 'F' are familiar ways of putting value on work done. These kinds of evaluation can also apply to a situation in a system (system evaluation) or to a person (personnel evaluation).

External assessment and external evaluation. External assessment was defined as meaning an assessment of (i) schools in a system or (ii) parts of that system or (iii) an assessment of personnel in schools by persons employed within the education system but not holding a position inside a school. Similarly, external evaluation was defined in the same way.

Internal assessment and internal evaluation. Internal assessment was defined as meaning an assessment of (i) a school or (ii) part of a school or (iii) an assessment of a person by personnel working within that school. Similarly, internal evaluation was defined in the same way.

School system external assessments or evaluations. These were defined as assessments and evaluations made by employees within a school education service but not employed within the school being visited. This definition would include experts organised within a national school education system although they might enjoy considerable autonomy, for example, national school inspectors, but it would not include independent firms employed by school systems whose credentials are not specifically educational, for example, management consulting firms.

Delimitation

The project concentrated on system assessment or evaluation rather than personnel assessment or evaluation.

Purposes of External Assessments and Evaluations

Five Aspects

In reviewing approaches to external assessment and evaluation, I suggest that at least five aspects need to be considered:

- first, approaches which are needed in cases of poor performance of individuals and institutions;
- secondly, controlling operations, which are needed to ensure conformity to norms or to identify satisfactory and unsatisfactory performance. These are coupled with mechanisms to ensure the implementation of methods to improve the situation;
- thirdly, assessment and evaluation as a normal developmental routine of a profession or organisation which reviews its own good, satisfactory or unsatisfactory performance in order to adapt, change, or improve a situation according to new needs or objectives;
- fourthly, as personnel employed in system-wide overseeing operations, inspectors, supervisors and advisers are often used to gather general information about the school system either for their own specific needs or on behalf of the Minister; and
- fifthly, the increasing awareness of the need for more accountability.

Disciplinary correction. Irrespective of the title inspector, school supervisor or adviser, when a special intervention is needed on isolated, disciplinary grounds, all systems make use of these experts to advise the appropriate authorities of their professional opinion on which a decision can be taken about a particular individual or institution. This theme was not part of our work.

Evaluation and control. In the most serious form of evaluation, blame, fault or negative criticism is attached to a school. Terminology such as 'weaknesses' and 'strengths' is used, balancing the negative criticisms with comments on positive aspects of the situation. The main emphasis is on the evaluator's perceptions. Sanctions are available, such as the threat of the withdrawal of funding, to force the responsible institution to take corrective action. It creates a threatening environment and is the cause of considerable anxiety. Conventional forms of inspection have inevitably evoked these responses. In the current economic climate the need to trim budgets is paramount and it is not surprising that there has been a shift towards the 'evaluation and control' model.

Assessment and development. Assessment for adjustment and development is a normal process carried out within school systems to monitor progress during a school year or over a period of years. An example would be the introduction of a new syllabus or a new organisational form which, after a trial period, may require additions or amendments. A more comprehensive approach within a school is an organisational development initiative involving the whole staff in assessment. In such assessments the apportionment of blame and an emphasis on failure are out of place. This kind of assessment takes place in a motivating environment where internal or external advisers within a school system make constructive suggestions to assist those working directly on an innovation or improvement.

Monitoring the system, policy-making support and policy implementation. In addition to their capability to spread information about good practice, in many countries, advisers, supervisors and inspectors are in an ideal position to carry out surveys on behalf of the Minister, the Chief Inspector or the Chief Adviser. They are not evaluative, but provide information about a situation or problem area which gives useful information for policy-making and possible action.

Accountability. Forms of accountability have been evident for many decades in European schools, but the methods for assuring good quality have not always been efficient or effective. In recent years, economic constraints, shrinking budgets and, in some cases, dissatisfaction with the performance of schools have all contributed to demands for more accountability.

The Spectrum of External Assessment and Evaluation Strategies

The second and third aspects of assessment and evaluation should not be seen as a dichotomy but rather as a spectrum, where parts of each merge with each other to greater or lesser degrees. The organisational climates in which these two processes take place are clearly very different and they strongly influence the relationship which is developed between all parties concerned.

Overview of Approaches in Selected Countries

In this section an overview of three countries is given – Denmark, the Netherlands and Germany – demonstrating strongly contrasting approaches to supervising and evaluating operations.

Management, Organisation, Evaluation and Assessment of Schools in Denmark. Upper Secondary Schools (Gymnasien) in Denmark

Management and organisation structure. The public upper secondary schools (*gymnasien*) are run and financed by the county councils which:

- establish, run or close down schools in accordance with securing capacity big enough to admit all qualified applicants;
- fix the grants for the operational expenses and investments of the schools;
- appoint headteachers after having obtained the opinion of the Ministry on the qualifications of the applicants; and
- appoint and dismiss teachers and other members of staff on the recommendation of the headteacher.

The Danish Parliament lays down the overall targets and framework for the upper secondary level. Curriculum and examination regulations are issued by the Ministry of Education, which is also responsible for controlling the quality of education through quality development projects, examination papers drawn up at the central level, general written guidelines, and advisory services.

The management of the advisory services is organised centrally from the Advisers' Section in the Department of General Upper Secondary Education in the Ministry of Education. It is responsible for 125 schools (*gymnasien*) and consists of a full-time Head of Division (Academic) and a Head of Division (Law), who report to the Director. There are nine other advisers in the ministry, six of whom are part-time and spend the remainder of their working time as teachers in schools. Each of these ministry advisers has a different field of responsibility such as in-service training, pilot projects, international relations, examinations, the Faroe Islands, Greenland, school visits, Quality

Development Project, etc. The 29 national subject advisers report to the Head of Division (Academic).

Approaches to evaluation and assessment of upper secondary schools (gymnasien) in Denmark. Upper secondary schools (*gymnasien*) have two kinds of external monitoring. Firstly, there is a system of monitoring whereby all subjects are monitored by advisers, who are practising teachers with a teaching workload of between one- and two-thirds of their time and who visit five or six schools per year to observe and assess the quality of teaching in their subject. At the central level there are a few full-time advisers who visit schools and observe general school aspects. During the visits by both these types of adviser, time is set aside to discuss their observations with the teachers and to listen to teachers' and headteachers' remarks about curricula and other matters. Reports are made to the head of the section in the Ministry responsible for the advisory service on their observations and on surveys they may be required to make.

The second approach takes place within the Quality Development Project whereby one school (until 1995 two schools) is visited by a group of advisers who assess all aspects of the operation of the school. The evaluation team spends 4 days at the school and makes observations of the following aspects: teaching, management, administration, students, and ways of cooperation. All these elements of the school are analysed, evaluated and described in a report. The report contains descriptions, emphasises strong and weak sides of the school and gives advice for ways of improving and changing. Aspects for improvement are drawn to the school's attention, but there is no intention of comparing schools on an evaluative scale as in England. The school has the opportunity to comment on a draft of the report, which is then printed and sent out to all upper secondary institutions for inspiration. Its purpose is to disseminate ideas of good practice gleaned from the visit. On the basis of the report, the school works out an action programme. After a year the evaluation team returns to the school for a 1-day visit, to ascertain the amount of change and improvement.

Primary and Lower Secondary Schools (6–16 years) (Folkeskole) in Denmark

Management and organisation structure. Primary and lower secondary schools (*folkeskole*) are governed by the national state law on these schools and the Minister of Education lays down regulations pertaining to them. However, the responsibility for the *folkeskole* rests with over 140 municipal councils.

The schools are run by school boards, each consisting of five or seven parents elected by and among the parents, two representatives of the teachers and other staff, and two pupil representatives elected by and among the pupils. The headteacher of the school serves as the secretary to the board.

A school board has a number of responsibilities, amongst which the most important ones are the responsibility to lay down the principles for the activities of the school, approve the budget of the school, submit recommendations to the municipal council regarding the appointment of headteachers and teachers and draw up a proposal for the curricula of the school for submission to the municipal council. Given these responsibilities, each school board takes part in different ways in assessing the school as an institution. Over and above this formal system of parental influence, there is also an informal assessment from the parents through close cooperation between the parents and the teachers, coordinated by class teachers.

Approaches to evaluation and assessment of primary and lower secondary schools (folkeskole) in Denmark. There is no formal system of external evaluation or assessment of primary and lower secondary schools in Denmark. This is partly explained by the closeness of the school to the municipal administration and the local community, including the parents. The schools are supported by district advisers who do not have assessing or evaluating functions, although occasionally a larger municipality, such as Copenhagen, might mount an evaluation study. Central advisers, working in the national Ministry, do not intervene in the schools, because, as I have said, each primary and lower secondary school (*folkeskole*) is controlled by the municipality and not by the central Ministry. Central advisers are engaged more in national matters such as curriculum development.

Management, Organisation, Evaluation and Assessment of schools in the Netherlands

Management and organisation structure. Dutch education is rather unique because of the existence of state and non-state education on an equal financial footing. Over two-thirds of Dutch primary and secondary schools are non-state institutions, founded by private foundations and governed by non-state school boards. Both types of school are financed entirely by the Government on the basis of the same payment formulae. The constitutional freedom of denomination and content of education offers immense opportunities to groups of people to have their children receive the education that conforms to their ideals and convictions. This freedom of education prescribes that the individual school will shape the education provided under its responsibility.

Responsibility for the provision of education rests with the competent educational authorities (school boards) working within a framework set out by the Government by means of several education acts. The school boards are responsible for evaluating education at the school level in order to maintain or to improve the quality of education on the one hand and to inform parents and students about quality matters on the other.

It stands to reason that, because of the autonomy of these schools, any measures taken by the Government in the field of education are looked upon critically by schools, school boards and parents, all the more so if such measures tend to enter the domain of content and form of education. Yet, conversely, this very autonomy of the schools also implies that the school boards must be accountable for the financial support they receive. Hence the need for an effective inspectorate.

Approaches to evaluation and assessment of schools in the Netherlands. The inspectorate in the Netherlands is autonomous through a contractual arrangement between the Minister and the Senior Chief Inspector of Schools. It has defined its tasks as follows:

- supervising compliance with statutory regulations (supervisory task);
- keeping up to date with the state of education, among other things by means of school visits (evaluating task);
- promoting the development of education by means of consultations with competent authorities and school staff, and with district or local governments (stimulating task); and
- reporting to and advising the Minister, either on request or on its own initiative (reporting task).

The inspectorate went through a major reform at the beginning of the 1990s and two main approaches to evaluation and assessment can be identified.

First, a system of evaluation was introduced, made on selected topics each year using scientific methods. A sample of schools is selected for investigation over a period of 2 years. New topics are started in another sample of schools every 2 years. These evaluations use scientific methods, which are designed by a research staff. On the one hand, these evaluations provide the Senior Chief Inspector and the Minister with concrete evidence on particular aspects of the school system. On the other hand, through the findings, the schools are provided with a 'mirror' in which to see outsiders' evaluations of their performance in those areas. School boards can then use those indicators to stimulate the drive for improvements in the schools. Moreover, the old evaluation forms can be used by schools to make their own internal evaluations. Inspectors I have met in the Netherlands say that they feel more satisfied with this first kind of evaluation, instead of the previous traditional method of visiting classrooms and simply talking to teachers about their teaching methods.

Secondly, in addition to the purely evaluative operations, supervisory control is maintained over the schools through the inspectors' duty to check compulsory documents like the School Plan and the Annual Report of each school for which they are responsible and to assure by assessment that the actual performance of the school conforms to these documents. It is also obligatory for the inspectors to visit annually every school in the group of schools for which they are responsible.

During the period 1996–99, the inspectorate had an important task of evaluating a new type of basic secondary education (12–15 year-olds), which was introduced in 1993. The evaluation of the implementation of this type of schooling was carried out by the inspectorate because it was capable of independently evaluating the state of education, since it does not participate in, nor bear joint responsibility for, the formulation of the government policy.

The 'Plan for the evaluation of basic secondary education' was drawn up by the Inspectorate and consisted of nine evaluation questions regarding school organisational aspects, the teaching–learning process and pupil performances. The questions were as follows.

- Do the educational content and the format of the teaching–learning process meet the characteristics of good education?
- Is there a favourable school climate?
- Is there proper guidance for all the pupils during the first years of secondary education?
- Are the pupils sufficiently prepared for the choice of studies and career?
- Are the results obtained in the first years of secondary education good?
- Is the school organisation aimed at adequately realising the educational content, the teaching–learning process and the results?
- Have the schools made arrangements to achieve a proper alignment between primary education and the first stage?
- Have the schools made arrangements to achieve a proper alignment between the teaching programme in the years in which basic secondary education is realised and teaching in the upper forms/secondary stage?

During the school year 1996–97, the school organisational aspects – school climate, school policy, provisions for pupils with special needs and educational and vocational orientation – were evaluated. The teaching–learning process was dealt with in the school year 1997–98. In order to be able to do this, the Dutch inspectorate developed an evaluation framework comprising 14 standards; developed instruments (forms for observations, discussions and oral and written survey); analysed textbooks; and set up in-service training for inspectors and staff. The inspectorate was attempting to achieve a number of objectives, each having a different purpose. In some cases, it carryied out both evaluation and assessment simultaneously. For example, during 1997–98 the teaching–learning process was evaluated in 120 schools by teams of

6–10 inspectors per school. The schools were to receive a written report. This was to specify the school's strong and weak points; also it was to contain recommendations to improve the weak points. Secondly, the inspectorate was making a system assessment for the purpose of policy-making.

The aim of the intended assessment and evaluation was to create possibilities for a social and political discussion on the desired further introduction and development of basic secondary education in the first stage of secondary education.

Management, Organisation, Evaluation and Assessment of Schools in Germany. A Federal System

Under the constitutional division of powers in the German Constitution, legal competence for school education is assigned to the individual states. The Federal Government only has powers allocated in the field of university and other tertiary education and in some aspects of technical and vocational education at the upper secondary school level (ages 16–19). As there are 16 states, there are many different organisational structures of school systems in Germany, although the same types of school are to be found in each state. Each state has its own school law and regulations and other laws relevant for other authorities or persons having a legal interest in schooling, such as district authorities and parents. In general, the state government regulates *internal* matters relating to schools, such as the curriculum, teaching materials and the employment of teachers. *External* matters, such as the construction and maintenance of buildings, and the employment of non-teaching personnel (caretakers, cleaners, secretarial staff, etc.) are the responsibility of district authorities. (In practice, districts receive subventions from the state to assist them with this financial burden).

In most states, except the city states of Berlin, Hamburg and Bremen, governmental administration is divided into three levels: central, regional and district. (The number of regions in each state varies according to the size of the state.) It follows that there is no *national* school system. However, the 16 states try to keep their school systems similar through the national *Ständige Konferenz der Kultusminister der Länder in der Bundesrepublik Deutschland* (the Permanent Council of the Ministers of Education). Even so, their decisions have to be unanimous and their intentions still have to be ratified and approved by their own state parliaments.

As there is no national system, there is neither a school inspectorate visiting the schools nationally nor a higher, central national inspectorate over regional inspectorates, such as that found in France (*inspecteurs généraux*), in Spain (*alta inspección del estado*) or in Britain (Her Majesty's Inspectors). It is not a decentralised system, but a federal system with rather highly centralised state school systems. Nevertheless, inspectors, principals and teachers in all states are paid according to the same national salary scales laid down for civil servants, depending on their position and seniority.

In spite of the multitude of systems, general practice tends to be similar, but significant differences do arise due to great differences in the political philosophy prevailing traditionally in each of the several states. The approach of the Christian Democrats (CDU) to schooling is very different from the Social Democrats (SPD). For example, organisation of schools strongly differs between Bremen (traditionally, SPD) and Bavaria (traditionally Christian Social Union [CSU], and aligned with the CDU). These basic differences also lead to divergences in the practice of school supervision (*Schulaufsicht*).

Moreover, differences can be identified in the general organisation of *Schulaufsicht* in each state. For example, school supervisors for the academic schools (*Gymnasien*) are located in some states at the central (state) level, in others at the regional level and, in another, even at the district level. Similarly, supervisors for the semi-academic schools (*Realschulen*) and non-academic schools (*Hauptschulen*) may be located organisationally at regional or district level.

In Germany, school supervision civil service officers (*Schulaufsichtsbeamte*) have the function of inspection as part of their general duties, but they are not inspectors in the sense found in other countries; rather, they are overseers of the administrative system. In the past two decades their work has become more and more oriented towards administration, but previously, as '*Schulrat*', (literally school adviser, but in reality very much the Inspector), they were seen more in the schools as controllers and advisers to teachers. Most of the school supervisors are drawn from the ranks of teachers, but a few at the district, regional and central governmental level have different backgrounds, e.g. a legal qualification, with no experience in schools. These civil servants assist in the interpretation and implementation of the myriad regulations in the German systems. Many of the educational school supervisors are dissatisfied with the growth of their administrative duties and would far prefer to have more time for what was previously their role as school inspector and adviser.

State Organisation and Functions

The states are organised into two or three administrative levels – Central, Regional and District, or Central and District, generally according to the size of the state. School supervision officers are employed at these levels in a hierarchical organisational system. Their functions are determined by the laws and regulations applying to school supervision.

227

A supervisor has responsibility for three branches of supervision, which are made up as follows.

- Subject area supervision (*Fachaufsicht*) ensures that the freedom teachers have in interpreting curricula guidelines is not abused. Changes and non-obligatory parts of the curriculum devised by teachers have to be approved.
- Service supervision (*Dienstaufsicht*) is overseeing that principals and teachers carry out all the responsibilities relating to their duties.
- Legal supervision (*Rechtsaufsicht*) relates to the duty of a supervisor to ensure that all laws and regulations are properly observed.

Supervisors also have to see that the administration and maintenance of the schools is carried out by the district authorities according to the established regulations. They are empowered to intervene at any time and inform themselves about matters relating to the schools and to visit lessons. Representatives can participate in school committee meetings of all teachers' and parents' formal meetings. They can also visit subject area meetings of teachers within the school or even order such a meeting to take place. They are responsible for coordinating inter-school cooperation, for the transfer of knowledge to teachers about new findings in subject areas and educational science and for implementing new approaches to fulfilling the educational mission of the school.

Internal hierarchy. There is a hierarchy of positions moving up from the district to the ministerial level, although the seniority of officers or a special position of responsibility (such as head of a district school office) may result in a senior officer at the district or regional level being at the same salary level as a junior ministry officer, although the name of the rank is different.

Specialisation. Supervisors are drawn from the ranks of teachers in the various school types at the primary and secondary levels and become supervisors for the type of school from which they originate. At the secondary level, schools are differentiated by the way young persons are channelled into different school types at the age of 10 years: *Gymnasium, Realschule,* or *Hauptschule.*

Secondary supervisors are subject area specialists, but primary supervisors are generalists. Moreover, at the secondary levels there are divisions according to the type of secondary school for which the supervisor is responsible (academic, vocational, and non-academic). A possibility for a supervisor to go into a different school type would only occur in those areas where there are comprehensive schools (*Gesamtschulen*), but one must bear in mind that only about 6% of pupils are in such schools in Germany.

When a supervisor has to visit a teacher with a subject area specialisation other than that of the supervisor, the supervisor will invite a teacher-adviser to assist him or her in making an assessment.

In view of the supervisors' many other formal tasks, it can be seen that the duties of the German *Schulaufsichtsbeamte* are a combination of those of an inspector and an education officer or of the pedagogical and administration inspectors found in France. In comparison with most other member states of the European Community, the supervisor does not carry the title of inspector and, indeed, it would be inappropriate. The Schulaufsichtsbeamte is an education officer with inspection as part of his or her duties.

Responsibilities

The evaluation of teachers. When teachers have completed their first phase of training at university and have passed their First State Examination (*Erste Staatsprüfung*), they become Probationary Teachers (*Referendare*). For an ensuing period of time (approximately 18 months), they undertake limited responsibilities in a school. During this period a supervisor visits them and makes assessments. At the end of the period the probationer takes a further examination – the Second State Examination (*Zweite Staatsprüfung*), which consists of written and oral examinations. Additionally, the teacher is visited formally by a supervisor and is evaluated on his or her suitability to become a permanent teacher. If successful, the new teacher will have yet a further period (about 1–2 years) as a probationary civil servant and, if, in the opinion of the supervisor and the school principal, this period is deemed satisfactory, the teacher becomes a civil servant for life.

A supervisor also has the responsibility of intervening in the event of a teacher defaulting in service responsibilities or, in a subject area, in deviating from the prescribed, but generous, limits of curriculum guidelines. Similarly, the supervisor oversees a principal's behaviour and will intervene if a situation in a school has become unsatisfactory due to a principal's shortcomings.

Supervisors in Germany do not work in teams, although, in special cases, such as observing a probationary teacher in a final examining visit, the principal may be present.

The non-evaluation of schools. Unlike practices in some other countries, schools are not inspected as institutions as a whole. Perhaps the reason for this is the assumption that, as the schools are so well governed by laws and regulations, they are assumed to be running equally well. A similar phenomenon is the absence of comparison or checking of standards as a regular function of supervision. Although supervisors do check teachers' examination standards when they set certain types of examination, e.g. the *Abitur*, the certificate of successful completion of the academic school, no effort is made to check the comparability of marking standards between neighbouring schools or schools in different cities and rural areas. The reason given is that the regulations set the standards. Questions of reliability and validity do not seem to be perceived as a problem.

The frequency and intensity of inspection visits. The frequency of inspection visits varies from state to state. In one state one finds the practice of visiting teachers every 4 years until they reach their fiftieth birthday, whereas in another state, teachers will only be visited for special reasons, e.g. a complaint against a teacher or in the case of a teacher seeking promotion in rank or to another position, such as principal. In many states, teachers rarely see a supervisor in their classroom after they have become permanent civil servants. The practice of using instruments to evaluate teachers varies from state to state. Occasionally, reports on the situation of a school are made by a supervisor to provide a general background when considering the suitability of new appointments to a school, but these should not be confused with a thorough school inspection for evaluation purposes. Checklists may also be used in the procedure for appointing heads of schools.

When a supervisor visits a teacher, he or she will take the opportunity to speak to a number of teachers in that particular subject area and to discuss general problems. The infrequency of supervisors' visits tends to blunt the effectiveness of any advice the supervisor might wish to offer in view of the lack of sufficient time to follow up such efforts. On the other hand, the visits do give the supervisor an opportunity to 'be advised'.

The ratio of supervisor to teachers is about 1:350. In practice this is often more, because one planned position may be occupied by two half-time teachers.

The contact a supervisor has with pupils, apart from seeing them in classroom visits, is very limited. Similarly, contacts with parents are rare, except in occasionally counselling parents who may wish to ask a supervisor about a particular problem or in the special case of children with disabilities being referred to schools catering for the handicapped.

The amount of time spent in talking to a teacher after an inspection is rather short, unless, in the case of probationary teachers, a more thorough discussion is warranted. Usually, the supervisor will take the opportunity of talking with the principal to discuss general matters relating to the school.

The consequences of visits to teachers. In the case of teachers performing unsatisfactorily, a supervisor will make suggestions about how improvements could be achieved and might recommend in-service training. A further visit on a future occasion would be planned. The influence of the supervisor in encouraging school teaching staffs to work more on pedagogical themes in the whole school committee and subject area committees can be of benefit to the school as a whole. On the other hand, as the inspections are more teacher-oriented (personnel evaluation) rather than teaching-oriented (system evaluation), the consequences for pupils are not observable.

Other Educational Responsibilities

Advising. A supervisor has a broad range of contacts, which enables him or her to be able to advise the teachers about sources for assistance to pupils in career counselling and special assistance from the psychological service. The supervisor has a key role in selecting new school principals and in allocating teachers to schools. Even in most recent laws, the inspector is also expected to give advice as an educational expert about the latest results in research, yet it is difficult to reconcile this expectation with the realities of a supervisor's actual work. Although they sometimes assist in the provision of in-service training for qualified teachers, this role has diminished. They must be informed about what is being offered at special institutions for this service and they are members of advisory committees deciding on priorities.

Reporting. When a supervisor visits a teacher, a report is made which goes into the teacher's personnel file at the regional offices. The teacher is entitled to see this report and to make written comments in response to it. Another important reporting activity of a supervisor is to make assessments about the suitability of new building sites, alternative accommodation for classes and the general state of maintenance of schools. These reports go to the district authority that has these responsibilities.

Links with other social and educational institutions. Supervisors are a link between the schools and other systems, such as health, social service, and legal authorities. They also liaise with universities in order to help place student teachers in schools for their practicum during their first phase of training.

Status and permanency of position. The supervisor is fully integrated into the legalistic-administrative bureaucracy of the state Ministry of Education at the central, regional or district levels. Therefore, the supervisors have no autonomy. They are accountable to the Minister and do not publish reports for the benefit of parents or the public. As civil servants, their loyalty is to the Ministry. On appointment, supervisors are already permanent civil servants by virtue of their position as teachers and this status continues for life. After a short period of probation, their position as supervisor is confirmed and, irrespective of which political party is in power, they retain this appointment. They have a notably higher salary differential, above teachers' salary scales, which are, apart from many other benefits, very satisfactory.

In their capacity as administrators, supervisors are indispensable in a system which is so heavily reliant on administrative procedures and, in keeping the wheels of administration moving, they are essential personnel. Their integrity in supporting and furthering the policies of future Ministers is unquestioned.

The only shifts that are observable are when there is a transition of power to another political party in government. Then, at the highest echelons of administration a senior ranking ministerial supervisor may be shifted from a key position, for example from responsibility for curriculum and school development, to another of seemingly less importance, such as international relations and pupil transportation. This reflects the reality that, although their integrity and competence as civil servants has brought them to high office, there are other hidden criteria which seem to be of advantage in promotion.

General Characteristics of School Supervision in Germany

It will be seen from this description that one cannot directly compare supervision in Germany with inspection in school systems of other countries. In such a highly regulated system, teachers, principals, and supervisors take their orientation for practice from regulations. The supervisory system is geared more to ensuring that these regulations are being followed rather than inspecting for evaluation and improvement. As the system as been predefined as ideal, it is for the practitioners to conform to it.

The change in profession from a teacher to a supervisor is considerable and for many supervisors the requirements of the position are at odds with the ideals they had at the time they chose the career, when they would have expected to be contributing to the improvement of the system rather than simply maintaining it.

In summarising, one can say that the role of the German supervisor includes duties carried out in other countries by education officers, pedagogical inspectors and inspectors of administration. Clearly, the duties are manifold and the work is a very demanding. Indeed, the hallmarks of the position are long working hours and dedication to the task. It is the multisided nature of the service which differentiates it from many systems of inspection and evaluation found in other countries.

Diversity of Approaches

In presenting these examples from Denmark, the Netherlands and Germany, it is clear that, together with what one knows about inspection in England, there are many ways of undertaking external evaluation and assessment of schools. Each country has devised its approach according to its own educational culture in order to achieve a satisfactory balance between evaluation and control on the one hand and assessment and development on the other.

Specific Characteristics Associated with Assessment and Evaluation Systems

Degrees of Autonomy

Amongst the countries reviewed in this project, the inspectorate in the Netherlands seems to have the most autonomous status. It has a clear responsibility to report on the results of its activities directly to the Minister and Parliament without any other official intervening in adjusting or negotiating about the contents. The inspectorate in Scotland and the Office for Standards in Education in England also manage their own organisations. In the other countries the advisory, inspection and supervisory services are parts of a Ministry and many operate within a legalistic-administrative bureaucratic organisation.

In those systems enjoying a high degree of autonomy, the controlling systems are stronger and are required to demonstrate how well the schools or school authorities are providing the services in their charge.

Lack of autonomy is particularly prevalent in 'administered' systems where internal administrative checks and balances are assumed to provide a guarantee of good quality. When a problem of dysfunctionalism arises due to convoluted administrative procedures, supervisors are not in a position to solve it. As they are part of the system, rather than evaluators of it, they simply become part of the problem.

The Separation of 'Inspection and Evaluating' from 'Advising and Developing'

In most countries where assessments and evaluations are made by inspectors, the question arises as to whether or not there should be a clear division between the two activities of controlling and developing. In conventional, formal approaches to personnel inspection, some inspectors feel there is no conflict between the two aspects of inspecting and advising. For others, there have been serious doubts about whether the intermingling of the two activities is desirable or effective.

In Denmark, single adviser visitations are not personnel evaluations and are purely advisory. Discussions take place between the advisers and the teachers. In Belgium (Dutch-speaking community), separation has been legislated, but it was argued that, in reality, when one looks at the activities of inspecting and advising, a somewhat different picture emerges. In practice, it is almost impossible to control activities without giving some indication about how to cope with some problem areas and it is likewise impossible to advise without including some control. It was concluded that a clear division between the two activities is not always possible. The only solution lies in good contact – formal or informal – on a general policy level between the inspection and advisory services.

In Germany, the situation depends on which state is considered, in particular where the practice of the regular evaluation of teachers still exists. In states where this has been dropped, most supervisors have agreed that teacher evaluation is not only enormously time-consuming but also of little value. However, supervisors' opinions in other states are divided and the theme is controversial.

In England, it is not the responsibility of inspectors to become involved with individual schools in the follow-up process. Their responsibility ends with the inspection, except where a later check is necessary after an unsatisfactory report. The use of inspectors in development is in another department, which is detached from the controlling role and the consequences of an individual inspection. In Scotland, there is systematic follow-up by inspection resulting in a further published report to ensure that the school and education authority take effective action on the recommendations in the original report. Traditionally, in Ireland in the primary sector, the inspector responsible for making one of the 6-yearly inspections for a school report would be further involved with the school because of the close association each inspector has with a set of schools. Principles of good management would suggest that inspectors can only be involved closely with individual school development if there is a sufficient number of inspectors to be able to be in close contact with schools over a long period of time. This is not usually the case.

Openness

The topic of openness revealed significant differences in practice between the countries under discussion in the extent to which the findings of assessments and evaluations are made known. Similarly, the range of authorities and persons who are entitled to know the results of quality assurance measures varies. The degree of openness depends upon either the autonomy of the supervision system or the acceptance of adverse comments by top administrators.

With regard to the accessibility and publication of reports about schools, the most open systems are found in Scotland and England. This stems partially from the relative autonomy of the assessment systems, but it is also partly due to the political agenda behind the increased emphasis on inspection, namely to assist parents in choosing a school for their children. There is also an assumption that the exposure of schools to public scrutiny will be a form of motivation to improve.

Reporting in the Netherlands is planned to move towards more openness, with the intention at some time in the future of publicly publishing reports which are at present only intended for the school boards and schools.

In other systems in the European Union with a legalistic-administrative bureaucratic tradition, assessment and evaluation remains a confidential matter and no publication is made of assessors' or evaluators' reports. The less autonomous a system is, the less open is the reporting. Another reason for confidential behaviour, especially in evaluation, was cited from Belgium (Dutch-speaking community). The decision not to publish the results of external evaluation is political, based on the argument that this could lead to a 'hit list' where the schools performing less successfully would not have the chance of rehabilitation in the eyes of the public.

In our considerations about openness, we were confronted with the different philosophy behind the idea of 'the state' in some countries. However, as there are many other parties interested in the quality of schooling in addition to the Ministry of Education, the Minister and 'the state', the theme provoked lively discussion. In other countries, the more these other parties are involved in mechanisms furthering accountability, the more those who have been traditionally controlling the system from the centre are being pressured to change practices.

Constraints on Effectiveness

There are many constraints on the effectiveness of assessment and evaluation systems; these were discussed in the report (Hopes, 1997) and are summarised here as follows.

1. Inadequate staffing
2. Inadequate preparation for the tasks (training)
3. Inadequate in-service education (professional development)
4. Out of touch with subject area specialisation
5. Absence of a plan reflecting the clear philosophy of main task
6. Lack of a regular management review of the mission
7. Absence of a management evaluation process
8. Infrequent presence in schools
9. Poor organisation or lack of coordination
10. Inadequate articulation between supervisors and evaluators responsible for different school types
11. Too many indirectly related tasks
12. Involvement with unrelated tasks
13. Assignment to other tasks before completion of current task
14. Lack of autonomy

The project did reveal that, during the past 5 years, the implementation of improved methods of assessment and evaluation processes and the introduction of reforms are leading to an amelioration of some of the problems encountered in assessment and evaluation approaches in the past. On the other hand, budgetary constraints are again imposing renewed strains on staffing.

International Comparisons

It is difficult to keep up to date in international comparisons, because somewhere within any one country there is a state of change. By the time the findings of any survey are published, some country or countries will have moved on and the analyses become partially invalid. This has certainly been the case in trying to keep up with current practice in system assessment and evaluation.

With regard to assumptions relating to introducing admired foreign practices, it is generally agreed that it would be extremely difficult, if not impossible, to transfer unadapted methods from one country into another country with a view to developing a school system, because the original practices are deeply integrated within other interdependent cultural characteristics. The usefulness of such studies, at least in the field of consultancy, is only relevant if the distilled generalisations can be applied over a longer period.

In comparing, there is a danger of seeking characteristics which seem to look the same as in our own country and dismiss differences as probably being insignificant anomalies. Yet if we unwittingly overlook significant differences, we blur the issues being discussed, because we all have different, hidden perceptions of the various concepts. We use the same words, for example, evaluation or accountability, but the interpretation behind them is different. Moreover, serious misunderstandings can be unintentionally or intentionally propagated.

Innocuous examples of abuses in comparative education misinterpretations are those such as an English inspector returning from a week's sojourn in Denmark who submitted a report on 'The Danish School Inspectors' and a former female Prime Minister who advocated the merits of 'the German school system'. More seriously, in the field of assessment and evaluation, an example of incongruent interpretation of criteria at the international comparison level is the word 'leadership' and what we expect of persons displaying it. In the English model, a strong, 'hands-on' approach, with responsibility for creating and communicating a clear direction, is normally expected. However, recent research has suggested that in Denmark, the good headteacher is expected to be more collaborative in building a vision with others, indicating a fit with the purposes of schools as contributing to the maintenance of a democratic society (Mahony et al, 1998). In a study of the differences in expectations of parents and teachers in both countries about the headteacher, a much greater emphasis on the need for 'strong leadership' or 'assertive leadership' emerged from the English data, whereas in Denmark the 'ideal' school leader was conceptualised as being cooperative and enabling. This problem opens up the whole question of specifying the criteria of aspects to be evaluated, because, although we may agree on a generic term, for example 'leadership', thereafter we can only anticipate a loss of consensus.

Another problem is the loose translation into another language of types of school or names for special positions of responsibility (*collège, Gesamtschule,* comprehensive school; *chef d'établissement, Schulleiter,* headteacher; *inspecteur,* inspector, *Schulaufsichtsbeamte*) as if they are equivalent. Closer examination shows great differences in the educational culture of the schools or the roles of holders of special positions. For example, a document came to my attention a few years ago written for the OECD in French about the *inspecteurs-généraux* in Nordrhein-Westfalen. There are, of course, no *inspecteurs-généraux* in Nordrhein-Westfalen. The writer was referring to the upper level *Schulaufsichtsbeamte* in the Ministry in that state. Many are former teachers, who have now become a kind of hybrid of an 'administrative education officer' and an 'inspector' or 'adviser'. The label *inspecteur-général* in the French language paper was quite inappropriate.

In the project working seminars, some clear differences emerged about the way setting up supervision and evaluation processes are organised. The examples of the Dutch inspectorate and German *Schulaufsicht* (school supervision) showed considerable differences, providing useful models for analysis and comparison. A Dutch inspector operates in an autonomous organisation separate from the Ministry, whose Director has signed a contract, on behalf of the Inspectorate, with the Minister, on behalf of the Ministry, to perform certain duties. The Inspectorate's autonomy allows them to criticise all aspects of education, to make recommendations and to be protected from interference from others. Their loyalty is to the public and the organisations which founded the schools.

When a German '*Schulaufsichtsbeamte*' says that the schools are under the supervision (*Aufsicht*) of 'The State', that does not just mean the *Schulaufsichtsbeamte* are supervising state schools. The concept of 'The State' is that of an all-pervading higher authority above government, which determines in detail the behaviour of the organs under its control and that means, technically, the very operations in a classroom of a school. These supervisors are the guardians of the right behaviours and proper administration of the schools. They owe their *direct* loyalty to the Minister, not to pupils or parents. Of course, indirectly through their operations they are shielding the rights of those being served by the state from external or internal abuse, but in such a system they cannot be held accountable to the public. Only the Minister is accountable in this manner. Whereas the Dutch Chief Inspector prepares a report for Parliament on the state of education based on the findings of the inspectorate, the work of the German *Schulaufsichtsbeamten* remains confidential and unknown to the public.

The German *Schulaufsichtsbeamte* cannot and probably would not have to compare the standards between schools of the same type or between the quality of marks awarded by teachers in one subject in one class or another class. Firstly, the teachers are allocated to the schools by the *Schulaufsichtsbeamte* and, theoretically, on an impartial basis and ensuring that all schools have a fair share of 'good' teachers. The supervisors themselves become the guarantors of 'good' schooling and schools of the same standard. Regulations about marking, if followed closely by the teacher, are assumed to determine that quality and standards are guaranteed. It is an exception for marking practice or standards to be questioned. The essential matter is to ensure that things are done correctly.

Whereas a Dutch inspector works in an autonomous organisation, a German civil servant supervisor is embedded in the closed structure of a state administrative hierarchy. For the foreign, bemused observer, the current, convoluted discussions about tentative approaches to school autonomy or limited self-management of schools in Germany and the consequences for school supervision and evaluation can only be understood by reference to the philosophical concept of 'The State'.

Professionalism

In addressing the question of the status of assessors and evaluators as 'professionals', reference might be made to some of the characteristics of professions, which can be defined as organisations which:

- possess a unique body of knowledge;
- select their own members;
- admit new members only after the attainment of specialised qualifications relating to the new assignments;
- have a clear code of conduct;
- exhibit a shared expertise; and
- set their own fees or salaries.

Some of these characteristics can apply to some groups holding positions of additional responsibility in school systems. In general, they can serve as a useful reminder of the way we think about such persons. Are they still teachers with a few additional responsibilities or have they moved on to some other occupation? If they have 'changed professions', what measures have been taken to ensure that they are properly equipped to take on the new role?

In many countries, supervisors and evaluators who started their careers in the classroom are now exercising new responsibilities far removed from the practice of teaching. In spite of this fact, one of the grave omissions in their career pattern is training or further 'professional development'. One hears such expressions as 'bringing their skills with them', which seems to assume that some innate additional skill which may not have been in use in the classroom with children can now be applied to working with adults. Additionally, 'demonstrated success in previous positions' (for example, head of department) will be accepted as a worthy acknowledgement of the potential for future success. Success as a teacher may even be regarded as equivalent to 'having the ability *to advise other teachers* about teaching' – a challenge which many teachers have experienced on having a student teacher arrive on the threshold of their classroom.

The problem is that all these characteristics are past rather than future oriented. One of the most frequent expressions of appreciation heard in 'planned learning experiences' for supervisors and evaluators, i.e. not just courses, is 'This is the first such planned event I have ever attended', an admission which is all the more surprising in view of the length of time they have already served in the position. Examples such as 'an annual meeting with the Minister' (who tells the inspectors what he or she expects them to be doing), 'a day's seminar on an innovation being introduced into the school system', 'three days per year for self-development', 'reading professional journals', or 'international seminars' were the standard answers about previous qualifying experience.

In brief, with regard to the criterion of being admitted as a new member of a profession only after the attainment of specialised qualifications relating to the new assignments, supervisors and evaluators in most countries would not qualify.

Concluding Remarks

Before we can start making conclusions about the advantages and disadvantages of particular education systems and the lessons we could learn from them, the philosophy, attitudes and values within the system have to be understood. However, in the first instance, basic practical information about the processes in foreign systems has to be discovered before research questions can be asked and our knowledge of the way a system works can be advanced.

The international seminars in the project were undertaken to contribute to the knowledge we have of other systems by providing reading materials about processes in several systems for those persons involved in personnel and system assessment and evaluation. If comparative education is linked to expertise in specific areas such as management and administration or assessment and evaluation, not only will research benefit, but professional development approaches can be enriched by the use of clinical analysis techniques applied to problems as seen against the background of practice in other countries. In this way, although the foreign system could not be adopted, more alternative solutions could be considered. These reflections can, in turn, contribute to new ideas for action and provide a means of breaking down the repetition of the same encrusted rituals that still hamper some parts of our school systems. For those persons engaged in supervision and evaluation, who may have simply adopted the practices of previous generations, a widening of their horizons through comparative studies of processes is an essential component of their professional development.

Acknowledgements

The projects mentioned in this chapter were made possible through the approval of the Chief Inspectors in the countries under consideration and the cooperation and commitment of many school supervisors and administrators, in particular in the countries mentioned in this article: Helle Høyrup and Aase Herskin (Denmark), Harmut Schrewe and Gernot Lückert (Germany), and Frans Janssens (Netherlands).

References

Hopes, C. (Ed.) (1991) *School Inspectorates in the Member States of the European Community – Belgium, England and Wales, France, the Republic of Ireland, Italy, Luxembourg, The Netherlands, Portugal, Spain.* Frankfurt-am-Main: Deutsches Institut für Internationale Pädagogische Forschung (DIPF).

Hopes, C. (Ed.) (1997) *Assessing, Evaluating and Assuring Quality in Schools in the European Union.* Frankfurt-am-Main: DIPF.

German version: Hopes, C. (Hrsg.)(1998) *Beurteilung, Evaluation und Sicherung der Qualität an Schulen in der Europäischen Union.* Frankfurt-am-Main: DIPF.

Mahony, P. & Moos, L. (1998) Democracy and School Leadership in England and Denmark, *British Journal of Educational Studies*, 46, pp. 302–317.

Educational Change and its Impact on the Work Lives of Teachers in Eight Countries

PAM POPPLETON & THEO WUBBELS

Introduction

Educational change has become commonplace in many countries and, over a number of years, it seems that teachers have faced accelerated and intensive educational change movements. Initiatives have taken many forms ranging from restructuring entire nationwide educational systems to small local efforts to involve parents in the school life of one individual school. These initiatives may lead to various results such as, in one country, more centralised educational planning, management, and control or, in another, to decentralising moves giving more freedom to schools to operate in the way they feel is most conducive for their students. Curriculum reform has taken many forms to adapt the curriculum to the current needs of society and students. There is in some countries, for instance, a shift toward less structured learning and assessment, whereas in others, rote learning is emphasised more strongly.

All of these movements have impact on the lives of teachers, and that is the focus of a study to be reported here, carried out under the auspices of the Consortium for Cross-Cultural Research in Education, a loose coupling of individual researchers from 16 countries. This consortium meets at conferences all over the world in order to plan and evaluate collaborative research in education. In 1995, researchers from eight countries agreed to take part in a research programme to examine the impact of educational change on selected dimensions of the teacher's working life in state secondary schools so as to throw light on the relationships between different types of change and the problems of implementation.

The research plan may be represented simply as an investigation of the effects of change on:

dimensions of the teacher's work life:
- school roles, responsibilities and working conditions;
- relationships with teacher colleagues, administrators, students and parents;
- professional development and own competence;
- student motivation and learning;

taking account of the:
- origin of the change;
- objective(s) of the change;
- teacher's role in the change; and
- forces affecting the implementation of the change.

The teacher's change of attitudes (disposition to change) connected to the educational change experienced was also investigated.

Rationale

A major aim of the project was to suggest ways in which change can be managed in order positively to enlist the teacher's efforts in the reform, innovation and implementation processes. 'Educational change depends on what teachers think and do – it's as simple as that' (Fullan, 1982).

The problems of implementation in educational settings have been thoroughly studied in recent years by scholars such as Fullan (1993), Fullan with Stiegelbauer (1991), Hargreaves (1994), Miles & Seashore Louis (1992) and Huberman & Miles (1984) in seminal books and hundreds of dissertations. Since these accounts have been based mainly on studies conducted in the USA and the United Kingdom, the Consortium for Cross-Cultural Research in Education felt that research should be more widely based to give access to an international perspective against which we can better understand our own problems. The results of the study would also enable teachers in any of the countries concerned to compare their experiences with those of teachers elsewhere and thereby develop a cross-cultural perspective on their work as well as promoting a sense of international professional identity. It also felt that change efforts described variously as reform, restructuring or innovation have generally been designed by persons and groups other than those in the teaching profession. Typically, these programmes of change are accompanied by the assessment of their impact on the learning and development of students but there has been little study of the relative effects of different types of change on the work lives of teachers. Teachers are key agents in the facilitation and implementation of change and the study of the quality of the teacher's life *per se* would seem to have its own intrinsic value. To focus on this aspect would also be complementary to other types of studies in the field.

Method

Initially, comparative study data were gathered by educational researchers from eight countries; Australia (Tasmania), Canada (Ontario), England (South Yorkshire and Oxfordshire), Hungary, Israel (Haifa), the Netherlands, South Africa (Pretoria) and the USA (Michigan). The actual geographical location of the schools is indicated where known and, although in the rest of this report, results are reported by country, it is important to note that the study was not conceived as a large-scale sample survey, but as a series of in-depth studies to be drawn together by both quantitative and qualitative procedures. In each country, the same semi-structured interview procedures were employed with approximately 50 secondary school teachers working in similar urban/suburban schools.

An interview schedule was developed by the consortium members in several rounds of piloting interview questions in different countries. The pilot schedule was used for interviews in several countries (if necessary, after translation) and the results, difficulties and the degree to which information related to the research question was gathered, were discussed. Consequently, the schedule was adapted twice to better serve the aims of the project. Eventually a schedule for every country evolved, identical, except for language, and the equivalence was tested by back translation.

All interviews lasted between 1½ and 2 hours and were taped and transcribed for subsequent coding and interpretation. An agreed coding system was worked out and applied to the transcripts in each country and is used here as the basis for international comparisons. In this interim report, the reported results are based on categorical data and comparisons made between countries according to the percentage of responses recorded in each category. Eventually, the extent to which teachers were actively engaged in implementing the proposed changes, and the extent to which they were now willing to participate in future changes will be treated as output or dependent variables on the basis of their correlations with the dimensions of working life outlined earlier. Full interview transcripts are available for those who wish to gain greater understanding of the teachers' perspectives and to illustrate the findings presented here.

To summarise, the decision was taken to plan a collaborative research which would be within the scope of all participating countries and inform them of the most probable effect on teachers of different types of change.

Results

This section presents the main findings, relating to the teachers' responses to questions concerning the *characteristics and antecedents of the changes* that they nominated (Table I), and their perceptions of the *impact of the change* on selected aspects of their work life, their feelings about the change and their willingness, subsequently, to envisage participation in future changes of the same kind (Table II).

Study Question	Percentage reponse *							
	Eng.	Aus.	Hun.	Can.	Isr.	USA	NL	S. Afr.
Domain of change								
School management	7	18	27	9	11	18	9	8
Teaching	67	20	46	21	56	40	70	41
Learning outcomes	–	42	–	2	5	18	6	14
Student experiences	26	20	27	68	28	24	15	38
Origin of change								
Teacher initiated	4	2	19	3	26	26	24	14
School initiated	7	12	44	19	50	28	23	19
Community initiated	4	2	16	23	5	16	3	14
Government initiated	85	83	22	54	19	30	50	54
Objective of change								
Improve education	39	36	62	48	54	44	52	27
Improve accountability	42	34	15	18	20	26	25	8
Social objectives	19	30	23	33	26	30	24	65
Teacher's role in change								
Resister	4	28	3	3	2	2	4	3
No role	7	4	15	11	2	12	1	38
Supporter	–	24	9	5	2	8	17	5
Implementer	48	32	24	45	28	36	57	30
Shared decisions	11	4	12	11	19	10	–	11
Planner	4	2	15	7	12	8	21	–
Initiator	26	6	24	17	35	24	–	6
*Forces helping implementation***								
Resources provided	22	9	46	29	42	35	41	38
Support provided	89	70	54	57	71	75	80	84
Professionalism	59	86	46	48	36	60	72	72
*Forces impeding implementation***								
System resources	48	67	48	67	65	60	52	78
Personal resources	48	83	16	3	19	36	70	47
Decision-making process	60	79	24	59	27	43	62	75
Opposition	20	19	32	31	15	23	25	44

* Percentage responses are rounded to the nearest whole number. ** Interviewees were allowed more than one response to these items.

Table I. Teacher perceptions of the characteristics and antecedents of change.

Study Question	Percentage reponse *							
	Eng.	Aus.	Hun.	Can.	Isr.	USA	NL	S. Afr.
*Impact on work life***								
None	22	24	27	11	–	24	3	5
Little	–	–	3	2	4	2	4	5
Some	7	–	3	13	3	8	21	8
Much	33	30	24	35	17	30	59	38
Almost all	22	14	21	22	38	30	14	24
All	15	32	24	17	40	6	–	19
*Impact on relationships***								
Negative	53	86	25	49	20	43	11	45
None or other	6	4	40	8	18	4	41	15
Positive	42	10	35	42	62	53	48	30
*Impact on professional development***								
Negative	37	56	27	52	5	22	41	54
No effect	–	22	–	20	–	–	7	41
Positive	63	22	73	28	95	78	52	5
*Impact on student learning***								
None	–	14	9	3	2	2	4	3
Little	11	20	9	6	–	6	13	–
Some	26	16	30	11	12	32	39	22
Much	37	24	24	58	25	38	40	46
Almost all	19	12	12	13	39	20	4	24
All	7	14	15	9	22	2	–	5
*Teacher's feelings about the change***								
Very negative	–	16	6	6	–	10	3	5
Negative	11	22	12	17	–	8	6	16
Somewhat negative	–	16	6	28	4	10	12	11
Somewhat positive	30	4	9	20	14	14	21	8
Positive	44	28	56	13	50	22	53	30
Very positive	15	14	12	16	32	36	5	30
*Willingness to participate in any future change***								
Negative impact	26	34	24	31	4	8	14	19
No impact	56	44	32	41	12	52	62	32
Positive impact	19	22	44	28	84	40	24	49

* Percentage responses are rounded to the nearest whole number. ** Interviewees were allowed more than one response to these items.

Table II. Teacher perceptions of the impact of change on the work life.

Nature of the Most Important Change (Domain of Change)

Teachers were asked to nominate the three educational changes (broadly defined) which had the greatest impact on their working lives, then asked to choose the one most important to them, and were told that the remainder of the interview would concentrate on this change alone. This gave the teachers considerable freedom. Across countries, teachers in six countries nominated, as their major choice, changes to do with some aspect of teaching (content, method or both), England and the Netherlands being outstanding in this respect with, to a lesser extent, Israel. Of the remainder, Hungary, South Africa and the USA (in that order) were also coping with changes in this area while Australian teachers most frequently nominated changes to do with student evaluation (learning outcomes) and Canadian teachers were most concerned with changes relating to student experiences.

The importance to teachers of changes in subject matter and/or teaching methods emerged as a major theme throughout the interviews, representing, as it does, the teacher's main source of occupational identity.

The Perceived Origin of the Change

There was a very strongly marked division between those countries which had experienced government-initiated, country-wide educational reform (England, Australia, Canada, the Netherlands and South Africa) and those for whom change had taken place in the form of innovations within a school or classroom context (Hungary and Israel). The research design was restricting in some ways. If we wish to know how teachers in different countries participate in and react to change, it would be misleading to compare the responses of the English teachers to the introduction of a national curriculum with those of the Israelis, the majority of whom reported changes that were school initiated. Cross-culturally, we need to compare like with like in terms of the origin of the change rather than the type of change alone but, by following through each type of change, it should be possible to say something about problems of implementation in each case.

Of the four categories that describe the origin of the change in each case, two refer to sources internal and two to sources external to the school. From responses to the item we may note the following.

(1) The prevalence of government-initiated changes in five out of eight countries, though these referred to national governments in England, the Netherlands and South Africa, but state governments in Canada and Australia. In either event, they may be regarded as instances of imposed change, which has been studied as a separate category in the literature (Sikes, 1985) and needs to be differentiated from teacher-initiated change.

(2) While the majority of teachers in Hungary and Israel attributed the change to school-initiated sources, the full analysis shows these to have been initiated by school administrators rather than classroom teachers. In

Israel, administrators might be principals or others who rarely have teaching duties. In all countries we need to know more about these people, their responsibilities and to whom they are accountable. The English data exclude headteachers from this analysis as their responses showed marked differences from those of the teachers and they are dealt with elsewhere.

(3) Attributions by American teachers were distributed fairly evenly over the four categories.

(4) Overall, changes initiated by teachers were nominated by only 15% of the total, and only 10% were thought to arise from the 'community', i.e. parents or community organisations. Thus, the majority of changes were seen by the teachers as being 'top–down', indicating that the attention given to the teacher as change agent in the literature varies inversely with the prevalence of teacher-initiated change.

The Perceived Objective of the Change

Judging from the even spread of nominations, the responses to this item show greater ambiguity of understanding on the part of the teachers. When in doubt, go for the more socially approved response – in this case 'to improve education' is pretty fail-safe with five out of eight countries combining it in England and Australia (where there have actually been significant changes in school management) with the objectives of greater accountability and efficiency. South African teachers were outstanding in the emphasis they placed on change being motivated by social (as well as political) objectives, though around a quarter of teachers in other countries rated these as quite important also.

The Teacher's Role in the Change

Following on from this theme, there were seven possible roles listed and coded: resister, no role, supporter, implementer, shared decisions, planner and initiator.

The role nominated by the majority of interviewees was that of implementer, except for Israel where the role of initiator took precedence. A substantial proportion of the teachers in England, Hungary, Israel and the USA also regarded themselves as initiators. Recall that, with the exception of England, these countries registered a high proportion of changes of internal origin. Australia had the highest proportion of teachers who claimed to be resisters and an equal proportion claiming to be supporters. They were the most polarised of any country about their roles. Some 38% of South African teachers said they had no role in their government-initiated change.

It should also be noted that the terms 'Implementer' and 'Initiator' are subject to ambiguity in the school context, where teachers who were given responsibility for implementing mandatory changes could see themselves as initiating the process of change within the school. It may be suggested that the number of 'resisters' would have been higher in England except for an early retirement programme that enabled teachers to leave before the reforms began to bite and the study took place. Many did so and this points to a difficulty for all change studies in that the dissatisfied leave before their views can be known.

Factors Seen as Helping or Hindering Implementation

'Helping' sources were ultimately classified into three categories to do with the provision of resources; support provided by school and colleagues; and one's own attitudes, competence and professionalism. Interviewees were allowed to nominate more than one source so that the responses do not add up to 100%. Of these, the provision of support and one's own professionalism were the most frequently nominated overall, especially in Australia where curriculum reform was making intense demands on the teacher's professionalism. Where more than 50% of responses fell into one category, they represented the development of an implementation plan oneself in Australia, and one's own attitudes in the Netherlands and South Africa. Collegial help was also high on the list, especially in England, the Netherlands, USA and South Africa. Sources seen as 'hindering' implementation were much more evenly distributed, both within, and between countries. English, Dutch and South African teachers made most mention of too many changes occurring together and, therefore, lack of time to concentrate on one. Australian teachers overwhelmingly claimed that lack of time was the predominant factor. Poor levels of resources (financial, human and physical) received widespread mention and lack of training and consultation were particular causes of concern in Australia. Overall, implementation decision processes and poor system resources were the main sources of difficulty.

Impact of the Change on Work Life

Around one-quarter of all respondents claimed that they had been relatively unaffected by the change, with the exception of teachers in Canada, Israel, the Netherlands and South Africa who had experienced greater impact. Over 30% of those in Australia and Israel claimed that all of their activities had been affected though, interestingly, changes had been predominantly either school- or teacher-initiated in Israel but either government- or state government-initiated in Australia. In other countries, responses were more evenly spread over the 'some' to 'all' effect categories. Taking these two countries as the most sharply contrasted in terms of the origins of change, it may be noted that their standing on the degree of impact on relationships and professional development were also contrasted.

Impact of the Change on Work and Social Relationships

Responses to this item show a degree of polarisation between England and Australia on the one hand (negative), and Israel and the USA on the other (positive impact). However, when one looks at the causes of the type of impact, a much more differentiated picture emerges. Quite often, a teacher would refer to instances of both more strained and more harmonious staff relationships; to greater formality but also greater communication with colleagues. These responses are not surprising in circumstances where curriculum reform in each of the countries concerned brought together colleagues who had not previously worked together to produce a whole school plan as well as a subject department plan. They also produced more restricted contacts with colleagues in other schools and markedly less time to spend with families under the stress caused, in some cases, by massively increased workloads. However, practically every country, with the exception of Australia, registered some degree of improvement in teacher–student relationships which could represent a kind of 'Hawthorn Effect'.

Impact of the Change on Professional Development

'Professional development' was generally treated as a taken-for-granted concept and very few interviewees reflected upon its meaning. It is one aspect of working life which interviewees generally thought to have been significantly affected in one way or another. However, both nationally and internationally, professional development is a much more problematic concept than it would appear, being variously defined by interviewees as acquiring new knowledge, having greater opportunities for career development, improving status, improving qualifications and raising the level of importance of the profession in the community.

Results showed that feelings tended to be polarised within countries as much as between them. No teacher in England, Hungary, Israel or the USA said that professional development had been unaffected by the nominated change and, generally, the effect had been overwhelmingly positive. On the other hand, teachers in Australia, Canada, and South Africa tended to feel that the effect on professional development had been negative, but were ambivalent. There were no differences, in this respect, between teachers in countries where change had been seen as either internally or externally initiated. This is a particular case where interpretation depends on being able to contextualise the process of change.

Amount of Student Learning Affected by the Change

Respondents rated this question on a scale of 1–6 from 'none of it' to 'all of it'. They were generally non-committal about the extent to which the change had affected student learning. A number of English interviewees observed that life goes on for students irrespective of the battles raging above their heads. Nevertheless, 62% of the total sample felt that much or most of student learning had been affected positively, 'much' being the modal response. In view of the high proportion of teachers in all countries selecting 'to improve education' as the prime objective of the change, they seemed to feel that the impact had been beneficial for the students.

Teachers' Feelings about the Change

Did the teachers themselves feel good or bad about the change? Respondents rated a category on a scale of 1–8 from 'very negative' to 'very positive'. Overall, 72% reported positive feelings, with teachers in Australia, Canada, the USA and South Africa being more ambivalent. There appears to be no difference in this regard between Hungary and Israel on the one hand (where the change was internally initiated) and England and the Netherlands (where it was government initiated). However, Fullan & Stiegelbauer (1991) reported that a change produced by fellow teachers was just as likely to be externally experienced as if it had come from government.

Impact of the Change on Willingness to Participate in Any Similar Future Change

Results show that more than half the teachers in England, the USA and the Netherlands reported no impact; in Israel, an overwhelming 83.7% reported greater willingness, with majorities in Hungary and South Africa also; and between countries, a decreased level of willingness appeared highest in England, Australia and Canada.

Summary and Conclusions

It is important to note that the findings reported still have to be related to the nature of the change as well as the change process before it will be possible to suggest ways in which change can be managed positively and constructively from the teacher's point of view. While in Hungary and Israel around 50% of respondents reported having been involved in school-initiated changes, the generally low proportions of those involved in teacher-initiated change suggest that the latter is a relatively rare event and, such as it is, occurs in classrooms and is to do with modifications or innovations in teaching methods. These appear to occur less frequently when a nationwide educational reform is introduced via a strict timetable for implementation, though there is no evidence that teachers would initiate change in its absence. In some countries, the involvement of administrators or administrative teachers is much more marked than in others and is a system characteristic.

This result mainly suggests that teachers, when asked what educational changes they have seen, concentrate on the wider issues and not on the day-to-day improvements they implement in their classes. Richardson (1990) has drawn attention to the fact that the change literature did not find many changes in teachers but that this result does not mean that teachers do not develop. On the contrary, there is evidence that teachers improve their lessons on a day-to-day basis frequently but, perhaps, do not regard such changes as sufficiently significant to be reported.

While 62% of respondents overall expressed positive feelings about the change they had nominated, there was much greater variation in attitudes towards participating in similar change in the future, which appeared to be related to the change's perceived origin. Teachers in Hungary and Israel, where changes had been predominantly internal to the school, showed a more positive attitude to participating in future change than teachers in England and the Netherlands, where change had been externally imposed by national governments. It may be that a major factor in the way that teachers felt about different kinds of change was the role they had played in it, which was almost universally that of implementer. This has important implications for the development of whole school policies, which require full support and involvement from all members of staff for the implementation of reform policies in schools – something which has particular relevance for South Africa, where only 9% of the total sample reported having played a role.

In the process of implementation, all countries, with the exception of Hungary, rated collegial working and the support of colleagues as a major factor in success and again, apart from Hungary, lack of time was the main factor cited in failure.

From special knowledge of the English teachers who went through a traumatic set of experiences with the introduction of a national curriculum and testing programme, we can say that a dramatic change of attitude occurred when, pending breakdown of the whole process, they were included in the revision process. Eventually, their involvement in the drawing up of curriculum plans for their own schools forced them into collaboration with colleagues from which they derived some satisfaction in spite of the often crippling workload that it created. But, along with the Australian teachers, it was the heavy workload factor that led a quarter of them to say that they would not wish to participate in any future change. It is suggested that the likelihood of participation increases, the closer its probable positive impact on the immediate environment.

There is great variation both within and between countries, which raises questions about the hazards of transferring 'borrowed' solutions to a culturally different environment. Teachers in Israel, Hungary and South Africa appear to be the most deviant in their perceptions and all are countries which have undergone social and political upheavals in the last 10 years.

No mention has been made of the qualitative analyses that have emerged from the full interview transcripts in several countries. These provide rich insights into the meanings that teachers attached to the changes they reported and will be the subject of further explorations in the near future.

Note

This paper is based on a presentation at the eighth Biennial Conference of the International Study Association on Teacher Thinking held at Kiel, Germany, 1–5 October 1997. An earlier version is published in the Proceedings of that conference under the title: 'Knowledge about Change and its Effects on Teachers' (Wubbels & Poppleton).

References

Fullan, M. (1982) *The Meaning of Educational Change*. Toronto: OISE Press.

Fullan, M. (1993) *Change Forces: probing the depths of educational reform*. London: Falmer Press.

Fullan, M. with Stiegelbauer, S. (1991) *The New Meaning of Educational Change*. Toronto: OISE Press.

Hargreaves, A. (1994) *Changing Teachers, Changing Times: teachers' work and culture in the postmodern world*. London: Cassell.

Huberman, A.M. & Miles, M. (1984) *Innovation Up Close: how school improvement works*. New York: Plenum.

Miles, M. & Seashore Louis, K. (1992) *Improving the Urban High School: what works and why*. London: Cassell.

Richardson, V. (1990) Significant and Worthwhile Change in Teaching Practice, *Educational Researcher*, 19, pp. 10–18.

Sikes, P.J. (1985) Teachers' Careers in the Comprehensive School, in S.J. Ball (Ed.) *Comprehensive Schooling; a reader*. Lewes: Falmer Press.

Postscript: policy perspectives from the sixth seminar

MARILYN OSBORN, COLIN RICHARDS, MERYL THOMPSON, GÉRARD BONNET & PHILIPPA CORDINGLEY

In the concluding part of this section of the book we open the debate directly to four people who came to the seminar with direct experience of the policy process. These résumés, produced from the tape-recorded proceedings, present their perspectives on the potential value of comparative education, its uses and abuses as well as their specific comments on the theme of comparing education professionals.

Colin Richards

I came to the seminar with two current preoccupations, for me, mercifully, not related to OFSTED (the Office for Standards in Education). I've got two particular interests at the moment, that is, in the light of the Green Paper, I came wondering whether the notion of teacher professionals – which is what we want to focus on – and the notion of the teaching profession were being redefined in England. My current preoccupation is whether the Government's attempts to, so-call, modernise the teaching profession, to establish a new culture of teaching, are likely to be successful. Those were the thoughts in my mind as I came, which somehow helped me begin to think those things through.

I enjoyed Harry Judge's contribution very much, particularly his obsession with nines; 1999, if you remember, had three nines in it. Remember 999 is the emergency phone number. I wondered if that was some sort of intimation that the teaching profession itself is in some sort of critical condition and needs that particular emergency service. I wondered whether comparative education or comparative studies would help give the notion of teacher professionalism a new lease of life in terms of its discussion currently in the English context. I liked Harry's analogy about the Church and God being pronounced dead. I wondered whether, in fact, in England at the moment we are being offered a new professionalism by the Government at the very time when that professionalism is being denied any significant meaning apart from some sort of sophisticated adherence or compliance with the central dictates of the DfEE (Department for Education and Employment). I like the idea of entering the Church just as God is pronounced dead – I just wonder, if he is pronounced dead, would the devil move into his place? I was encouraged by what I heard from the comparative studies perspective – I do think it offers the opportunity to be, in Harry's terms, an optimistic and knowledgeable sceptic. I don't think it has the potential, and some of the other contributions today have revealed that, to dispel illusions (which I think was Theodor Sander's notion) but I wonder how far comparative study is also creating illusions of its own. It has the possibility of uncovering assumptions and debunking myths. But what of the assumptions themselves underlying the field of education studies which vary from context to context and country to country? Comparative study certainly offers the possibility of penetrating official rhetoric – but it has a rhetoric of its own. So there are some interesting issues there.

I do think that, unlike school effectiveness research, at least comparative studies do acknowledge, understand and almost celebrate, complexity – and probably add to it. There were some memorable words from various people today, which I shall long remember – Theodor's quote, 'The English road is a strange one', in terms of the way we're going in the redefinition of teacher professionalism. I liked his reference in his paper when referring to the English ITT (initial teacher training) curriculum as 'a mass of vague and hollow (I can't read my writing there) ... written by ignorant technocrats'. And I was concerned by this thought that perhaps the way we're moving in England, we might be losing this notion of teacher professionalism. As Theodor said, 'I hope nothing is forever'.

I enjoyed some memorable concepts – from Lynn Davies in particular – she talks, for example, about 'fragile societies with a cultural fear' – it didn't seem to be too far removed from the situation facing us currently in England. I liked the notion of there being 'an edge of chaos' – it seems to be a summary most of the time of my current predicament – teaching in classes, inspecting schools. Governments trying to change the bulk of teaching professionals I suspect are taking us on that edge. I liked her view in criticising school effectiveness research that 'you can't impose a factorial risk on an institution'. I just hope the current Government realises that by putting a factorial list of so-called objective stamps on teacher professionalism they are not able also to impose professionalism that way.

It was good to be reminded by Clive Hopes that there is more to inspection than OFSTED. I did, in fact, grade OFSTED in terms of Clive's last overhead in terms of the various constraints on effectiveness of the inspection/evaluation system for 14 constraints and for things like 'poor training' and so on, and I marked OFSTED as having 12 out of those 14. I was encouraged, lastly, by the fact that it is certainly possible to learn from comparative study. Clive's paper implicitly gave me that piece of information. Why? Clive explored the Danish system of what I would call school inspection. I was delighted to find that two of three Danish inspectors, who I invited over in 1993 for in-depth examination of the English inspection system, clearly learned so much from it that they decided not to implement it in Denmark!

Meryl Thompson

I will take a somewhat different approach, rather than reviewing the programme of the day. I also find it very difficult to embrace the day as a whole. What I have found very interesting is that the basis of learning from comparing is that what we must do is to go back to the cultural context of the society. That seems to me to be so valuable and useful that it is something which we should really celebrate and save. Like Bruner, I would agree that it only makes sense if we view education in this broader context. We must see education as a function of how one perceives a culture too. What's been intriguing me for a while is, in fact, and to some extent it's a rather undisciplined interest, in the underlying and unconscious assumptions that underpin so much of what we do – we never bring to the surface and we never discuss – similarly with the idea of the mean, the unit of cultural information that underpins so much of what we do. We can use these assumptions and in a first sense they're useful, but after a time they so affect our actions and thoughts that they become ambiguous and are really definitely not in our interest, because we do not examine them. I think that in comparative education, what it will force everyone to do is to begin to expose those means and their unconscious assumptions that underpin everything.

Just let me offer some which I think are the themes throughout the day, and possibly an idea that will challenge all of us. There are many conflicts that underpin all that we do and this is the reason that we can't abandon anything – we can't abandon looking at professionalism because it's there and will influence us always. All of these things we constantly examine. But what in different societies are the mental constructs of teacher, education, child, and the rights of a child? How do you reconcile the difference between the conception of the highest standard in Denmark that in fact sees life coming first and learning to follow, and that schools should offer knowledge that enables children to understand the world that surrounds them? And the conception by Chris Woodhead that education demands above all else the willingness to submit oneself to something hard, and often unforgiving, to persevere in the face of failure and accept one's weaknesses with humility on the way to success? What differences do those two underlying conceptions make, or to what extent do they reflect differences in the cultures that they're actually evolved from and with what's going on? What impact does that have on our conceptions, for example, of the management reorganisation of schools? Does this influence, in a sense, the notion of the kind of charismatic leader in education that we seem to have adopted in the United Kingdom, which may not be the case in other societies.

Are we using definitions of matters that are influencing fundamentally the way that we think and are making us unable to move from an idea where the individual matters to one where the organisational culture as a whole matters? And I think that they certainly are. And also, as well, in terms of the classroom, are we looking at, and I think this is probably happening very little anywhere – what concept of mind do teachers have that underpins education? Bruner again has said that if you think about education you had better take account of the folk theories that teachers are engaged in and the folk pedagogy. I would suggest that perhaps, at the moment, we have not thought sufficiently about how teachers' conceptions of merging the mind of understanding and children's abilities are actually influencing the cumulative education across the whole system whether we compare things or not.

I have been very interested in some of the information on 'brain-based research', which would very much suggest that we should radically overhaul the education system in almost all countries, because what we are not doing, in fact, is teaching in accordance with the way children learn best and learn naturally. So I think comparative education has a lot to offer, but at the same time, perhaps, we also ought to look at many of the assumptions that are underpinning education more generally. I think, in particular, in relation to the United Kingdom, it is very easy to be very ethnocentric, because at the moment I believe we have a great deal to gain from the comparison of those who will in fact look at the strengths of the system. English teachers, at the moment, are being told, in many ways, that they are not professionals – that they have not responded professionally. But, in fact, what they're not aware of is actually what the comparison is with any other culture. And, equally, I think, they're not aware of whether it has to come in and even what it is.

Some research from ATL (the Association of Teachers and Lecturers) has shown us how dispirited and disempowered the teaching profession has become because, although they're presented with this new Green Paper which is about modernising the teaching profession, very many of them are not even bothering to read it because their feeling is that everything has been imposed on them so far and this will be no different. And yet it is known to be the vehicle by which the profession is modernised. Now, just to give you a flavour, for those of you perhaps who don't know the Green Paper, and going back to what Colin was talking about – the Government sets out in here the case for modernising the teaching profession, developing information technology; classroom support and school buildings; opening up new possibilities of raising standards; and then they go on to say, 'this needs to be matched by a new vision of the teaching profession, good leadership, centres for excellence, a strong cultural professional development, and better support for teachers to focus on teaching to improve the image and status of the profession'. Of course, what they're not revealing is that those centres for excellence are to be pay-related. But in encapsulating that you can see what a challenge there is at the present moment in comparative education in looking at what's happening in the English education system, whereas any one of those can be unpacked comparatively. If there were to be a research project to look at the impact of the Green Paper on change in teacher professionalism in England, not necessarily in Scotland, it would be a most interesting research project. So, above all, I think we very much need researchers like you to investigate all these and offer for us the exposure of these means that underpin the policy of education. Particularly, we need to emphasise the importance of revealing the political dimensions of some of these things too and in so doing offering the teaching profession, in many ways, the way forward. Because that, I think, is another thing that researchers can reveal.

Gérard Bonnet

Well, I'm glad you said that – that someone actually needs comparative research because I was going to ask the question – what for? Why do we need comparative research? Listening very closely to the discussion that took place here today, I think this is the question that perhaps we should try and answer. I have one answer that I can put to you. Of course, I am not saying that you will all agree with it, but I'm trying to find some way from the policy perspective, you understand. I'm not speaking as a researcher, which I'm not, but more like somebody who works within a context of policy-making and who advises people on policies. One of the criticisms, which, as you well know, we've often levelled at academic research, is that it is really of not very much use in the real world for policy-makers. I'm not saying that I agree with that, I clearly do not, but this is something which you hear a lot of people saying. So I think it is very useful, indeed indispensable, to point out very clearly to people to what uses this kind of research can be put, in a very practical, i.e. policy-making, sort of way. So, clearly, what we've heard this morning and this afternoon shows that there is no question of comparing the education systems for the mere sake of trying to transfer one system into another country. We've heard, and this has been repeated several times over and I think it is absolutely fundamental, that all this, that has to do with education, is obviously cultural-specific, and there is no way that you can pick up bits of what is going on here or there and try and implant it somewhere else – indeed, it doesn't work within the same country. This business of trying to promote 'good practice' from one school to another obviously has its limits.

So, what is it that comparative research could do for us then? I think it would certainly be very useful in helping policy-makers to identify trends that are common to a lot of countries that are bound together for those reasons – and there are a lot of countries that are bound together. You can take the European Union and there is one kind of bond there, or you take the global internationalisation of societies, which would be another kind of bond. You really need to take what is emerging in terms of trends and difficulties to try and see how you can reconcile the specificities of the systems with the current world evolutions. And I'm not saying that you need necessarily find the same answers and the same policies, but let me just take one example to make myself perhaps a little clearer. We've just heard about the Green Paper on teachers in the twenty-first century – or whatever it's called – there is an interesting bit in it that I read about recently in an article by Peter Mortimore in the Education Supplement of *Parliamentary Brief* in which he says that one of the things that is in the Green Paper is that there should be help made available to teachers in the classroom for administrative purposes. Now, that's interesting. Because in France – and I promise I'm not going to talk about France only – in France we find that we are in the same situation, that indeed there is a definite move now to put into the school people that weren't there before, i.e. people who are not teachers, people who either are specialists in other fields like music, painting, sports, whatever, or people who come to support teachers in their work and should not themselves teach. Now, this is extremely interesting, that obviously for very different reasons two countries like England and France, which we know have very different systems, should, in fact, be contemplating the same sort of policies.

I can think of one specific area in which research is very helpful to point out these emerging issues. I'm not obviously passing any kind of valid judgement on those issues – they may be red herrings or whatever – but they are things that are taking place in different countries at the same time and there must be a reason for it. The reason clearly in the case of teachers is that for different reasons we feel in France that teachers are not actually doing enough talking about teacher professionalism in the way of looking after the pupils. And you feel that in England, presumably, that they are too bound by administrative duties to look properly at their teaching. So, starting from opposite ends, you end up trying to find the same solutions. But having said that, I feel that we have to be very careful in defining policies that would arise out of international comparative research, because one thing we do not want to be is to be manipulated by certain types of international bodies with a political agenda. This has been said at least on two occasions today – the OECD (Organisation for Economic Cooperation and Development), for example, is a case in point. The OECD organises research but that research has a political agenda quite clearly. We do not necessarily wish for that agenda through the methodology imposed by the OECD to become an international agenda that would be valid for the whole of, say, the European Union. So we need a different methodological approach to research than that which is being promoted currently by bodies such as the OECD as the universal model.

Another difficulty that arises, of course, is that when you try to compare professional people in education, i.e. teachers, headteachers, not so much inspectors, but certainly the (former) categories, that you are very much at a loss to decide really how you are going to compare which system is best, because what makes a good teacher here does not necessarily make a good teacher there. Here and there being two different countries or cultures. And the difficulty, and this is probably why we haven't so much heard about this today, is that the outcome of good teacher education or good professional development for headteachers, for example, can only be in the last analysis the outcome of pupils in the case of teachers, and the outcome of schools in the case of headteachers. So, in fact, what you need to measure then is not so much the performance of teachers and headteachers, but the performance of pupils in terms of their results at exams or national testing or whatever, and the outcome of schools and headteachers in terms of perhaps value added and other types of measures. So this business of education professionals is, in fact, more removed from the mere process of evaluating than other aspects of education that were discussed in previous seminars, particularly the assessment of pupils.

Having said all this, I really wish to emphasise again that there is great value in research, certainly from the point of view of policy-making. The only thing is that research has to be seen to be something that would be valid in other contexts than that of the professionals, of teaching. Research has to be seen to apply very directly to identify the needs of society by the needs of the education system. And in so doing, the choice of methodologies, as I hinted, is not at all indifferent and we must be very careful that not one single type of methodology is used, because one type of methodology will obviously, to some extent, constrain the results of research, so it is diversity that we want to see in research and methodological approaches to research – something that was pointed out today and I think it is extremely important to emphasise it again.

Philippa Cordingley

I do think international comparisons can be helpful with all the important provisos that Harry Judge and Theodor Sander in particular highlighted, for example:

- the principle of limitation or focusing on a highly specific aspect; the need to work out from the specific to the general;
- being clear how someone from outside a country can contribute something which an informal researcher could not contribute more effectively and efficiently;
- being clear that the purpose of comparing is to contrast changes over time;
- the importance of capturing change over time;
- the need to avoid an affirmative approach which takes diversity as a given;
- the need for depth in critique and analysis and the data to be calculated, including (and especially from a TTA [Teacher Training Agency perspective) a stakeholder input;
- the strong links between politics and comparative studies.

Most of these safeguards take as read the virtue of pursuing studies as a given, even if the virtue of comparison is challenged – we do need to take on board the comment about the risk of being seen to 'try to establish the sex of angels' and the questions about 'who asks the questions?'

Certainly I feel that any teacher who had been present would have been confused, cynical or depressed, including, perhaps even especially, in the chaos and complexity session. Perhaps this is simply because comparative study is not an appropriate method of enquiry in relation to pedagogy. It isn't that teachers aren't interested in theory or rigour – it's that they take as their starting point questions about improving teaching and learning.

Perhaps the strongest message I took from the day was my increasing inclination to oppose labelling teacher engagement *with* research as research at all. This simply implies that teaching isn't a good enough label for professional practice rooted in enquiry. It also puts teachers in the position of very junior participants with half a step on another professional ladder. Many teachers engage with research as a means of developing their own practice. This can perfectly properly be described as teaching. A few teachers can and do engage *in* research which has the capacity to inform the profession as a whole. The latter should be labelled as research and gain the credit it deserves.

Postscript: Marilyn Osborn

These four contributions bring together many of the issues emphasised in this section of the book. In considering the potential and value of comparing education professionals across national contexts, they have revisited the central theme of the seminar series as a whole, the nature and purpose of comparative education itself. Here and in all the seminars we have posed the question of what particular contribution comparative education can make to our understanding of and our capacity to resolve educational problems and questions, both those which are particular to one national context and those which are more universal. The contributors to this section of the book have tried to be clear about the limitations and challenges posed for comparative education research, as well as the opportunities. As Robin Alexander argued in his concluding comments to the seminar, on occasions, we have drawn perilously close to deciding that there is no future for comparative research but each time we have drawn back from the brink of that decision. This is largely because the opportunities and potential contribution we have identified still vastly outweigh the limitations. Certainly, in this volume, in spite of the caveats and concerns expressed, a number of fruitful ways forward have been suggested and some new challenges posed for comparative research in the twenty-first century.

To take up the particular challenge posed by Philippa Cordingley's comments on the value of comparative research to teachers in developing their practice, the contributions here would suggest that such research can help teachers by highlighting to policy-makers the importance of consulting and involving teachers when trying to implement change. More than that, however, in terms of teacher development, there may be great value in research which can demonstrate both the centrality and universalism of some teacher concerns and practices, regardless of the system in which they work, as well as the particular features which are unique to one education system. Such awareness of what is enduring and universal about being a teacher and what is unique to a particular situation or national context (i.e. the situatedness of some concerns and practices) may help to highlight the taken-for-granted features of our beliefs and practice and thus facilitate further professional development.

Notes on Contributors

Robin Alexander is Professor of Education and Director of the Centre for Research in Elementary and Primary Education, University of Warwick, United Kingdom.

Terry Allsop is Senior Educational Advisor, Department for International Development, currently based at DFID Central Africa, Zimbabwe.

Gérard Bonnet is adviser to the director of development and planning at the Ministère de l'Education Nationale, Paris, France.

Colin Brock lectures in comparative education at the University of Oxford, United Kingdom.

Nadine Cammish lectures in comparative education at the University of Hull, United Kingdom.

Cheng Kai-Ming is Professor of Education and Pro-Vice Chancellor, University of Hong Kong.

Philippa Cordingley is at the Teacher Training Agency, London, United Kingdom.

Michael Crossley lectures in the Graduate School of Education, University of Bristol, United Kingdom.

Lynn Davies is Professor of Education at the University of Birmingham, United Kingdom.

Clive Hopes is Senior Research Fellow at the Deutsches Institut für International Pädagogische Forschung, Frankfurt-am-Main, Germany.

Harry Judge is a Fellow of Brasenose College and former Director of the Department of Educational Studies, University of Oxford, United Kingdom.

Mary-Louise Kearney is a specialist in the Higher Education Division of UNESCO, Paris, France.

Joanna Le Métais is head of the International Centre, National Foundation for Educational Research, United Kingdom.

Marilyn Osborn is Reader in Education at the Graduate School of Education, University of Bristol, United Kingdom.

David Phillips is a Fellow of St Edmund Hall and Reader in Comparative Education at the University of Oxford, United Kingdom.

Pam Poppleton is Professorial Research Fellow, Department of Educational Studies, University of Sheffield, United Kingdom.

Rosemary Preston directs the International Centre for Education in Development, University of Warwick, United Kingdom.

Colin Richards is Professor of Education at St Martin's College, Lancaster and a former member of Her Majesty's Inspectorate (HMI), United Kingdom.

Val D. Rust is Professor of Education in the Graduate School of Education and Information Studies, University of California, Los Angeles, USA.

Theodor Sander is Senior Lecturer at the Institut für Erziehungswissenschaft, Osnabrück, Germany.

Michele Schweisfurth lectures in comparative education at the University of Birmingham, United Kingdom.

Meryl Thompson is at the Association of Teachers and Lecturers, London, United Kingdom.

Theo Wubbels is Professor of Education at Utrecht University, the Netherlands.